Professional Powers

A Study of the Institutionalization
of Formal Knowledge

Eliot Freidson

The University of Chicago Press
Chicago and London

ALBRIGHT COLLEGE LIBRARY

ELIOT FREIDSON, professor of sociology at New York University, is the author of numerous books, including *Doctoring Together*, also published by the University of Chicago Press. His classic study, *Profession of Medicine: A Study of the Sociology of Applied Knowledge*, received the American Sociological Association's Sorokin Award and has been issued in Dutch, French, German, and Spanish editions.

The University of Chicago Press, Chicago 60637
The University of Chicago Press, Ltd., London
© 1986 by The University of Chicago
All rights reserved. Published 1986
Printed in the United States of America
95 94 93 92 91 90 89 88 87 86   5 4 3 2 1

LIBRARY OF CONGRESS CATALOGING-IN-PUBLICATION DATA
Freidson, Eliot.
  Professional powers.

  Bibliography: p.
  Includes index.
    1. Professsons—United States—Sociological aspects.
2. Power (Social sciences) I. Title.
HT690.U6F76 1986   306'.42   85-20789
ISBN 0-226-26224-3

LF

Professional Powers

301.444
F 911 p

203731

For Helen

What do I need line for, when I have color? To me the whole universe is a gigantic theater, and I am the only member of the audience who hasn't glued opera glasses to his eyes. The orchestra is playing the overture to the third act; the stage is far away, just as in a dream; my heart swells with ecstasy. I see Juliet's purple velvet, Romeo's lilac silk, and not a single false beard. And you want me to blind myself with forty-copeck spectacles!

Kerensky in Isaac Babel's "Line and Color."

Contents

Preface

Over the past few decades there has been increasing concern with the role that knowledge plays in human affairs. Some writers have voiced that concern by reference to knowledge in and of itself—writing about the impact of technology and physical and biological science on our society or that of social science, pedagogy, psychiatry, and medicine. Others, particularly recent historians of the American Progessive Era but also contemporary critics, have focused not on knowledge alone but on the professional groups representing disciplines or bodies of knowledge that claim the right to control particular areas of social policy that affect particular areas of human life—schooling, child rearing, health care, welfare, city planning, the organization of factory work, and the like. Professional groups, including scientists and academics, are often represented as the creators and proponents of particular bodies of knowledge that play important roles in shaping both social policy and the institutions of everyday life. Thus they and their knowledge are said to have power. Knowledge becomes power, and profession stands as the human link between the two.

But there are two profound deficiencies in most of the literature dealing with the power of knowledge. First, the terms of analysis are often used so vaguely that it is almost impossible to determine precisely what people and activities they refer to. Key words are often undefined, or they are defined so loosely that one can never be sure what they mean. In much of the literature they are used as part of a colorful rhetoric that exercises the imagination by its connotations but that does not allow actual connection with concrete human events and experiences in the real world. Second, even when denotations are specified, key terms are usually not grounded in human activities. Knowledge, for example, is most often treated as a disembodied entity: it is "Taylorism," or "social science literature on the family," or "medicine," its content constructed by quoting textbooks, speeches, or articles in professional or lay periodicals. Whether the knowledge constructed from such published material is in fact employed by those who administer schools, social agencies, hospitals, or other institutions and by those who perform the daily work in them is rarely investigated, let alone demonstrated. It is merely assumed that knowledge is impressed like some ghostly rubber stamp on a passive humanity, and by force of rhetoric terms like *hegemony, dominance, monopoly of discourse,* and *social control* are invoked to sustain the assumption.

Given those two deficiencies, questions about evidence supporting assertions about the power of knowledge or of professions cannot even be raised, let alone answered. There is no reliable way to refine the question or to introduce qualifications about conditions that facilitate or discourage the use of knowledge to influence human affairs. One must accept or reject the discourse solely on the basis of one's willingness to believe and fill in the details by imagination alone. One can, like Kerensky in Isaac Babel's "Line and Color," quoted as the epigraph of this book, regard the world as a spectacle, thrill to the color of the grand words, and even be contemptuous of those who want to see clearly the line, the detail, the evidence. One may even claim that seeing the detail distracts from envisioning the grand whole. But if one wishes to undertake responsible and successful action in the real world, no longer a mere spectator or entertaining commentator, colorful visions fail as a guide. This is the moral of the end of Babel's little story:

> Six months later I saw Alexander Fyodorovich once more; it was June, 1917, and he was now supreme god of our armies and arbiter of our destinies.
>
> That day the Troitsky bridge had been dismantled. The workers of the Putilov Factory were marching on the Arsenal. Streetcars lay like dead horses in the streets. A rally had been called at the House of the People, and there Alexander Fyodorovich made a speech about Russia—Russia, mystic mother and spouse. The animal passion of the crowd stifled him. Could he, the only mem-

ber of the audience without opera glasses, see how their hackles were rising? I do not know. But after him, Trotsky climbed to the speaker's tribune, twisted his mouth, and in an implacable voice began:

"Comrades!"

In this book I wish to clarify the relations between knowledge and power by grounding them in the institutions of professionalism in the United States. Such grounding requires detailed analysis of how those institutions are put together, how they work, how the people participating in them are differentiated by position and perspective, and how those institutional positions influence their work of creating, transmitting, and applying their knowledge. I assume that knowledge cannot be connected to power without becoming embodied in concrete human beings who in turn must be sustained by organized institutions. By those means knowledge can influence affairs systematically. My basic thesis is that the actual substance of the knowledge that is ultimately involved in influencing human activities is different from the formal knowledge that is asserted by academics and other authorities whose words are preserved in the documents that are so frequently relied on by historians and other documentary analysts. Down at the level of everyday human experience, in schools, prisons, scientific laboratories, factories, government agencies, hospitals, and the like, formal knowledge is transformed and modified by the activities of those participating in its use. Thus the paradox that, while the institutionalization of knowledge is a prerequisite for the possibility of its connection to power, institutionalization itself requires the transformation of knowledge by those who employ it. The analysis of scientific and scholarly texts can be no substitute for the analysis of the human interaction that creates them and that transforms them in the course of using them in a practical enterprise.

A grand view unaided by opera glasses that allow a close look at the institutions involved cannot see that transformation and certainly cannot understand how it occurs. It is that grand view I seek to correct. For that reason much of this book is detailed analytic description of the institutions of professionalism in the United States—particularly the legal-political institutions that sustain the positions of those who speak and act for a body of knowledge and that both permit and constrain the exercise of organized power. Since no work presently exists that brings together in a coherent way the information that is available on the legal, political, and organizational status of the professions, I presume that at the very least this book can serve as a resource for those seeking a broad overview of the formal institutions of professionalism in the United States today. In addition, by setting out in some detail the character of those institutions and the manner in which they influence the creation and use of knowledge in human affairs, I hope to provide materials that larger, more colorful theories might feel challenged to take into account if they wish to be taken seriously as plausible guides for understanding and action.

While this book is concerned more with an analytic description than with creating a theory, it cannot avoid commenting on theories designed to illuminate the position of knowledge and the professions in our society. In the first chapter I attempt to sort out the variety of efforts to delineate the characteristics of those who may be said to be agents or carriers of formal knowledge. In the second chapter I attempt to clarify the issues connected with the idea of profession, choosing to use it as a historic rather than an abstract, analytic concept. Taking it as an American social category for distinguishing a group of occupations, I consider the usefulness of thinking of professions as a class, whether a "new class" or a "professional class." In the light of the heterogeneity of the occupations in the category I reject such concepts and treat professions merely as those occupations that have in common credentials testifying to some degree of higher education and that are prerequisites for holding jobs. Higher education presupposes exposure to a body of formal knowledge, a professional "discipline."

Turning to the credential system characteristic of the professions in the United States, I show how it works to establish positions both for ordinary practicing professionals and for those members of the professions who serve in administrative and in teaching and research positions. In the light of that characteristic, system-supported differentiation within professions, and in light of the professions' place in the legal system, I turn to evaluating another set of theories about them—namely, those asserting that they have lost or are losing their powers.

In the course of discussing the absence of empirical support for the theories of deprofessionalization and of proletarianization I point out that employment, not self-employment, is the characteristic position of professionals. To appraise the powers available to them therefore requires analysis of their position as employees. By analysis of U.S. labor law and of an important legal decision involving the relationship of professional employees to management I show that the concept of the industrial proletariat has little analytic value—even as a suggestive analogy—for understanding the position of professional employees. Indeed, I show how rank-and-file practitioners have important discretionary powers to determine how work is to be done, what services and benefits clients receive, and the like, the limits to their power being established in large part by other professionals serving as administrative superiors in their employing organizations.

Finally I turn to the broader impact of the professions on political, economic, and technical decisions that form the framework within which rank-and-file professionals must deal with their work. I discuss the formally constituted associations that organize and focus the political activities of professions, the prominent individual professionals who are sometimes very influential even though not officially representative of the profession, and the other individuals who serve in government staff positions and on the quasi-governmental committees that make policy recommendations and establish both personnel and product standards to guide the production of goods and services. I point out that the professions participate in but rarely dominate the process of policy formation, the administrative implementation of legislation and the establishment of official standards or norms. And in assessing how formal knowledge figures in the exercise of power I show that it is an unstable element. Practitioners, administrators and teacher-researchers are each in a position to exercise different powers over client services and material production. Each has a different perspective on the relevance and use of the profession's formal knowledge in the different tasks each performs. This creates differences in what knowledge is actually employed. The outcome is sufficiently variable and indeterminate to require us to adopt an interactive view of the relations between knowledge and power and of the role of the professions as the actors. Neither domination nor impotence may be ascribed to either the professions or their disciplines.

Finally, I must acknowledge that there are matters of importance that could not be addressed in more than a passing way in a book of this length. Perhaps my greatest regret lies in being unable to discuss the fine empirical and theoretical work on the professions that has been done in the United Kingdom over the past decade or so. Excellent work from France, Chile, and, more recently, Canada and Australia has also had to go undiscussed. This omission is purely a function of my reasoned choice to do an idiographic study of professions in one nation and to emphasize analytical description over abstract theorizing.

Other omissions stem from the limitations imposed on what can be discussed reasonably well in a book of this length. There is, for example, little discussion of the systematic discrimination that women, blacks, ethnics, and other minorities have suffered in the professions or of the place of the professions in the class system of the United States. Nor is there much discussion of the theoretical and moral issues that both guide and justify social policy toward the professions. My primary task of bringing together the materials that are necessary for understanding how professions can be what they are, of grounding the knowledge and skill of our society in professional institutions, has had to take precedence.

The analytic strategy I have chosen is also a function of my primary task. Though I have taken pains to cite relevant historical work, I have made little effort to analyze the history of American professions and their institutions. I believe that, were I to have undertaken a history, I would not have been able to analyze in detail as many contemporary institutions as I have. Ultimately, both historical and contemporary studies are essential for a full understanding of the world, the one to follow the course of various streams of events flowing toward the present and the other to examine the contemporary pool into which all those separate streams flow. By my analysis of the contemporary pool I hope I have succeeded in dredging up objects of interest and useful ways of looking at them whose development over times past future historians may find it useful to study.

Acknowledgments

This book is indebted to a variety of sources of institutional and intellectual support. Before it was even conceived, the Russell Sage Foundation provided a small grant that allowed me to begin exploring issues in the social organization of occupations in the human services. Subsequently, the Center for Advanced Study in the Behavioral Sciences indulged my still unfocused needs for exploratory reading by making available to me its extraordinary messenger-photocopying service, which looted the libraries of the Bay Area for my growing file of materials. Still later, while conducting a Summer Seminar for College Teachers on the topic of the professions and supported by the National Endowment for the Humanities, my interaction with the participants drew things into first focus. During that time, one of the seminar participants, Jay Gold, led me to see how much grist for analysis is provided by the law. Finally, Cambridge University provided me with the opportunity to present a course of lectures on the professions that showed me what I did not want to write and set me on the track that led to this book. A subsequent sabbatical from New York University in conjunction with a fellowship from the John Simon Guggenheim Foundation provided me with the opportunity to finally begin sorting and shaping my accumulated ideas and data into coherent written form.

Over the years during which this book was pursued I received enormous stimulation, encouragement, and aid from many more people than I can remember, some making their mark with an offhand remark during the course of a conversation about ostensibly irrelevant topics. Those whom I do remember wrote me comments that have rescued me from disorganization, inaccuracy, illogic, and unnecessarily peevish

xvii

rhetoric by their friendly but critical candor as they commented on various draft segments I had sent them. Chapters in various stages of incoherence were read and commented on by Howard S. Becker, Arlene K. Daniels, Wolf V. Heydebrand, Barbara Heyns, Derek L. Phillips, and Daniel Walkowitz. Samuel Estereicher, Matthew Finkin, and Marc Rauch gave generously of their time in commenting on chapters that dealt with law. Steven G. Brint and Terence C. Halliday provided exceptionally detailed and critical commentary and suggestion for a great many chapters, while Helen Giambruni cast a helpfully cold eye on my style. And Pat Hartman's intelligence and precision were responsible for getting everything together into tangible form.

All authors who are conscious of the social process by which their work emerges into the world must make such acknowledgments. The process is so common that, in most cases, the form of acknowledgment tends to seem perfunctory and stereotyped or, for those who wish to avoid that appearance, overly extravagant. I have not attempted to solve that stylistic problem in the hope that my observation of it will lead those to whom I owe so much to ignore the form and take my thanks sincerely and literally. Of course they deserve none of the blame for any deficiencies in this final version.

Chapter One

Formal Knowledge, Power and the Professions

Knowledge is power, it is said. If we consider the overwhelming growth of knowledge—particularly scientific knowledge—over the past hundred years, we might be inclined to think that the power of knowledge has grown as well. And surely there is ground for that. The power to render whole continents, if not the entire planet, virtually uninhabitable has grown out of the physical sciences, while unprecedented power over the shape of life itself seems to be developing out of the biological sciences. These are the most widely known and widely feared bodies of knowledge, but there are also others that seek the sources of power over personal and social as well as physical and biological existence. Such knowledge is said by many to constitute a new form of domination over our lives, to create a new form of pervasive social control hiding its face behind a mask of benevolence but leaving us helpless and dependent on others for guidance in the conduct of even our intimate lives in our families (cf. Lasch 1979).

The question is, What is the relationship between those who create, transmit, and apply that knowledge and the actual exercise of power? Can it be said that scientists are a "new priesthood" (Lapp 1965) or "new Brahmins" (Klaw 1969)? Can we speak of the "tyranny of the experts" (Lieberman 1970) without hyperbole? Do people actually come to rule by virtue of their knowledge? Or, what may come to be the same thing, do they influence so completely the way we think about the world and conceive of solutions to our problems that, while politicians may nominally rule, their decisions are predetermined by the authoritative knowledge of their expert advisers? In what way can it be said accurately that knowledge is power? That is the broad question around which this book revolves.

In order to answer that question usefully, it is necessary to understand how knowledge gets translated into action, which means understanding the human institutions that mediate between knowledge and power. The largest portion of this book will be devoted to an analysis of those institutions, in part because many of them have not received the attention they deserve and so are not to be taken for granted as commonly understood and in part because of my belief that no analysis of the relation between knowledge and power can possibly be persuasive without showing how the two are linked and translated into action by human beings in their institutions. In this first chapter, however, I shall attempt to lay out the elementary groundwork for the analysis of those institutions. First, I shall attempt to identify the special kind of knowledge—formal knowledge—that has been linked with power in modern times. Then I shall discuss the agents of knowledge—the people who create, transmit, and apply it—and the problem of identifying them as a group in a fashion that allows us to discern the concrete institutions in which they act. My choice will then permit closer focus on them and their institutions in the chapters that follow. But first let me discuss knowledge itself.

The Rise of Secular Formal Knowledge

Knowledge is intrinsic to human culture, embracing the facts believed to compose the world, the proper methods or techniques by which to cope with them in order to gain a particular end, the attitudes or orientations that are appropriate to adopt toward them, and the ideas or theories by which one makes sense of facts, methods, and attitudes, explaining and legitimizing them. All human beings everywhere may be said to have some sort of knowledge.

But not all people have the same body of knowledge. Obviously, the substance of the knowledge of people in one culture can be quite different from that of people in another. Furthermore, within any particular culture of any complexity and size one can locate both a body of knowledge common to all and specialized knowledge that is available only to some. The social division of labor, constituting the interlinked system of specialized activities in a society, represents diverse bodies of specialized knowledge manifested through those activities. Thus we commonly distinguish everyday or commonsense knowledge shared by all normal adults in the course of the activities they all perform from specialized knowledge shared by particular groups of people who perform activities on a regular basis that others do not.

In the ancient great civilizations, however, and in our own today, yet other distinctions arise—distinctions between sacred and profane knowledge, theoretical and practical knowledge, elite and popular or mass knowledge, and higher and lower knowledge. In the West, higher knowledge was formalized into theories and other abstractions, on efforts at systematic, reasoned explanation, and on justification of the facts and activities believed to constitute the world. Formalization so distinctly marks modern higher knowledge that it is appropriate to call it formal knowledge. Formal knowledge remains separated from both common, everyday knowledge and nonformal specialized knowledge. Originally rooted in arcane lore and in texts in ancient languages known only to a few, higher knowledge is now still expressed in terms unfamiliar to and impenetrable by the many and discussed by techniques of discourse that are opaque to outsiders. Those who developed modern higher knowledge—the secular scholars of the Renaissance, for example—addressed each other and members of the ruling elite who shared some of their knowledge and belief in its virtues. They did not address the common people or the common, specialized trades. So it is in our time.

If there is a single concept by which the nature of formal knowledge can be characterized, the most appropriate is likely to be *rationalization*, a concept that is central to Max Weber's analysis of the development of Western civilization. Rationalization consists in the pervasive use of reason, sustained where possible by measurement, to gain the end of functional efficiency. Rational action is organized to address both the material and the human world, and it is manifested most obviously in technology but also in law, the management of institutions, the economy, indeed, in the entire institutional realm of modern society. It is intimately associated with the accounting and management methods that developed with capitalism and the administrative methods of developing predictable social order that rose along with the modern state in the form of "rational-legal bureaucracy." Above all it is intimately associated with the rise of modern science and the application of the scientific method to technical and social problems. Much of the formal knowledge developed in universities over the past century may not have the capacity to control its object of study that the natural sciences have gained—that is to say, may not be adequately scientific—but it nonetheless adopts the same technical or functional rationality, the same effort to develop rational theories on which to base practice and to codify "knowledge with abstract systems of symbols that, as in any axiomatic system, can be used to illuminate many different and varied areas of experience" (Bell 1976, 20). There can be no doubt that formal knowledge, so defined as the subjects of research and teaching in the modern university, has increased at an extraordinarily rapid rate over the past century, with a parallel increase in specializations or disciplines (ibid., 177–78).

FORMAL KNOWLEDGE AND DEMOCRACY

There is a tendency for prestige and respect to be given to formal knowledge by those who lack it. At least since Francis Bacon's *New Atlantis* there has been a strong belief in the capacity of science to improve human life. Indeed, that belief has been expressed frequently and forcefully from the latter part of the eighteenth century down through our own day. But there is also a tendency to fear it, a tradition that goes back long before the rise of modern science and that, with perhaps better justification than before, continues into our day. Formal knowledge is arcane to everyday people, and some of it can be thought to be powerful and dangerous. It is true that not all formal knowledge is feared: dusty scholars studying obscure minutiae that have no perceptible connection with everyday life are more an object of ridicule than respect even though their knowledge is arcane. But science, like alchemy before it, is thought to be consequential knowledge and therefore potentially dangerous.

By definition, formal knowledge is not part of everyday knowledge. This means that it is elite knowledge. And insofar as it is used to direct human enterprises, decision making on its basis is not democratic, not open to the active participation of all. Thus formal knowledge can be seen as a threat to democracy. Since formal knowledge has grown enormously over the century, and since it is increasingly used in the advanced industrial societies in virtually every sphere of life, it can mean that democracy itself may be at risk. Some visionaries, such as Saint-Simon early in the nineteenth century, have actually argued in favor of a society that is ruled by "objective" knowledge in the face of which opinion is irrelevant and democracy meaningless. Most writers, however, seem concerned with maintaining democracy, and many of them have considered growth in the importance of formal knowledge to human affairs to be a threat to democracy.

Perhaps the most direct and unqualified statement of the importance of such knowledge to modern societies has been made by Jacques Ellul, who characterized the essential spirit of its application to human concerns as "technique"—the state of mind and method of procedure of the scientifically oriented. The "intervention of reason and consciousness . . . can be described as the quest for the one best means in every field. And this 'one best means' is, in fact, the technical means" (Ellul 1964, 21). Technique is seen to be an irresistibly developing force, similar to Weber's "rationalization" and by no means limited to the natural sciences and technology. It embraces the methods used by the police, the management of factories, of education, and of medical care, and in politics the management of the public by propaganda and other techniques. The outcome is order: "Technique has only one principle: efficient ordering. Everything, for technique, is centered on the concept of order" (ibid., 110). Insofar as technique is the one best means, then there is really no choice on the part of politicians but to accept the solutions offered by technique. So it is that Ellul can see a society in which police technique in suppressing crime has been advanced to the point of true efficiency as a concentration camp and can see technique as the boundary of democracy (ibid., 209; for a summary of Ellul's work, see Kuhns 1973, 82–111).

Other commentators have also considered knowledge to be a tool employed for the purpose of controlling or dominating everyday lives, shaping them to the purposes of the state. The technique or rationalization inherent in such formal knowledge so orders and structures the possibilities for choice and action on the part of ordinary people that true choice is prevented. People become a function of the system created by others to control them. The most sweeping and complex statement of this emerges from the work of Michel Foucault. His historical analysis tries to show how domination, or imposed order, was generated in the course of the development of a variety of institutions from the ideas growing out of a number of formal or scientific disciplines. The formal knowledge of the disciplines shapes the way human institutions are organized and the way the behavior of human beings is conceived, providing justification for particular methods of interpreting and disposing of a wide variety of human behaviors. They "define how one may have a hold over others' bodies, not only so that they may do what one wishes, but so that they may operate as one wishes, with the techniques, the speed and the efficiency that one determines. Thus, discipline produces subjected and practised bodies, 'docile' bodies" (Foucault 1979, 138).

Discipline has a double meaning; it is both a segment of formal knowledge and the consequence of its application to the affairs of others. Such disciplines establish the power of the norm, statistical or otherwise, which is used as a "principle of coercion" in a variety of standardized institutions—in education, in health care, and in industrial work, for example. "Normalization becomes one of the great instruments of power" (ibid., 184). Power becomes no longer simply physical coercion but something much more comprehensive, "working to incite, reinforce, control, monitor, optimize and organize the forces under it: a power bent on generating forces, making them grow, and ordering them, rather than one dedicated to impeding them, making them submit, or destroying them" (Foucault 1980, 136). The disciplines are powerful enough to mold human beings to their will and to the will of the state.

FORMAL KNOWLEDGE AND POWER

The use of formal knowledge to order human affairs is of course an exercise of power, an act of domination over those who are the object. Ellul might regard such domination as an inevitable outcome of the dynamism of technique. Others, however, would distinguish formal knowledge and technique themselves from power and argue that those who hold the power of decision making are not necessarily the same as those who possess formal knowledge and technique. Politics and politicians hold the power, and it is they who decide what formal knowledge to apply and to what. Daniel Bell is quite firm in asserting that it is the politician who ultimately holds the power: "The control system of the society is lodged . . . in the political order, and the question of who manages the political order is an open one" (Bell 1976, 374; see also 360). Given the growing importance of formal knowledge, however, Eulau (1973) postulates a change in the nature of political decision making in which a complex consultative relationship develops between politicians and those with the relevant skills. Lane (1966) argues that some decisions will be entirely removed from politics and thus from the process of democracy by virtue of having become objectively technical instead of political in character.

Habermas, following Marcuse and others of the Frankfurt School, adopts a critical rather than a descriptive perspective on the matter. He agrees that the growth of formal knowledge during this century has been so great as to create a qualitatively new situation. To him the present represents a second, new stage of the process of rationalization analyzed by Weber, for "the exercise of power . . . [has] been structurally transformed by the objective exigencies of new technological strategies" (Habermas 1971, 62). He does not see formal knowledge as a threat to democracy because of an intrinsic tendency inevitably to preempt political decisions and democratic participation. He denies the inevitability of the influence of technique. The threat he sees is the inappropriate and fallacious use of technique as ideology to justify decisions that are actually not technical or scientific in character. He argues that reason expressed through technology is only one dimension of knowledge and action and cannot adequately legitimate "practical decision in concrete situations," which is a different dimension (ibid., 63). For this reason he asserts that, "as little as we can accept the optimistic [belief in] the convergence of

technology and democracy, the pessimistic assertion that technology [inevitably] excludes democracy is just as untenable"
(ibid., 61).

The danger is that, whatever may be the logical case for the
difference between formal, rational knowledge and "practical
decision in concrete situations," it is entirely possible, as
Habermas observes, that the former can be used as a false but
politically effective justification for the undemocratic exercise
of power. Under such circumstances political decisions are not
subject to popular debate because they are presented as "technical" decisions. People are not allowed to choose among a
variety of alternatives because the issue is presented as a technical one that involves the necessary use of the "one best
method." Thus, as formal knowledge grows in magnitude and
complexity, and as it is developed into disciplines addressed to
an increasing number of areas of human life, one can see an
increasing tendency toward rule by technique rather than by
public debate about and participation in political decision making. One can see a tendency, in short, away from democracy
and toward technocracy.

TECHNOCRACY

Apart from programmatic or wishful statements like
the utopian *New Atlantis* of Bacon or the scientifically based
society of Saint-Simon, the concept of technocracy is rather
opaque and its thrust uncertain and ambivalent. (For summa-
ries of the "technocratic" utopians like Saint-Simon, Comte,
and Veblen and some historical material, particularly on engineering, see Armytage 1965.) Meynaud (1969), who provides a balanced review of various conceptions of technocracy,
himself arrives at a somewhat equivocal conclusion addressed
particularly to France, in which elected representatives who
nominally wield political power become a kind of reflex of the
decisions that are prepared in advance for them by technical
experts. In this sense, what he sees and what, for that matter,
writers such as Sarfatti-Larson (1972–73) see is not literal rule
of the polity by those with formal knowledge but rather a
position in the structure of rule that mediates, qualifies, and
sometimes directs the actions taken by those who actually rule.
The "technocrat" is a high-level adviser perhaps, or a high-

level member of the staff of the politically powerful, or a high-level administrator with technical training (cf. ibid., 4). But the technocrat is not the one who makes the ultimate decisions of the polity.

Beyond programmatic writers who are not describing the world as it is, then, there is little inclination to postulate anything more than a "tendency" to technocracy. Formal knowledge is an instrument of power, a source for guiding and facilitating the exercise of power, but not power in itself. Insofar as those with access to formal knowledge are in power, they are politicians rather than literal technocrats, as Bell (1976, 79) indicates, and must operate like politicians. What we must do if we wish to understand better the relation between formal knowledge and power, therefore, is to avoid the trap of assuming that knowledge itself is a system of domination that controls the ultimate power of the polity, as Foucault seems to imply. Furthermore, we must avoid the trap of assuming that there is only one method appropriate for making all political decisions, as Ellul seems to imply. Both writers treat knowledge and method as forces that are independent of human action and choice.

THE AGENTS OF FORMAL KNOWLEDGE

The question we must ask is, How is it possible for formal knowledge to have an impact on anything? In and of itself knowledge is an abstraction. Insofar as it is tangible, its "growth" over the past century or so can be "measured" by counting the number of books and journals that were published (Price 1961), but in order to exist in books and journals knowledge must have human creators and consumers. How does knowledge establish a consequential relationship to the everyday world? To have any impact on either the natural or the social world knowledge must have human agents or carriers, and the impact it makes must be influenced in part by the characteristics of those agents. Thus we cannot understand the role of formal knowledge in our world without understanding the character of those who create it and apply it. This, then, raises another question, namely, What are the characteristics of those who are the carriers or agents of formal knowledge? Who are they? and What are the characteristics of the institutions that make their activities as agents of knowledge viable? In identifying the agents of knowledge the literature is somewhat confusing, for it has employed a number of different terms to characterize them. Sometimes the word *expert* is used for them and sometimes *technician*, sometimes the word *technocrat* and sometimes *professional*, sometimes *intellectual* and sometimes *intelligentsia*. Let us examine those terms.

The term *intelligentsia*, apparently first used in Poland in 1844 (Gella 1976, 12), was widely used in Poland and Russia by the 1860s and is still used widely, though in a different manner, in the Soviet Union and its surrounding Central European countries. In its traditional use in those countries, Gella argues persuasively, it referred to a social stratum joined together by a common education that, while secondary, was "higher" and "academic" in character. It was not a stratum composed of all those with a *gymnasium* education, however. The stratum was distinct from others with the same education in the middle and upper classes because it shared a "specific combination of psychological characteristics, manners, style of life, social status and, above all, value system" (ibid., 13). That value system, with roots in the ideals of the landed nobility, emphasized the obligation to serve the nation and lead it to what was defined as its destiny through fundamental sociopolitical change (cf. Konrád and Szelényi 1979, 85–142).

Members of the intelligentsia were active in the Russian Revolution and in the government of the Polish Republic between 1918 and 1939 but were supplanted by the new *working intelligentsia* of eastern Europe, a much broader stratum. The term became an official government label for all people who performed white-collar rather than manual labor and who had more education than the general population. As Churchward (1973) shows, it is a very heterogeneous category. In eastern European state socialist regimes today, which are based on state-directed "rational redistribution" of resources to the population, Konrád and Szelényi (1979) argue that an elite segment of the working intelligentsia has developed that in essence directs the process of redistribution and is developing into a technocratic class. Bailes (1978) paints a somewhat more complex and qualified picture of the technical intelligentsia of the Soviet Union, but he would certainly agree that they exercise important influence on policy.

If *intelligentsia* is the eastern European word for the carriers and disseminators of formal knowledge, *intellectual* is its western European and North American analogue. While it may be a function of the translation from Hungarian to English, it is nonetheless a happy coincidence that Konrád and Szelényi alternate during the course of their analysis between the use of *intelligentsia* and the use of *intellectuals*. Who are the intellectuals? and What are their characteristics?

The term *intellectual* as used to designate a special group of people is even more modern than *intelligentsia*, having first been used widely in France at the end of the nineteenth century (cf. Feuer 1976, 48–49; Nettl 1969, 95). Those writers who have attempted to identify or define intellectuals tend to employ two criteria. On the one hand some emphasize the kind of knowledge that intellectuals pursue and transmit and the orientation of that knowledge. To those writers, it is not all formal knowledge that concerns intellectuals but only that which in some sense transcends the practical affairs of daily life. As Coser (1970, viii) put it, "Intellectuals feel the need to go beyond the immediate concrete task and to penetrate a more general realm of meaning and value." Thus intellectuals do not characteristically address the pursuits of everyday life as a practical problem and cannot be considered to be synonymous with, let us say, technocrats. In a sense they are concerned with ideas rather than with systematic bodies of knowledge or intellectual disciplines.

Furthermore, a number of influential writers have portrayed intellectuals as being somehow detached from or marginal to their societies and intrinsically critical of them (cf. Nettl 1969, 88). In his superb essay on the sociology of intellectuals in capitalist societies, Schumpeter (1950, 145–55) characterized them as those "whose interest it is to work up and organize resentment, to nurse it, to voice it and to lead it" (ibid., 145). Dahrendorf put that detached, critical perspective of the intellectual more mildly and, through his reference to the earlier role of the court jester, in a more ironic context: "All intellectuals have the duty to doubt everything that is obvious, to make relative all authority, to ask all those questions that no one else dares to ask" (Dahrendorf 1969, 55). Shils, however, in his broad, comparative view, analyzes the intellectual's dissent from and distrust of authority as a secondary characteristic that is comparatively recent in history (Shils 1969, 46–51; Shils 1982, 224–72).

Lipset employs functional criteria to distinguish the "hard core" of creators and distributors of culture from a peripheral group "composed of those who apply culture as part of their jobs—professionals like physicians and lawyers" (Lipset 1963, 311). Similarly, Shils (1982, 224) distinguishes the creation, cultivation, and transmission of knowledge as the primary role of the intellectual, with the secondary role being "the performance of intellectual-practical (or intellectual-executive) actions in which intellectual works are intimately involved." This distinction between those who are "pure" and those who are "applied" is in fact an important one in the literature. Parsons (1969, 13) adopts it along with distinctions between those affiliated with the lower ranks of society and those with the upper ranks and between those employing humanistic knowledge and those employing scientific knowledge.

On the whole, those who see intellectuals as having a singular mission in the employment of their knowledge would agree with Coser in ruling out scientists as a group and ruling out as well the practicing professions "unless they talk or write about subjects outside their [strictly defined] professional competence" (Schumpeter 1950, 146). But that discrimination presupposes accepting as the critical mark of intellectuals a particular preoccupation with transcendent values and ideas, including the aims or goals of the society they speak for. In that view, the knowledge of intellectuals is not technical in character but deliberately "teleological" with "cross-contextual" significance (cf. Konrád and Szelényi 1979, 6–9, 29–35). To accept that criterion would of course shrink the population of intellectuals into a very small segment of all who can be appropriately considered agents of formal knowledge and markedly shrink the corpus of knowledge they represent.

However, the distinction between the technical and the teleological leads us to recognize other terms that have been used to designate the creators and carriers of formal knowl-

of Konrád and Szelényi (1979, 74–142). In spite of those differences, however, the modern intelligentsia of eastern Europe can be defined as professionals who are trained and gain their living as "lawyers, physicians, economists, teachers, scientists, engineers, journalists, artists and others" (Bailes 1978, 15), just as Parsons, Bell, and Lipset could describe as professionals the intellectuals of the United States and other capitalist countries. Economic support for the agents of formal knowledge is provided in modern times most often by professional pursuits.

A reasonable method of identifying the agents of formal knowledge in modern times in such a way as to be able to discern how they can gain the living that is necessary to allow them to serve as such agents is to identify them as members of professions. Explicitly connected with the idea of profession is training in higher education, the institutions of which are without doubt the major source of the transformation of the source and role of agents of formal knowledge in all advanced countries (cf. Parsons 1969, 15–18; Shils 1969, 38–39). But the university's importance does not lie solely in its role in training those who engage in knowledge-based pursuits in the world outside, many of whom compose the practicing professions. Perhaps more important for the substance and role of formal knowledge is the fact that the university itself provides a professional pursuit to most of the intelligentsia and the intellectuals who are concerned with the transcendent and the teleological. That profession is university teaching.

In contrast to schoolteachers in "lower" educational institutions, university professors are granted enough time free from teaching to make it possible for them to do scientific, scholarly, and intellectual research and writing that does not generally have sufficient market value to provide a living by itself. Some can work as extremely specialized scientists or humanistic scholars who report their obscure investigations in academic journals and monographs (cf. Coser 1970, 249–96). By virtue of their sinecures they are free to address only each other rather than the general public, on whose support they would otherwise depend, as Bender (1984, 84–106) notes. Others, however, are made similarly free by their sinecures to spend much of their time serving as critical intellectuals in nonscholarly journals of opinion. They can address the general public on broader subjects as "intellectuals" if they so choose but without having to depend on the public's economic support because they gain their living from teaching. This subsidization of activities that have little monetary value in the marketplace is what makes it possible for academics to play such a strategic role in the creation rather than in mere transmission of formal knowledge. By virtue of being members of the profession of teaching they gain the opportunity to be preoccupied with the pure, the transcendent, and the teleological, none of which are ordinarily considered to be strictly professional issues.

Understanding that the professions include many people of a sort that some analysts would not be willing to admit into the ranks of the elect, I nonetheless argue that as a term or a category profession constitutes the most useful source for identifying the agents of formal knowledge in our day. Furthermore, it includes most, if not all, of the elect. Being members of professions provides intellectuals, the intelligentsia, experts, and others represented as agents of formal knowledge with a living and therefore makes it possible for them to function as agents of formal knowledge, whether pure or applied.

If we accept this mode of grounding formal knowledge in the economy, we have moved toward identifying the agents empirically, but we have not moved far enough. Granting that the agents of formal knowledge can be described as professionals, the problem still remains of delineating the position of professions that gives them access to power, the institutional complex that creates and sustains that position, and the activities by which it can be said that professionals exercise power. Many recent histories purporting to show how some professional powers developed and shaped society have been rather unpersuasive because they have paid little or no attention to those institutions, discussing the ideas and rhetoric produced by selected spokesmen for the professions without indicating how they could have any impact in the Babel of ideas and rhetoric of the real world (cf. Bledstein 1976; Lasch 1979).

THE TASK AHEAD

Without understanding the nature of the institutions by which professions are created and sustained, the nature of other institutions within which professionals perform their work, and the nature of still other institutions through which professionals attempt to exercise power, the possibilities for exercising any significant and consistent power by those agents of formal knowledge remain entirely obscure. In order to understand how formal knowledge can influence the social world around it, therefore, one must understand both the professions that serve as its carriers and the institutions that make those professions possible. That is the task of this book. I shall attempt to illuminate the role of formal knowledge in our time by presenting an analysis of the professions, their composition, their organization, and, more extensively, the institutions that sustain them and provide them with opportunities for the exercise of powers. But first I must clarify the issues involved in identifying the professions themselves.

References

Armytage, W. H. G. 1965. *The rise of the technocrats.* London: Routledge & Kegan Paul.

Bailes, K. E. 1978. *Technology and society under Lenin and Stalin.* Princeton, N.J.: Princeton University Press.

Bell, D. 1976. *The coming of post-industrial society.* New York: Basic Books.

Bender, T. 1984. The erosion of public culture: Cities, discourses and professional disciplines. In *The authority of experts,* edited by T. L. Haskell, 84–106. Bloomington: Indiana University Press.

Bledstein, B. J. 1976. *The culture of professionalism.* New York: W. W. Norton & Co.

Churchward, L. G. 1973. *The Soviet intelligentsia: An essay on the social structure and roles of the Soviet intellectuals during the 1960s.* Boston: Routledge & Kegan Paul.

Coser, L. A. 1970. *Men of ideas: A sociologist's view.* New York: Free Press.

Dahrendorf, R. 1969. The intellectual and society: The social function of the "fool" in the twentieth century. In *On intellectuals*, edited by P. Rieff, 53–56. New York: Anchor Books.

Ellul, J. 1964. *The technological society.* New York: Vintage Books.

Eulau, H. 1973. Skill revolution and consultative commonwealth. *American Political Science Review* 62:169–91.

Feuer, L. S. 1976. What is an intellectual? In *The intelligentsia and the intellectuals*, edited by A. Gella, 47–58. Beverly Hills, Calif.: Sage Publications.

Foucault, M. 1979. *Discipline and punish: The birth of the prison.* New York: Vintage Books.

———. 1980. *The history of sexuality.* Vol. 1, *An introduction.* New York: Vintage Books.

Gella, A. 1976. An introduction to the sociology of the intelligentsia. In *The intelligentsia and the intellectuals*, edited by A. Gella, 9–34. Beverly Hills, Calif.: Sage Publications.

Habermas, J. 1971. *Toward a rational society.* Boston: Beacon Press.

Klaw, S. 1969. *The new Brahmans: Scientific life in America.* New York: William Morrow & Co.

Konrád, G., and I. Szelényi. 1979. *The intellectuals on the road to class power.* New York: Harcourt Brace Jovanovich.

Kuhns, W. 1973. *The post-industrial prophets.* New York: Harper Colophon.

Lane, R. E. 1966. The decline of politics and ideology in a knowledgeable society. *American Sociological Review* 31:649–62.

Lapp, R. E. 1965. *The new priesthood: The scientific elite and the uses of power.* New York: Harper & Row.

Lasch, C. 1979. *Haven in a heartless world.* New York: Basic Books.

Lieberman, J. K. 1970. *The tyranny of the experts: How professionals are closing the open society.* New York: Walker & Co.

Lipset, S. M. 1963. American intellectuals: Their politics and status. In *Political man*, edited by S. M. Lipset, 332–71. New York: Anchor Books.

Meynaud, J. 1969. *Technocracy.* New York: Free Press.

Nettl, J. P. 1969. Ideas, intellectuals, and structures of dissent. In *On intellectuals*, edited by P. Rieff, 57–134. New York: Anchor Books.

Oxford English Dictionary. 1971. Vols. 1, 2, compact ed. New York: Oxford University Press.

Parsons, T. 1969. "The intellectual": A social role category. In *On intellectuals*, edited by P. Rieff, 3–26. New York: Anchor Books.

Price, D. 1961. *Science since Babylon.* New Haven, Conn.: Yale University Press.

Sarfatti-Larson, M. 1972–73. Notes on technocracy: Some problems of theory, ideology and power. *Berkeley Journal of Sociology* 17:1–34.

Schumpeter, J. A. 1950. *Capitalism, socialism and democracy.* 3d ed. New York: Harper Torchbooks.

Shils, E. 1969. The intellectuals and the powers. In *On intellectuals,* edited by P. Rieff, 27–51. New York: Anchor Books.

———. 1982. Intellectuals and the center of society in the United States. In *The constitution of society,* edited by E. Shils, 224–72. Chicago: University of Chicago Press.

Znaniecki, F. 1968. *The social role of the man of knowledge.* New York: Harper Torchbooks.

Chapter Two

Identifying Professions

In chapter 1 I noted some of the scholarly controversies surrounding what one means when one uses the
words *intelligentsia* and *intellectual* and then offered *profession* as
the more desirable alternative for identifying the carriers of
formal knowledge. *Profession* was offered not because there is
any less controversy surrounding its meaning but only because
it more particularly implies a method of gaining a living while
serving as an agent of formal knowledge and implies as well
the fact that bodies of formal knowledge, or disciplines, are
differentiated into specialized occupations. Since there is considerable controversy surrounding the usage of *profession*,
however, and since that controversy implies that not everyone
can agree in identifying what are professions and what are not,
it is essential to establish a procedure of identification at the
outset of my analysis. Only that will avoid the fatal vagueness
and inconsistency that characterizes some of the work on the
topic. Here, then, I shall first review the history of contradictory connotations and denotations connected with the word—
a semantic history that prepares us for understanding the
foundation for varied usage. Then I shall discuss the scholarly
work on the concept of profession, including some of the
controversies characterizing it and the issues underlying them.
Finally, I shall indicate the choice I have made of the source of
identifying the professions. This will establish the parameters
of the analysis to follow in later chapters.

Portions of this chapter are reprinted from Eliot Freidson, "The Theory of
Professions: State of the Art" in *The Sociology of the Professions: Lawyers,
Doctors and Others.* ed. R. Dingwall and P. Lewis, (London: Macmillan Press,
1983), 19–37.

A Semantic History of "Profession"

There are very good reasons why there is so much confusion in English-language writing on professions, reasons that go far beyond theoretical propensities. As a word, *profession*, along with other words having the same root, has a number of overlapping denotations and connotations, few of which are sharply distinct from the others. Furthermore, contrary to so many modern writers who associate it only with high status and prestige, there are negative as well as positive evaluations connected with it. This bewildering and contradictory variety is clearly reflected in the comprehensive collation of historical usage in the *Oxford English Dictionary* (1971, 2:2316–17) and the less comprehensive but nonetheless valuable *Webster's Third New International Dictionary* (1967, 2:1811). Guided by these sources, but avoiding mechanical summary and employing my own ear for the contemporary language, let me look at those meanings.

Unlike those relatively modern terms *intelligentsia, intellectuals, technicians*, and *experts*, the word *profession* has a long history in all European languages with Latin roots. The oldest usage in English is today relatively uncommon—*profession* (and *profess*) as a declaration, avowal, or expression of intention or purpose. This was the primary denotation of the word before the sixteenth century, originally connected with taking consecrated vows and stemming from the clerical foundation of the medieval university. In that usage, the word is evaluated positively, implying religious and moral motives to dedicate oneself to a good end. However, there is also connected with it the notion of insincerity and lying, of claiming in words what is not done in fact. Such usage as "He professes to know nothing about it" appeared in the sixteenth century, when the word *profession* came to be applied to secular occupations as well as to that of the clergy. Today, I suspect that only the connotation of insincerity would be attached to the usage of the verb *profess*.

The noun *profession*, referring to an occupation rather than an avowal or a claim, also elicited contradictory evaluations as far back as the sixteenth century. At that time, it was used to refer to the university-educated occupations of divinity, law, and medicine (but not surgery) and, less commonly, the gentlemanly occupation of the military. These pursuits were not only learned in character but also distinctly, indeed, almost exclusively, activities of the well born. High status was therefore attached to those occupations, more perhaps because of the status of those who filled them than because of any deep respect for the skills and activities involved in their practice. Positive evaluation was therefore intrinsic to the usage, as was narrow and exclusive reference to only three, at best four, of the entire range of occupations to be found in those times.

However, quite another usage developed during the sixteenth century by which the word referred not to a few exclusive occupations but rather to the whole range of occupations by which people were identified and made their living. Thus one could properly ask anyone what his or her profession was without assuming that the answer had to be limited to medicine, law, the clergy, or the military or to other exclusive, highly prestigious occupations. The occupation in this sense could be modest or even degraded—a haberdasher, a tailor, saddler, barber, or waterman, as in a passage from 1616 cited in the *Oxford* (1971, 2:2316). Thus even as early as the sixteenth century the word *profession* could be used to mean either a very exclusive set of occupations or the exact opposite—any occupation at all.

The gentlemanly or, in latter-day usage, prestigious connotation of *profession* is carried on into another usage that essentially reverses connotations—that is, one in which *professional* carries the connotation of the ungentlemanly, the crass, the inappropriately labored or excessive. This occurs in one context of the contrast between *professional* and *amateur*, in which prestige is associated with being an amateur who performs some activity for the sheer love of it and without interest in its capacity to provide a living. (Indeed, to be an amateur is to have a living already at hand and to need no income from the activity.) In contrast to the amateur, "professionals" earn money from their activity, and this makes their motives for undertaking the activity potentially suspect and belies their status as "gentlemen" or men supposed to be economically independent. As the *Oxford* puts it, the term is "disparagingly applied to one who 'makes' a trade of anything that is properly pursued from higher motives, as a *professional politician*" (1971, ibid.).

Beyond that, there is another disparaging usage that does not imply commercial motives so much as bad form—employing an unseemly amount of energy and attention in an activity, as in being a professional partygoer, a professional beauty, or whatever. Interestingly enough, this usage is first recorded in the nineteenth century at the same time as the word *profession* came to be used to refer to a number of new or refurbished and reorganized middle-class occupations as exclusive and prestigious and also as gentleman scholars began to be seriously threatened by the full-time, professional scholars and scientists in universities. Indeed, the period during which the development of specialized training began to replace "liberal" higher education in both America and England was marked by this semantic turn. Veysey notes that researchers did not want to be considered to be people who made their living by their activities. Quoting the *Johns Hopkins University Register* (1877–78), he noted that, in its initial public portrayal of its graduate programs, "'The Johns Hopkins University' . . . announced [that it] 'provides advanced instruction, *not professional*, to properly qualified students in various departments of literature and science'" (Veysey 1965, 149; italics added). That is, it should not be expected that a graduate program would train people in a pursuit from which a living might be expected, as is the case for a professional school.

The contrast between *professional* and *amateur* that I have already noted makes the dedication and motivation of the professional suspect, and so it expresses devaluation. There is another contrast between the same words, however, that precisely reverses evaluations, in that it contrasts the quality of the work or activity that one may expect of each. To characterize something as an amateurish job, or the work of an amateur, implies poor work, while to characterize something as a professional job implies good, reliable work of skill and quality. This distinction has kinship with and supports yet another usage of *professional* that is also positive in valuation. If someone works as a professional actor or musician rather than as an amateur, earning a living by the work, the presumption may

203731

ALBRIGHT COLLEGE LIBRARY

be that, unlike the amateur, the person is sufficiently accomplished at the acting or playing to warrant being paid for it and earning a living from it. And in that context it may be implied that the amateur either lacks skill or lacks sufficient dedication to cultivate what skill he or she possesses to its fullest possible extent. The amateur is a dabbler at a mere pastime, a Sunday painter; the professional is dedicated to practice and refinement of his or her skill during the working days of the week and so seeks support for it. In this sense, the professional is an accomplished expert, a full-time specialist cultivating a particular kind of skill and activity.

The professional-amateur distinction is one that is in some sense universalistic, contrasting all those who regularly perform a particular kind of work for a living with those who perform that work for other rewards and, as often as not, irregularly. In that context, *profession* thus refers to all kinds of occupations that one engages in for a living, without making invidious distinctions among them. It refers to any kind of work undertaken for a living and thus to a great variety of skills. The more narrow denotation of *profession*, however, which stems from those occupations that developed out of the medieval university, contains within it a considerably more specific notion of the skill connected with professional work. Indeed, *profession* may be defined by reference to a particular kind of training and skill.

The narrowest meaning of *profession*, which underlies some of the connotations of derived words like *professional, professionalize, professionalism,* and *professionalization,* is one that makes much of the special nature and source of the knowledge or skill involved in specialized work, locating it in abstract concepts most often taught today in universities. So important are the details of this narrow meaning that, however tedious, one must quote two authoritative sources of English definition. The *Oxford* definition is most parsimonious: "A vocation in which a professed knowledge of *some department of learning or science* is used in its application to the affairs of others or in the practice of an art founded upon it. Applied *spec.* to the three learned professions of divinity, law and medicine; also to the military professions" (1971, 2:2316; italics added). The *Web-*

ster's Third definition is much more elaborate, informed, no doubt, by reference to the work of academic sociologists of the 1960s. It refers both to the type of education and to the way knowledge and skill are institutionalized: "A calling requiring specialized knowledge and often long and intensive preparation including instruction in skills and methods as well as in the *scientific, historical, or scholarly principles underlying such skills and methods*, maintaining by force of organization or concerted opinion high standards of achievement and conduct, and committing its members to continued study and to a kind of work which has for its prime purpose the rendering of a public service" (1967, 2:1811; italics added).

It is important to note that these dictionary definitions are socially authoritative. That is, people in our society who want some clarification of what a profession is go to these sources or an abridged version of them. They do so not only because they might regard the editors of major dictionaries as singular arbiters of usage in and of themselves but also because dictionaries are made up by collating and refining the varied usages that are found in both the everyday and the scholarly, intellectual, and artistic discourse of a society. Dictionary definitions do not represent merely *ex cathedra dicta* about "correct" meanings, usage, and spelling; they also document the history of usage of the society they represent. While they may not reproduce timeless verities, they do reflect many of the consequential and influential ideas of their time. And, like the work of academic theorists, they reflect what people, both laypeople and those who wish to call themselves and be called professionals in this special sense, have in mind when they use a word in a particular context.

One way to clarify this special, narrow sense of *profession* is to oppose it to the broader sense that refers to all occupations in which people work for a living and in which they develop proficiency or skill. In both cases there is specialized expertise or skill that sets them apart from amateurs, so that people in both cases can be considered "pros" or even experts. But the expertise of the former is qualitatively different from that of the latter because it is based on some branch of higher learning and because it is thought to be of special benefit to society in some more than ordinary way, thought, in short, to be in some sense distinct from and superior to the work of those engaged merely in commerce or the ordinary trades. As we shall see in later chapters, this has encouraged the support of a special status in various bodies of law. By virtue of being "trained and skilled in the theoretic or scientific parts of a trade or occupation, as distinct from its merely mechanical parts . . . , [one] raises his trade to the dignity of a learned profession" (*Oxford* 2:2316). The expertise or skill of this special kind of profession is thus intellectual in character even if, as in the case of dentistry or surgery, the activity is manual, for it is based on training in the higher learning. Since the nineteenth century this has meant that some kind of formal higher education marks professionals off from other workers, distinguishing both the nature of their training and the nature of their skill. Such education is a basic credential for professionals; it delineates the foundation of their expertise. The distinction has lain at the root of thinking about professions as a special class or category of occupations.

The latter portion of the *Webster's Third* definition suggests a more complex conception of professions. They are not solely occupations whose members are trained in institutions of higher education but also occupations that are organized into special institutions that are thought to influence the conduct and commitment of their members. It refers to more than dignity, prestige, or status and the possession of formal knowledge, implying a process of social control of professional behavior as well as institutions by which that process is carried out.

THE FRUIT OF SEMANTIC AMBIGUITY

I trust that my discussion of the various denotations and connotations attached to the word *profession* and those related to it has shown the contradiction and confusion intrinsic to it in the English language. In one context it refers to high prestige or status and in another to low status. In one usage it is widely inclusive of all occupations, in another broadly exclusive, and in still another narrowly exclusive. In one circumstance of use it implies exalted motives and moral probity, but in another it implies crass motives and deceptiveness. If it is accurate today to say that the public and those who speak for it look on the professions with some ambivalence, it is no less accurate to say that the semantic ambiguity of the word itself both encourages and reflects that ambivalence. Indeed, it is not just the public that has been confused. Scholars and intellectuals have not been immune to the heavy and diverse semantic freight of the word: some of their controversies about professions and professionalization have stemmed as much from emphasis on different connotations and denotations as from issues of fact, logical inference, or analytic concern. Let us look at some of their controversies.

THE ACADEMIC WRITERS

Intellectual interest in the professions has a long tradition in the English-speaking world. Substantial commentary extends back into the nineteenth century. Until the 1940s, the most important voices were British. Late in the nineteenth century no less eminent a scholar than Herbert Spencer (1896) devoted considerable space in his *Principles of Sociology* to showing how various professions function to augment human life by the application of specialized knowledge to human problems and by the practice of artistic skills. Beatrice and Sidney Webb (1917), with the assistance of George Bernard Shaw, devoted themselves to a sustained analysis of the performance of professional associations, which were analyzed as "associations of producers" that might serve as an alternative to capitalism in controlling and organizing work in the public interest. R. H. Tawney (1920) saw so many virtues in the presumed orientation of professionals to serving the public interest that he argued that industry should be professionalized. The monumental volume by E. M. Carr-Saunders and P. A. Wilson (1933) attempted to make a comprehensive analysis and comparison of all the occupations in England that might conceivably be called professions in order to evaluate what they all had in common and how they differed among each other and to assert their positive role in both present and future society. T. H. Marshall's fine essay (1939) represented the culmination of the long British tradition that saw the professions as a hopeful sign of a new altruism that could transform the social and political world of industrial capitalism.

After World War II American academics dominated writing on the professions for some twenty years. (The most frequently cited work from that period is probably Wilensky 1964; Greenwood 1957; Barber 1963; the work of Talcott Parsons [e.g., 1939, 1968] and W. J. Goode Jr. [e.g., 1969]; and W. Moore 1970. The work of Hughes [e.g., 1971] was very important but difficult to classify with the others.) While all those postwar scholars adopted a far more structured, analytic stance toward the professions than that held by their English predecessors, one in consonance with the effort to develop general concepts applicable to more than one historic period or nation, I think it is fair to say that, on the whole, their dominant emphasis was on the special character of the knowledge and skill of the professions and on their special ethical or altruistic orientation toward their clients. This is not to say that they, any more than their predecessors, were mere apologists for the professions. In the writings of virtually all of them we can find overt recognition and criticism of deficiencies in the performance of professions and most particularly of the degree to which economic self-interest rather than the common good can motivate the activities of professionals and their associations. Nonetheless, the general tenor of their analyses has represented professions as honored servants of public need, occupations especially distinguished from others by their orientation to serving the needs of the public through the schooled application of their unusually esoteric and complex knowledge and skill.

In the 1960s, however, a shift in both emphasis and interest developed both in the United States and in the United Kingdom. The mood shifted from one of approval to one of disapproval, from one that emphasized virtue over failings to one that emphasized failings over virtues. The very idea of profession was attacked, implying, if not often stating, that the world would be better off without professions. Furthermore, the substantive preoccupation of the literature changed. In the earlier literature, the major scholarly writings focused primarily on the analysis of professional norms and role relations and on interaction with clients in work settings. While all writers acknowledged the importance of political and economic factors, they did not analyze them at any length. The more recent scholarly literature, on the other hand, focuses on the political and cultural influence of professions (e.g., Freidson 1970), on the relation of professions to political and economic elites and the state (e.g., Johnson 1972), and on the relation of professions to the market and the class system (e.g., Larson 1977).

This shift in evaluation and emphasis was reflected in a shift in conceptualization. The academic sociologists of the 1940s and 1950s were prone to emphasize as the central characteristics of professions their especially complex formal knowledge and skill along with an ethical approach to their work. These and other traits were used to set professions off from other occupations and to justify the protective institutions and high prestige that also distinguished them. Writers from the late 1960s on, however, emphasized instead the unusually effective, monopolistic institutions of professions and their high status as the critical factor and treated knowledge, skill, and ethical orientations not as objective characteristics but rather as ideology, as claims by spokesmen for professions seeking to gain or to preserve status and privilege. The earlier effort to develop an analytically coherent definition of professions was attacked as merely apologetics on behalf of the status quo (e.g., Roth 1974). Indeed, the very enterprise of definition was attacked. Instead of expertise, *power* became the key word for both academic and nonacademic writers on the professions, though it was usually employed in a vague and global manner (e.g., Klegon 1978).

But while there have been significant changes in the evaluative and substantive emphasis of sociological writings on the professions, they are changes only in the content and not in the nature of theorizing. This has been the case even though some of the recent criticism of the traditional approach has been metatheoretical in character. Unfortunately, those metatheoretical critiques have addressed either false issues or issues that are essentially insoluble because of the very nature of the concept of profession itself. For this reason there has not been any significant advance in developing a theory of professions over the past decade or so that does not have as many deficiencies as past theories.

THE PROBLEM OF DEFINITION

Much debate, going back at least as far as Flexner (1915), has centered around how *profession* should be defined—which occupations should be called professions and by what institutional criteria. But while most definitions overlap in the elements, traits, or attributes they include, a number of tallies have demonstrated a persistent lack of consensus about which traits are to be emphasized in theorizing (cf. Millerson 1964, 5). No small part of the criticism of the traditional literature on the professions has been devoted to pointing out a lack of consensus. Because we seem to be no nearer consensus than we were in 1915, and because usage varies substantively, logically, and conceptually (cf. Freidson 1977), some analysts have given the impression of condemning the very practice of seeking a definition. In order to think clearly and systematically about anything, however, one must delimit the subject matter to be addressed by empirical and intellectual analysis. We cannot develop good theory if we are not clear about what we are talking about.

One method of attempting to solve the problem of definition has been to deprecate the value of defining the characteristics of professions as "inherently distinct from other occupations" (Klegon 1978, 268) and to urge instead discussing the process by which occupations claim or gain professional status. The outcome of such a position, however, is to avoid entirely any conscious definition while in fact covertly advancing an implicit and unsatisfactorily vague definition of a profession as an occupation that has gained professional status. What is professional status? How does one determine when such status does or does not exist? What are its characteristics?

A closely related suggestion is to shift from a "static" approach that focuses on the conception of profession as a distinct type of occupation to one that focuses on the process by which occupations are professionalized (e.g., Vollmer and Mills 1966). However, as Turner and Hodge (1970, 23) and Johnson (1972, 31) have correctly noted, an emphasis on process rather than on structure, on professionalization rather than on the attributes of professions, does not really solve the problem of definition. To speak about the process of professionalization requires one to define the direction of the process, to define the end state of professionalism toward which an occupation may be moving. Without some definition of *profession* the concept of professionalization is virtually meaningless, as is the intention to study process rather than structure. One cannot study process without a definition guiding one's focus any more fruitfully than one can study structure without a definition.

Thus the issue of definition for a theory of professions cannot be dealt with profitably either by denial or by avoidance. A word with so many connotations and denotations cannot be employed in precise discourse without definition. One can avoid the issue of definition only if one adopts the patently antianalytical position that all occupations—whether casual day labor, assembly-line work, teaching, surgery, or systems analysis—are so much alike that there is no point in making distinctions of any kind among them. That all forms of work share some common elements of analytic importance cannot be denied. That there are no differences of any analytic importance must be firmly denied.

Given the necessity, one may note that the character of an adequate definition must be such as to specify a set of referents, that is, attributes, traits, or defining characteristics, by which the phenomenon may be discriminated in the empirical world. Unfortunately, there has been a tendency in the recent critical literature to confuse these defining characteristics with the particular characteristics specified by earlier writers. One can criticize a definition because of the analytically and empirically ambiguous traits it singles out (Freidson 1970) or because its traits have no systematic interrelations and no theoretical rationale (Johnson 1972). But it is not the fact that a definition is composed of traits or attributes that can be criticized justifiably.

It would seem, then, that in the present state of theorizing about professions recent comments on the issue of definition miss the mark. The definitional problem that has plagued the field for over half a century is not one created by squabbling pedants, to be solved by eschewing definition entirely. Nor is the problem created by the adoption of a static "structural" or "functional" approach, to be solved by a "process" or "conflict" approach. Nor is the problem created by including traits or attributes in a definition. The problem, I suggest, lies much deeper than that. It is created by attempting to treat *profession* as if it were a generic concept rather than a changing historic concept with particularistic roots in those industrial nations that are strongly influenced by Anglo-American institutions.

THE ANGLO-AMERICAN PROFESSIONS

Occupations called professions in English have had a rather special history. As we all know, the medieval universities of Europe spawned the three original learned professions of medicine, law, and the clergy (of which university teaching was part). Those occupations could be delineated conceptually by the characteristics they shared as a result both of their origin in the universities and of their special status within preindustrial societies in Europe. Elliott (1972, 14, 32) has suggested the term *status professions* for them, pointing out quite accurately their marked difference from the more recent *occupational professions*. Before the nineteenth century, the identity and characteristics of those professions were clear and nonproblematic in both western Europe and in England. As the occupational structure of capitalist industrialism developed during the nineteenth century in a variety of national circumstances, general terminological consensus about the nature and identity of those original "learned," "liberal," or "free" professions was strained and distorted, perhaps, but nevertheless survived down to our day.

In England, however, and then later in the United States, terminological consensus became greatly confused by the efforts of newly reorganized or newly formed middle-class occupations to seek the title *profession* because it was connected with the prestigious gentlemanly status of the traditional learned professions rather than with the lowly trades and could therefore dignify the trades so denominated (cf. Reader 1967; Larson 1977). The aim and strategies of those occupational movements to organize and gain respectability by being recognized as professions perforce took shape within the specific national history and political economy of England and, later, the United States. While there were very important differences between the two nations, they had in common a market economy, a comparatively passive and decentralized state apparatus with a strong but by no means unambivalent laissez-faire philosophy, and a small civil service.

Occupations seeking a secure and privileged place in the economy of those countries could not do more than seek state support for an exclusionary shelter in the market in which they had to compete with rival occupations. They had to organize their own training and credentialing institutions since the state played a passive role in such affairs. Unlike other countries, the title *profession* was used to establish the status of successful occupations; it became part of the official occupational classification scheme in the United States and in England, expanding its coverage slowly by including more occupations in the same category, with the same title, as the original status professions of the medieval universities (cf. Reader 1967, 146–66, 207–11; and see Davies 1980). Gaining recognition as a "profession" was important to occupations not only because it was associated with traditional gentry status but also because its traditional connotations of disinterested dedication and learning provided political legitimation for the effort to gain protection from competition in the labor market. Given laissez-faire philosophy, only quite special excuses could justify the state-sanctioned creation of a market shelter. The ideologies of "higher" learning and moral probity provided by the traditional concept of status profession, sustained by occupational institutions, and advanced in the political arena by occupational associations provided just such a basis for legitimating protection.

In England and the United States the tendency was for each occupation to have to mount its own movement for recognition and protection. Its members' loyalties and identities were attached to their individual occupation and its institutions. The situation was much different in continental Europe: there the state was much more active in organizing both training and employment, although, as Konrád and Szelényi (1979) rightly noted, the system was by no means monolithic, its structure depending on whether the political economy involved was capitalist or not. The traditional status professions of medicine and law maintained their occupational distinctiveness in Europe as they reorganized their associations and workplaces, but the new, middle-class occupations of Europe did not seek classification as *professions* to gain status and justify a market shelter: such an umbrella title imputing special institutional characteristics to them was not employed to distinguish them (cf. Hughes 1971, 387–88). Rather, their status and security were gained by their attendance at state-controlled, elite institutions of higher education, which assured them elite positions in the civil service or other technical-managerial positions. Their economic protection lay in sinecures in bureaucratic organizations, not in a privileged competitive position in the labor marketplace.

In nineteenth-century Russia and Poland, merely to be a graduate of a *gymnasium* was what was important, not one's occupation (Gella 1976). In Germany, what was important was to be a university graduate, an *Akademiker* (Reuschemeyer 1973, 63–122; Ringer 1979, 411). In France, one's fortunes flowed from attending one of the *grandes écoles* (e.g., Ben-David 1977, 38–46; Suleiman 1978). Primary identity was given not by occupation but by the status and connections gained by elite education no matter what the particular specialty. As Ben-David noted for France, "the technically competent . . . whom the [*grandes écoles*] system was . . . designed to produce . . . do not primarily identify themselves by their professional qualifications, but by their employment. If they are in private practice, they tend to consider themselves part of the *bourgeois entrepreneur* class, and if they are salaried, they consider themselves officials of a certain rank, rather than chemists or engineers" (Ben-David 1977, 46). This is a far cry from Anglo-American professions, which gain their distinction and position in the marketplace less from the prestige of the institutions in which they were educated than from the substance of their particular training and their identity as credentialed members of particular, corporately organized occupations to which specialized knowledge, ethicality, and importance to society are imputed by influential members of the polity.

From this discussion we can see that profession can be more

than an occupation with prestige attached to it because of its formal knowledge. It can also be an occupation that has special forms of protection from competition in capitalist labor markets, one that benefits from a "social closure" (Parkin 1979), "sinecures" (Collins 1979), or "labor market shelters" (Freidson 1983). This protection can vary in its source and in its strength, with different outcomes for members of what are nominally the same occupations in different countries (cf. Orzack 1978; Johnson 1973). In the United States, and probably to a lesser extent in the United Kingdom, the means lie primarily in political activity on the part of occupational associations that seek to organize a loyal membership identified with the occupation itself and that negotiate with the state for the official support of market shelters for that occupation (cf. Gilb 1966). The institutions connected with that enterprise and the nature of the shelters themselves vary in their relative importance between those two nations. The Anglo-American pattern taken together varies even more from that of European nations with more centralized governments that take considerably more initiative in shaping the shelters. In turn, all capitalist nations taken together vary in many important ways from the process of shelter formation in the state socialist countries of eastern Europe, where the stability, substance, and strength of the occupational interests of the "working intelligentsia" are significantly different (cf. Konrád and Szelényi 1979).

All in all, I would argue that, as a concept capable of dealing with more than prestige and the fact of formal knowledge, with the way professionals can gain a living, and with the institutions that shape the way they gain a living, *profession* must be used in a specific historical and national sense. It is not a scientific concept generalizable to a wide variety of settings. Rather, to use Turner's epithet, it is a historically and nationally specific "folk concept" (Becker 1970, 92).

The Phenomenology of Profession

If *profession* may be described as a folk concept, then the research strategy appropriate to its investigation is phenomenological in character. One attempts to determine not so much what a profession is in an absolute sense as how people in a society determine who is a professional and who is not, how they "make" or "accomplish" professions by their activities, and what the consequences are for the way in which they see themselves and perform their work. This is not, however, a simple undertaking, for we cannot realistically assume that there is a holistic folk that produces only one folk concept of profession in societies as complex as ours. What a profession is phenomenologically, then, is not determined solely by any single group—neither by members of an occupation, nor by those of the other occupations they deal with in the course of their work, nor by their clients or employers, nor by sociologists, nor by the state. There are a number of different perspectives, no one of which may be thought to be better grounded, phenomenologically, than any other. If this be granted, then it follows that there is no way of resolving the problem of defining *profession* that is not arbitrary.

However, while there are a number of different perspectives in a society, some are more consequential than others if only because they stem from positions of substantial political and economic power. While they are not authoritative in any ultimate epistemological or scientific sense, they are authoritative in the pragmatic sense of setting the legal, political, and economic limits within which everyday professional work can go on reasonably securely and of guiding the provision of the political and economic resources without which the circumstances and opportunities for work cannot exist. Though such pragmatically authoritative "definitions" are themselves negotiated and changed by the efforts of organized occupational groups and other agencies and thus are not so rigid and stable as the terms *official* and *formal* imply to the naive, they cannot be dismissed as somehow less legitimate than those of other elements of the society. They in fact represent the official legitimacy of the present, something those concerned with a different conception of profession try to change in order for their conception to be legitimized.

It is for this reason that I choose to focus in this book on the formal or official conceptions of profession and on the formal institutions that sustain and elaborate them. I shall not impose on them any academic conception of profession thought to be more scientific or intellectually elegant. Rather I shall try to distill out of the concrete materials expressing those conceptions what seems to be their essential character and then go on to connect those conceptions to the circumstances under which professionals work to gain their living and to those features of professional organization that are in interaction with the legislators and jurists who create and clarify official conceptions. By this means I hope to establish a foundation of description and analysis that will allow me to delineate the varied powers that it is possible for the professions to exercise. Given the national and historical variation in conceptions of profession and in the institutions sustaining and realizing them, it follows that I shall focus on one time in one country—namely, on the past few decades in the United States. Some of what I deal with no doubt has relevance to other times and other nations, but to draw that out systematically is a task I shall not undertake here.

Identifying Professions in the United States

Given the strategy of focusing on official conceptions of profession, it follows that professions will be identified by reference to official sources. In the United States, the major source of information about the professions in the labor force is the Bureau of the Census. Virtually anyone who wishes to learn anything about the kinds of professions that exist, the number of professions, the number of members each has, their members' education, income, and employment status, and the like must use the decennial census or the Current Population Survey for national statistics. Without these sources, one is at the mercy of anecdote and personal impression. Those agencies collect, collate, and publish what is taken to be official knowledge about the professions and other occupations in the labor force.

However, it is apparent to anyone familiar with the census that, while it represents the only available source of information that is at all comprehensive, even if imperfectly so, it is a frail vessel. Its classificatory system has changed from decade to decade, so that occupations classified as professions in one census may not be so classified in another. And in any single decade, the collection of occupations included in any single category, including the category *profession*, may not seem to be reasonably homogeneous. Patently, what is needed for us to be able to make better use of such a frail vessel are studies of the history of occupational nomenclature—some small movement toward which has only just begun (cf. Scoville 1965; Katz 1972; Derosieres n.d.; Sharlin 1979; Conk 1978—and, in the present context, studies of the category of profession itself and of how and why it has changed over the past century (cf. Reader 1967; Davies 1980; and for some relevant absurdities in the 1940 census, see Halliday 1949, 531). But here, all I can do is to use—albeit cautiously—what is available. Let me turn to that task in the next chapter, in which I shall take a close look at the content of the relevant census categories to see if it is possible to use them as an empirical representation of a "professional class."

References

Barber, B. 1963. Some problems in the sociology of the professions. *Daedalus* 92 (Fall): 669–88.

Becker, H. S. 1970. The nature of a profession. In *Sociological work*, edited by H. S. Becker, 87–103. Chicago: Aldine Publishing Co.

Ben-David, J. 1977. *Centers of learning: Britain, France, Germany, United States*. New York: McGraw-Hill Book Co.

Carr-Saunders, E. M., and P. A. Wilson. 1933. *The professions*. Oxford: Clarendon Press.

Collins, R. 1979. *The credential society*. New York: Academic Press.

Conk, M. A. 1978. Occupational classification in the United States census: 1870–1940. *Journal of Interdisciplinary History* 9 (Summer): 111–30.

Davies, C. 1980. Making sense of the census in Britain and the U.S.A. *Sociological Review* 28 (August): 581–609.

Derosieres, A. n.d. Elements pour l'histoire des nomenclatures socio-professionelles. In *Pour un histoire de la statistique*, vol. 1, edited by F. Bédarida et al., 155–94. Paris: Institut National de la Statistique et des Etudes Economiques.

Elliott, P. 1972. *The sociology of the professions*. London: Macmillan Press.

Flexner, A. 1915. Is social work a profession? *School and society* 1:901–911.

Freidson, E. 1970. *Profession of medicine*. New York: Dodd, Mead & Co.

————. 1977. The futures of professionalization, 14–38. In *Health and the division of labor*, edited by M. Stacey, M. Reid, C. Heath, and R. Dingwall. London: Croon Helm.

————. 1983. Occupational autonomy and labor market shelters. In *Varieties of work*, edited by P. L. Stewart and M. G. Cantor, 39–54. Beverly Hills, Calif.: Sage Publications.

Gella, A. 1976. An introduction to the sociology of the intelligentsia. In *The intelligentsia and the intellectuals: Theory, method and case study*, edited by A. Gella, 9–34. London: Sage Publications.

Gilb, C. L. 1966. *Hidden hierarchies: The professions and government*. New York: Harper & Row.

Goode, W. J., Jr. 1969. The theoretical limits of professionalization. In *The semi-professions and their organization*, edited by A. Etzioni, 266–313. New York: Free Press.

Greenwood, E. 1957. Attributes of a profession. *Social Work* 2:45–55.

Halliday, R. W. 1949. Problems involved in the classification of professional occupations. *Occupations* 27 (May): 530–34.

Hughes, E. C. 1971. *The sociological eye*. Chicago: Aldine Publishing Co.

Johnson, T. 1972. *Professions and power*. London: Macmillan Press.

————. 1973. Imperialism and the professions: Notes on the development of professional occupations in Britain's colonies and the new states. *Sociological Review Monograph* 20:281–309.

Katz, M. B. 1972. Occupational classification in history. *Journal of Interdisciplinary History* 3 (Summer): 63–88.

Klegon, D. 1978. The sociology of professions. *Sociology of Work and Occupations* 5: 259–83.

Konrád, G., and I. Szelényi. 1979. *The intellectuals on the road to class power*. New York: Harcourt Brace Jovanovich.

Larson, M. S. 1977. *The rise of professionalism*. Berkeley: University of California Press.

Marshall, T. H. 1939. The recent history of professionalism in relation to social structure and social policy. *Canadian Journal of Economics and Political Science* 5 (August): 325–40.

Millerson, G. 1964. *The qualifying associations*. London: Routledge & Kegan Paul.

Moore, W. E. 1970. *The profession: Roles and rules*. New York: Russell Sage Foundation.

Orzack, L. 1978. *Professions in different national societies*. Paper presented at the Ninth World Congress of Sociology, Uppsala, Sweden.

Oxford English Dictionary. 1971. Vol. 2, compact ed. New York: Oxford University Press.

Parkin, F. 1979. *Marxism and class theory*. New York: Columbia University Press.

Parsons, T. 1939. The professions and social structure. *Social Forces* 17:457–67.

————. 1968. Professions. In *International encyclopedia of the social sciences*, vol. 12, edited by D. Sills, 536–47. New York: Macmillan Publishing Co. and Free Press.

Reader, W. J. 1967. *Professional men: The rise of the professional classes in nineteenth-century England*. New York: Basic Books.

Reuschemeyer, D. 1973. *Lawyers and their society*. Cambridge, Mass.: Harvard University Press.

Ringer, F. K. 1979. The German academic community. In *The organization of knowledge in modern America 1860–1920*. edited by A. Oleson and J. Voss, 409–429. Baltimore: Johns Hopkins University Press.

Roth, J. A. 1974. Professionalism: The sociologist's decoy. *Sociology of Work and Occupations* 1:6–23.

Scoville, J. G. 1965. The development and relevance of U.S. occupational data. *Industrial and Labor Relations* 19:70–79.

Sharlin, A. 1979. From the study of social mobility to the study of society. *American Journal of Sociology. 85:338–60.*

Spencer, H. 1896. *Principles of sociology*, vol. 3, pt. 7, Professional Institutions, 179–324. New York: Appleton & Co.

Suleiman, E. N. 1978. *Elites in French society*. Princeton, N.J.: Princeton University Press.

Tawney, R. H. 1920. *The acquisitive society*. New York: Harcourt Brace.

Turner, G., and M. N. Hodge. 1970. Occupations and professions. In *Professions and professionalization*, edited by J. A. Jackson, 19–50. Cambridge: Cambridge University Press.

Veysey, L. R. 1965. *The emergence of the American university*. Chicago: University of Chicago Press.

Vollmer, H. W., and D. J. Mills, eds. 1966. *Professionalization*. Englewood Cliffs, N.J.: Prentice-Hall, Inc.

Webb, S., and B. Webb. 1917. Special supplement on professional associations, Parts 1, 2. *New Statesman* 9, no. 211 (April 21): 1–24; 9, no. 212 (April 28): 25–48.

Webster's Third New International Dictionary of the English Language Unabridged. 1967. Vol. 2. Springfield, Mass.: G. & C. Merrian Co.

Wilensky, H. L. 1964. The professionalization of everyone? *American Journal of Sociology* 70 (September): 137–58.

Chapter Three

The Category *Profession*

In chapter 1, I indicated that many terms have been used to single out the agents of formal knowledge and argued for the usefulness of the concept of profession in identifying those agents both because of their presumed training in the higher learning and because, unlike those individuals referred to by the other terms, they imply a set of institutions that allows us to connect them and their formal knowledge to the political economy. By focusing on those agents, I argued, one is considerably more likely to be able to trace the relationship between formal knowledge and power by examining the ways concrete professional institutions are constituted and operate than by trying to trace the fortunes of selected and ill-defined groups of intellectuals with no visible means of support or by trying to examine the massive stratum of the intelligentsia. The problem is how to identify professions as a group, and there I noted the scholarly controversies surrounding definition and specification and argued that resolution is unlikely to occur. Taking only the traditional status professions, the differences between medicine and law are very great, and they are in turn quite different from university teaching, the ministry, and the military. Add architecture, dentistry, accounting, and engineering, among the older occupational professions, and one can argue that the differences among them are too great to allow generalization. Indeed, part of the course of disagreement among scholars about the attributes to be used in defining *profession* arose from the fact of those differences. Scholarly controversy, however, has not succeeded in discouraging others from the use of *profession* as a social category or folk concept. Indeed, controversy among scholars specializing in the study of the professions has either not penetrated to or, if it has, not discouraged other scholars concerned with broader issues like the class system of modern society. Some have seen higher education (if not necessarily the formal knowledge one might assume is its product) as the key to the formation of a "new class" that has a special position in the class system of advanced societies.

PROFESSIONS AND THE NEW CLASS

There are a number of different orientations underlying the idea of a new class. The first to become concerned with the possibility that a new kind of middle class was developing was Emil Lederer early in this century (for sketch of Lederer's work, see Bell 1976, 69–72). Subsequent development of the idea involved the notion that the old middle class of the nineteenth century, which was composed largely of small businessmen and members of traditional status professions like law and medicine, was being supplanted, or at least pushed aside, by a rising new middle class composed of salaried members of the administrative or managerial staff, the specialized professions, and, depending on the writer, the clerical and technical staffs of large public and private organizations (for historical sketches of the development of the notion, see Mills 1951; Crozier 1971, 21–40; and Giddens 1973, 177–97).

At its broadest the new class is an undifferentiated, broad white-collar class, its members sharing only its ostensibly "clean" work. That is essentially the way Mills (1951) conceived of it. At its narrowest in present-day writings it is conceived of as composed solely of intellectuals who are professionals in the arts, journalism, and academia and of others involved in government regulatory and welfare activities (for a delineation of how major notions of the new class vary in their inclusiveness, see Brint 1984). Historians who have used the idea have similarly differed in their conceptions of the class, Lasch (1979) apparently including only some academics and the personal service professions and Bledstein (1976) including everyone, including baseball players, who may be said to hold a "culture of professionalism" that is oriented toward careerism and mobility (cf. Lederer's discussion of the "life rhythms" of the civil servant in Bell 1976, 70; and for a cogent critique of historians' use of the idea of profession, see Veysey

1975). On the whole, as Bell put it, it is a "muddled concept" (Bell 1979).

It is my opinion that, even though new class theory is very much alive today, C. Wright Mills's comments on its status made more than thirty-five years ago are still accurate and deserve quoting:

These various arguments are difficult to compare, first of all because they do not all include the same occupations under the catchword, 'new middle class.' When we consider the vague boundary lines of the white-collar world, we can easily understand why such an occupational salad invites so many conflicting theories and why general images of it are likely to differ. . . . At given times, different theorists in pursuit of bolstering data have spotlighted one or the other groups composing the total. So contrasting images of the political role of the white-collar people can readily exist side by side [and perhaps both be correct]. Those, for instance, who believe that as the vanguard stratum of modern society they are slated to be the next ruling class do not think of them as ten-cent store clerks, insurance agents and stenographers, but rather as higher technicians and staff engineers, as salaried managers of business cartels and big officials of the Federal Government. On the other hand, those who hold that they are being proletarianized do focus upon the mass of clerklings and sales people. . . . Their views are based not on an examination of this [entire white collar] stratum as much as on, first, the political program they happen to be following; second, the doctrinal position . . . they have previously accepted; and third, their judgment in regard to the main course of the twentieth-century industrial society. [Mills 1951, 291–92]

My task here is not to debate new class theory, though I think that by clarifying the problem of identifying the professions as a group or class and of delineating and analyzing their institutions I can introduce some useful cautions into the debate. What I wish to note here is that in virtually all conceptions of the new class at least some professions figure as prominent members and that in most conceptions they are central members of the new class. That European analysts do not make much reference to professions or dismiss tham as part of the anachronistic petite bourgeoisie (cf. Carchedi 1975;

Poulantzas 1975) I would explain by a reminder of the different character of the professions on the Continent and of the different connotations emphasized in the word itself in other languages than English. In Anglo-American writings, however, one cannot deny the importance of professions to new class theorists.

How is it possible to speak of the professions collectively, as a category if not a class? Scholars are in sufficient disagreement about definition that they differ in the occupations they would include as professions and those they would exclude. However, the official category of the U.S. census does exist as a social reality and, what is more, forms the framework for the collection of comprehensive empirical information about the labor force in the United States and the delineation of those occupations that taken together are classified as professions. By its decision to include some occupations as professions and to exclude others it presents us with an official categorical portrait of professions. For those new class theorists who are concerned with determining who are members of the new class and how they are distributed through the labor force, the census provides an official collation and classification for the nation. Can it be used to represent the professions productively? Obviously, since it *is* used, we should know more about it in any case. But by examining what some new class theorists postulate to be important about a class in which professions are prominent we can also generate some criteria by which to evaluate the intellectual usefulness of the category. Let me sketch two interesting and related new class theories, show what issues they are concerned with in considering professions an important part of the new class, and then go on to examine the relevant census categories in sufficient detail to appraise their usefulness in representing the issues. This will lead me to conclude by suggesting the criteria by which I shall identify the social category *professions* in the chapters to follow.

TWO THEORIES

Two related versions of new class theory employ the U.S. census as a source for identifying the members of that class and estimating their number in the labor force. I refer to the notion of the "Professional-Managerial Class" created by the Ehrenreichs (Ehrenreich and Ehrenreich 1977a, 1977b) and the notion of the "New Class" of intellectuals and technical intelligentsia created by the late Alvin Gouldner (1979). First the Ehrenreichs.

After reviewing some of the efforts at defining the new middle class by previous Marxian writers, the Ehrenreichs advance the notion of the Professional-Managerial Class, so named in order to signal the exclusion of sales and clerical workers, who are classified by them with the working class, and in order to avoid confusion with the old middle class of self-employed professionals, tradesmen, farmers, and the like. The Professional-Managerial Class is seen to have been created by a process that began in the last half of the nineteenth century. According to the Ehrenreichs' theory, the capitalist class sought to quell working-class unrest by improving its methods of control of workers in both the workplace and the community. It supported the development of science, engineering, education, and health and welfare services toward that end. This meant encouraging the growth of occupations to staff the activities of such services. Thus the extraordinary growth in number and importance of such workers as teachers, social workers, engineers, nurses, lower- and middle-level managers, journalists, advertising personnel, experts in child rearing, truant officers, city planners, writers, accountants, lawyers, and physicians, who, among others, compose the Professional-Managerial Class.

That class cannot be considered part of the working class because, even though it is salaried by the capitalists, as is the working class, and thus in an objective position of antagonism to them, it can exist "only by virtue of the expropriation of the skills and culture once indigenous to the working class" (Ehrenreich and Ehrenreich 1977a, 17) and by exercising control over the working class in the interest of the status quo. It is neither working nor capitalist class, those professionals and managers in it having in common both their structural position between capital and labor and their common function of organizing the means of production and reproducing the class relations of capitalism.

The typical way in which the occupations of the Professional-Managerial Class are organized is as professions that claim commitment to public service and possession of an esoteric body of specialized formal knowledge and that seek freedom from evaluation and control by others. But since specialization is divisive, the occupations of the class are not unified by their class position and do not act as a class. The deepest division is between managers and administrators who are tied to business and industry and professionals providing personal services. That division is easy to overemphasize, however, for both managers and professionals partake of higher education, and their children tend to go to college together and to intermarry. Members of the class have a common life-style, part of which is rooted in anxiety about assuring that their children gain "decent" jobs under circumstances in which jobs can no longer be directly inherited.

Finally, it is essential to note the conflicting interests of the Professional-Managerial Class. On the one hand, its dependence on the capitalist class for its employment creates antagonism; so also is antagonism to capitalism created because the efforts of members of the class to rationalize and reform their work is frustrated by "capitalist greed, irrationality and social irresponsibility" (Ehrenreich and Ehrenreich 1977b, 7). On the other hand, since, "in daily life, its function is the direct or indirect management and manipulation of working-class life—at home, at work, at school" (ibid., 7–8), it also has an antagonistic relationship to the working class. "Their actual attitudes often mix hostility toward the capitalist class with elitism toward the working class" (ibid., 8).

A related conception of the Professional-Managerial Class was elaborated by Alvin Gouldner in *The Future of the Intellectuals and the Rise of the New Class* (1979). While he refers to the New Class instead of to the Professional-Managerial Class and attempts to make his argument relevant to Europe as well as to the United States (and relevant as well to much broader theoretical interests), he emphasizes the importance of the role of the ideology of professionalism and the demand for professional autonomy as a central characteristic of the class. The members of the New Class constitute a class by virtue of the formal knowledge that they gained from their higher education and on which they depend for their living in the marketplace. He also emphasizes the commitment of that class to developing its technical and intellectual skills and producing worthy goods and services, which is its own "cultural capital" and which creates one part of its antagonism to traditional capital. While it is the class that performs technical services for capital and that legitimizes contemporary social arrangements as modern and scientific, it also as a class resists its subordination and seeks greater control over the institutions in which it works in order to advance its own material and ideological interests. Indeed, one of its basic strategies is to cultivate political alliances with the working class in order to institute a "welfare" or "socialist" state.

Gouldner elaborates the Ehrenreichs' reference to the education and life-style of this class, discussing its education as its "capital" and its ideology as an assertion of the social value of science and technology—that is, of the formal knowledge obtained from its education. He characterizes its cultural capital as "the culture of careful and critical discourse," which constitutes the rules of argument and evidence that underly and unify all the various technical specialties (and their language) that ostensibly divide the members of the class. In his view, this careful and critical discourse serves as a common bond between the humanistic intellectuals and the technical intelligentsia, creating a special solidarity that makes it possible to participate in a common life-style, share the same social circles, and the like. Considerable attention is paid to the role of public education—elementary, secondary, and most especially higher education—in secularizing students and otherwise inculcating critical discourse and the attitudes that go with it.

These are the essentials of the theories advanced by the Ehrenreichs and Gouldner identifying a new class of which professionals are an important part. I have not done their theories full justice because I am concerned not so much with new class theory as with the identification of the actors the theory deals with and the analysis of their institutions. Identification is a prerequisite to singling out their supportive institutions for analysis. Both theories are far more interesting and provocative than my account may imply, and both are concerned with a different problem—namely, how to sort and characterize shifting political currents in a time when past conceptions of the class system have come to seem inadequate to the task. This summary exposition, however, should give a reasonable idea of the social, attitudinal, and experiential characteristics they single out so that we can turn to the census categories to see how the occupations included in them may be seen to share them.

IDENTIFYING THE NEW CLASS IN THE CENSUS

In their efforts to estimate the size of the new class, the Ehrenreichs apparently employed census data on the *professional, technical, and kindred worker* and the *managers and administrators, except farm* categories. They did not indicate how they arrived at their conclusion when they estimated the Professional-Managerial Class to constitute close to 25 percent of the U.S. labor force. It appears, however, that they combined the numbers in the two categories, for taken together, the two constitute 23 percent of the *experienced civilian labor force 16 years and older* in the 1970 census, to which they had access when writing their essay. Gouldner implicitly endorsed this method by citing the Ehrenreich's estimate of the size of the Professional-Managerial Class and by reproducing it in his essay.

It is true that the criterion of specialized knowledge and skill as such is not at the bottom of new class theories, for specialization may be divisive and fragmenting rather than unifying, Durkheim notwithstanding. Rather, at the bottom is the fact of higher education, which, even though permeated with specialized training, can be seen as a common cultural experience of some significance to one's outlook on the world and one's place in it. And this is what a great many writers have been concerned with in connecting the new class with political attitudes that may underly political alignments of segments of the population that influence the shape of the future of industrial societies. For example, the question is whether they have common attitudes toward the redistribution of income so as to increase equality, whether they are more or less permissive toward civil liberties, and the like. (For a thorough review of the evidence on differences in political attitudes, see Brint 1985.) Even though it is higher education in general that is at the bottom of the matter, however, many writers employ professional and managerial occupations as an index of such education, and some, like the Ehrenreichs and Gouldner, employ the official census categories as the source of delineating professionals and managers.

In order to justify the use of those census categories as empirical representations of special types of occupations, one must establish that important homogeneity exists among the occupations in them. And in order to do that one must look closely at the individual characteristics of those occupations, something that apparently none of those who use either the categories or the occupational titles included in them to represent the new middle class has done. Both for the information a close look yields and for discerning the problems of identifying a consequential category *profession*, let us do so now. Since virtually all the writers I comment on use data from the 1970 census, it is obviously inappropriate to evaluate their referents by examining the recently available 1980 census, and in any case the categories of the 1980 census do not vary very much from those used in 1970.

THE OFFICIAL CATEGORY "MANAGERS AND ADMINISTRATORS"

Since new class theorists are concerned with managers and administrators as much as with professionals, some to show their commonalities and some to show their differences, it is useful to understand what is included in the broad census category representing them. Perhaps it is more important to know what is included in the category in the light of the argument I shall make in later chapters—namely, that some administrative and managerial positions are mandated to members of professions and must be classified as professions. They are a function of professions' efforts to preserve their control by using their own members to mediate between practitioners and the surrounding social environment. Let us begin by examining the content of the 1970 census category *managers and administrators*, employing an asterisk (*) to identify those occupations in the category that are large enough to include more than 100,000 people.

Assessors, controllers, and treasurers, local public administration

* Bank officers and financial managers

Buyers and shippers, farm products

* Buyers, wholesale and retail trade

Credit men

Funeral directors

Health administrators

Construction inspectors, public administration

Managers and superintendents, building

Officers, pilots and pursers, ship

* Officials and administrators, public administration not elsewhere classified

Officials of lodges, societies, and unions [and professional associations]

Postmasters and mail superintendents

* Purchasing agents and buyers not elsewhere classified

Railroad conductors

* Restaurant, cafeteria, and bar managers

* Sales managers, except retail trade

School administrators, college

* School administrators, elementary and secondary

* Managers and administrators not elsewhere classified, salaried, subdivided by industry

* Managers and administrators not elsewhere classified, self-employed, subdivided by industry

Close scrutiny of this list is sufficient in and of itself to lead to doubt that the general category *managers and administrators* is sufficiently homogeneous to sustain generalization. But for the skeptical, more detailed examination of the characteristics of the occupations should be persuasive.

The *Occupational Outlook Handbook* (U.S. Department of Labor 1978) presents the official picture of several hundred American occupations, a picture that seems to emphasize the positive and ideal characteristics of those occupations more than it does the actual norm. For most occupations, it describes the nature of the work performed, the places of employment, training and other qualifications required for employment and advancement, the employment outlook, average earnings, and working conditions. Not all occupations named by the census are included in it, but for those that are it is instructive to compare them to each other. Let us examine the "usual," though probably overstated, educational requirements and the range of salaries (1976) for those occupations discussed in the *Handbook*.

> *Bank officers and financial managers*: Generally requires a liberal arts degree from a four-year college. $800–$900 per month was the starting salary in 1976, with a B.A. The annual salary range was from $9,600 to $28,800.
>
> *Buyers, wholesale and retail trade*: High school, trade school, junior college, and four-year college training are all possible qualifications for employment, depending on the industry and the firm, the annual salary range running between $15,000 and $25,000 in 1976.
>
> *Purchasing agents*: "No universal educational requirements for entry-level jobs," but most large companies now require a college degree and prefer applicants with an M.A. in business administration, small companies having more variable requirements. Salary range, $9,300 to $50,000.
>
> *Restaurant, cafeteria, and bar managers*: The *Handbook* addresses only the more specialized *hotel manager and assistants*. Experience is the most important qualification for employment. Where formal education is relevant, junior college, technical institutes, and the rare B.A. program in hotel and restaurant administration are equally useful qualifications. No salary information.

As we can see merely from this small selection of those of the occupations in the official category for which we have data, there is great variation in the type and amount of education required for entry and great variation in income. The *Handbook*, in commenting in general on "administrative jobs," states that "nearly all administrative jobs require a college degree, although employers vary in the specific area of study they prefer. Some seek business administration or liberal arts graduates; others want a background in a technical area such as engineering or science" (U.S. Department of Labor 1978,

130). We should note, however, that even this broad and varied educational requirement by employers is not likely to hold true for self-employed managers and administrators who made up 14 percent of *managers and administrators* in 1970 and about 25 percent of *managers and administrators not elsewhere classified*. Even among top executives, ranging from vice-presidents to chief executive officers in 1979, with an average annual salary of $134,500, only 25 percent had an M.B.A. (The organization man 1980, 96). Higher education is in fact a far less marked characteristic of the managerial occupations in this category than it is for those in the professional category (Ginzberg 1979).

Turning from the limited number of occupations discussed in the *Handbook* to the larger number in the census category, we may note that, of all the occupations listed in the census category, very few had training or educational requirements that were mandatory—that is, requirements other than at the option of the employer's or customer's preference for filling a job. Funeral directors require licenses in the vast majority of the states, though higher education is not a necessary qualification. Ship's officers also require licenses, but no standard educational requirements exist for them either. It is in the census classification *professional, technical, and kindred workers* that a far greater proportion of occupations are licensed, certified, registered, or otherwise distinguished by specific credentials that are considerably less dependent on the employer's or customer's variable preference in filling positions. It is also a considerably more populous category; in the 1970 census it was almost double the size of the *managers and administrators* category. But it too contains great variation in educational requirements for entry to the occupations and, as we shall see, in prestige and income.

OFFICIAL CATEGORY "PROFESSIONAL, TECHNICAL, AND KINDRED WORKERS"

Let us examine the occupations included in the category, again employing an asterisk to distinguish those that had 100,000 or more members and indicating educational requirements where information is available from the *Occupational Outlook Handbook*.

* *Accountants*: In 1976, about one-third were CPAs or CIAs, most of whom had college training. Qualifications of the remaining two-thirds are far more variable.

  Architects: All states require a license, but many architects work without a license. Most states accept experience in lieu of higher education.

* *Computer specialists*: (Includes *programmers and systems analysts.) Higher education is not a requirement, though most have it.

* *Engineers*: Bachelor's degree acceptable for beginning job.

  Farm management advisers: No information.

  Foresters and conservationists: B.A. necessary with a major in forestry and conservation.

  Home management advisers: Degree necessary.

* *Lawyers and judges*: Degree usually necessary.

* *Librarians, archivists, and curators*: Professional library degree necessary in large organizations and libraries, but these employ a distinct minority of all librarians. A large proportion need meet no degree requirements.

  Mathematical specialists: (Includes actuaries and statisticians.) B.A. with major required.

* *Life and physical acientists*: Degree necessary.

  Operations and systems researchers and analysts: No information available.

* *Personnel and labor relations workers*: College important but not necessary.

* *Physicians, dentists, and related practitioners*: (Includes chiropractors, optometrists, *pharmacists, podiatrists and veterinarians.) Higher education required for all.

* *Registered nurses, dietitians, and therapists*: B.A. required for dietitians but not for others.

* *Health technologists and technicians*: (Includes *clinical laboratory technologists [B.A. necessary] and technicians, dental hygienists [vocational school required], health record technologists and technicians [two years of college required], radiologic

technologists and technicians [two years of college required], and therapy assistants [two years of college or vocational school or on-the-job training].)

* *Religious workers*: Denominational postsecondary education required, save for fundamentalists.
* *Social scientists*: Higher education required.
* *Social and recreation workers*: Social work degrees required for some but not all (e.g., social work aides).
* *Teachers, college and university*: Higher education required.
* *Teachers, except college and university*: Higher education required.
* *Engineering and science technicians*: Subdivided by a variety of criteria. Includes *draftsmen (high school, two-year college, or vocational school) and surveyors (high school, two- and four-year college, and vocational schools).
* *Technicians*: Except health, engineering, and science. Includes air-line pilots, air traffic controllers, embalmers, flight engineers, radio operators, and tool programmers, for none of whom is higher education required.
* *Vocational and educational counselors*: No standard requirements.
* *Writers, artists, and entertainers*: Includes actors, athletes and kindred workers, authors, dancers, *designers, *editors and reporters, musicians and composers, *painters and sculptors, photographers, public relations and publicity writers, radio and television announcers, very few of which have higher educational requirements.
* *Research workers*: Not specified.

The data on these occupations are not complete. Furthermore, the occupational titles themselves include too many different circumstances of work to allow sensible generalization about educational requirements except when licensing, certification, registration, and other formal criteria are involved. And many occupational titles mask important variations within the general occupation—as *accountants* includes about one-third who must meet explicit training or examination standards, while two-thirds need not. The census category is clearly very heterogeneous. Insofar as formal general education is a prerequisite at all, only high school is required for some, like airline pilots. For others trade or vocational school without any connection with liberal arts institutions of higher education is required, as is the case for embalmers, drafters, artists, and entertainers. For still others simply prior experience is required, as is nominally the case for athletes even though in some sports many players go through college on the way to joining "professional" teams, and for others two-year "associate" degrees in vocational programs that may or may not be connected with colleges or universities are required, as is the case for dental hygienists, surveyors, and therapy assistants. For others a four-year liberal arts college degree with or without a vocational major is required, while for still others a graduate professional program following the liberal arts degree is required. In the vast majority of cases, even though there is licensing, certification, or registration, such alternatives to formal higher education as extensive work experience are available, with an examination serving as the arbiter of qualification: this is the case, for example, for lawyers, vocational counselors, and architects.

It is true that, taken as an aggregate, the occupations assigned to this category do produce an average education that is higher than any other if only because the substantial number for whom some graduate education is standard raises the average for the entire aggregate. However, the average level of higher education of an aggregate cannot be used sensibly without reference to the range of variation, for the question is what the members of this category have in common, what they share. To speak of them even loosely as a group requires them to have enough education in common to make it plausible that they have, in Gouldner's terms, a common way of looking at and responding to the world outside the narrow and specialized confines of their work—a "culture of careful and critical discourse." On the sheerly mechanical ground of the degree of exposure each has to higher education, this is very dubious. If such a common culture as Gouldner describes exists, surely it is likely to be restricted only to those with extensive exposure to higher education. I estimate that only half of all those people to be found in this category have had a minimum of four years of college.

The same may be said for other criteria delineating strata and classes. It is true that the range of average income in this category is not as wide as that in the labor force as a whole since it does not extend down to the lowest reaches of unskilled labor. But it reaches pretty far down toward the bottom. The average income of members of occupations in this census category is fairly high because it is raised, as an average, by the presence of physicians, dentists, and airline pilots, whose occupations rank among the best paid. But the physicians' economic interests have little connection with those of people with a very much lower income and in different areas of work—little connection with, for example, drafters or surveyors.

In the matter of prestige, as measured by the standard National Opinion Research Center survey, the range within the professional-technical category is also extremely wide, running from the first rank position of the U.S. Supreme Court Justice (an exalted career possibility for lawyers, who, more generally, rank fifteenth in prestige) down to the seventy-fourth rank (out of ninety), *singer in a night club*. Here, as in the case of income and education and for the same reason, it is true that the average prestige of all occupations in the category is high, perhaps higher than the average for any other category. But the range is so wide that it strains credibility to suggest important common interests joining all its members so that all occupations will act together in the light of their common prestige as "professionals." Indeed, it is far more plausible to think that members of occupations that work in the same industries or situs have, as Bell (1979) noted, broadly common material interests that separate them from those in other industries and that within the same industry—for example, the health industry—members of occupations may very well be in competition with each other for economic and symbolic rewards rather than joined together in a common cause.

Finally, I may note that there is also wide variation in the political orientation of members of the occupations in the category. The microcosm of the professoriate might serve to indicate such variation since it includes members engaged in the teaching of the disciplines of a great many professions. As Ladd and Lipset's (1975) analysis indicates, the members of the professoriate can be politically radical at one extreme, conservative at the other, or in-between. These are not merely individual positions, however, for political attitude is closely correlated with the discipline, occupation, or professional school to which the professors are attached. Even though they may be more liberal than the practicing engineers employed by industry, professors in engineering schools, for example, like professors in business schools, tend to be politically conservative compared, for example, to professors of sociology or psychology, who are more likely to be liberal. Professionals as a group have moderate to conservative political attitudes, but there are important variations among them, from artists, journalists, and academics at one extreme, through school-teaching, social work, and nursing, to industrial scientists, engineers, and accountants at the other extreme (cf. Brint 1985).

The Value of the Census Categories

All in all, close scrutiny of the composition of both census categories raises serious doubt about their usefulness in serving as analytically salient groupings of occupations. Looking at the range of education, income, and prestige of the occupations in question and taking into account the different interests connected with the quite different industries in which various occupations work, it is very hard to imagine them sharing a common culture of any significance, a common set of material interests, and a common inclination to act politically in the same fashion and direction. In the case of higher education and exposure to formal knowledge, those occupations that presuppose some higher education—and, as we saw, not all do—require anywhere from one to eight years, a range that is double the difference between elementary and secondary education. Variation in the qualities of the experience connected with postsecondary education is similarly very large, including education in general liberal arts programs at four-year colleges, highly specialized vocational programs, tiny rural denominational colleges, and world-renowned universities.

One must conclude that the official categories of the census cannot be used to delineate a grouping of either professional or managerial occupations in any fashion that matches the intellectual interest and intent of those who are interested in new class theory. The range of variation among members of both categories may not be so wide as that of the entire labor force, from unskilled workers up to high-level executives, but it is wide enough to give pause. A common culture in more than the most superficial and vague sense cannot be inferred from such an occupational and educational salad, nor can common political position, common prestige, or common economic interest. It is not by critical inspection of a minority of cases that I arrive at such a conclusion. Only in a minority of the occupations in both categories can we find the characteristics asserted or implied by those who talk of managers and professionals as theoretically important classes or groups.

But this should come as no surprise, for official classificatory schemes are no less subject to social influences than are others—indeed, they may be more subject to them than many others. The census categories, after all, have changed over time (cf. Conk 1978), and in various decades as much as 30 percent of the labor force was not even classified. The categories are inevitably a partial function of the political processes they serve. Given the fact that official classification as a profession can confer at least symbolic and sometimes real economic benefits on members of an occupation, it is not surprising that active political lobbying may have as much to do with the inclusion of an occupation in the professional category as do the objective educational qualifications of its members. Airline pilots and nurses, neither of whom are required to have college training, lobbied for the elimination of the *semiprofessional* category in which they were both classified in the 1940 census so that they would be classified in the professional category subsequently (cf. Scoville 1965). The census categories must be seen as a complex and analytically heterogeneous product of the historical interplay among a variety of political, economic, and administrative forces. While they do maintain some rough, common thread from decade to decade, their content varies as those forces vary with an inevitably confounding result for their use as analytic categories.

DELINEATING THE PROFESSIONAL CATEGORY

If we cannot find a reasonably homogeneous set of occupations in the official census category, and if we cannot find consensus among scholars' methods of discriminating professions that employ easily available and reasonably reliable information, how can we identify that group of occupations we can call collectively *professions?* Let us agree, first, with new class theorists and students of intellectuals and the intelligentsia that a critical criterion lies in some degree of exposure to higher education and the formal knowledge it transmits. But remembering the importance to potential understanding of the professions' capacity to exercise power and of the problem of gaining a living, let us add the criterion that they are occupations for which education is a prerequisite to employment in particular positions. Formal education creates qualification for particular jobs, from which others who lack such qualification are routinely excluded (Collins 1979). Such a circumstance is likely to mean that those occupations have developed a coherent organization that effectively undertakes a "market project" (Larson 1977) that succeeds in carving out a labor-market shelter, a social closure, or a sinecure for its members in the labor market.

In the occupations listed in the census category bearing on professions we have already seen the amount of variation in that criterion. Among the traditional professions, medicine, but not law, the clergy, or university teaching, comes close to complete social closure, but so does a profession of considerably lesser prestige, income, and education—schoolteaching. Engineering is close in a de facto fashion, but hiring on the basis of credentials is discretionary for employers, and there is the constant likelihood that some jobs held by engineers can be given instead to drafters and lower-level technologists. There is nothing to prevent employers from doing that. The vast majority of all nurses, librarians, accountants, and, depending on how they are defined, social workers do not have to have any specific number of years of specialized training in institutions of higher education for their jobs. In this book I shall include them, however, because the leadership and upper tier of those occupations do have higher education and specialized training and are pressing for "higher" standards. For that reason, too, as well as for their history, I would include architects. Furthermore, by this criterion we must also include some managers as professionals—namely, those managers and administrators for whose jobs specific educational credentials are required. It is no accident that Wright et al. (1982, 719) found that, by their "class location" criteria, conventionally classified "professionals" were "managerial" in 52 percent of the cases. Among those managers listed separately in the census it might be appropriate to include health administrators as members of the professions and certainly necessary to include school principals and superintendents among the *administrators, primary and secondary schools.*

It should be apparent from the criterion I am using that a number of the occupations listed in the census category are excluded from the narrower category I am attempting to define here. I exclude from my category all those occupations in which it is normally the case that working does not depend on possessing credentials based on higher education. Thus airline pilots are excluded, along with most of the technicians in health, engineering, and science. Computer programmers are also excluded, as are most of the occupations in the *writers, artists, and entertainers* grouping.

It should be apparent that this criterion has the virtue of singling out higher education and exposure to formal knowledge as a central element and also that it employs that education and exposure to identify the manner by which livings are gained. Insofar as one does use it, one is immediately led to inquire into the nature of the system by which professions produce those credentials of education and the nature of those credentials themselves. That is what I shall turn to in the next chapter. In the course of analyzing the credential system of the professions, one can begin to see the structure that provides them with a living, some of the dimensions of the activities of organized occupations, and the way those occupations are differentiated internally by virtue of the credential system itself.

References

Bell, D. 1976. *The coming of post-industrial society*. New York: Basic Books.

———. 1979. The new class: A muddled concept. *Society* 16 (January–February): 15–23.

Bledstein, B. J. 1976. *The culture of professionalism*. New York: W. W. Norton & Co.

Brint, S. G. 1984. "New class" and cumulative trend explanations of the liberal attitudes of professionals. *American Journal of Sociology* 90 (July): 30–71.

———. 1985. The political attitudes of professionals and managers. *Annual Review of Sociology* 11:389–414.

Carchedi, G. 1975. On the economic identification of the new middle class. *Economy and Society* 4 (February): 1–86.

Collins, R. 1979. *The credential society*. New York: Academic Press.

Conk, M. A. 1978. Occupational classification in the United States Census: 1870–1940. *Journal of Interdisciplinary History* 9 (Summer): 111–30.

Crozier, M. 1971. *The world of the office worker*. Chicago: University of Chicago Press.

Ehrenreich, B., and J. Ehrenreich. 1977a. The professional-managerial class. Part 1. *Radical America* 11 (March–April): 7–31.

———. 1977b. The professional-managerial class. Part 2. *Radical America* 11 (May–June): 7–22.

Giddens, A. 1973. *The class structure of the advanced societies*. New York: Harper & Row.

Ginzberg, E. 1979. The professionalization of the U.S. labor force. *Scientific American* 240 (March): 48–53.

Gouldner, A. W. 1979. *The future of the intellectuals and the rise of the new class*. London: Macmillan Press.

Ladd, E. C., and S. M. Lipset. 1975. *The divided academy*. New York: McGraw-Hill Book Co.

Larson, M. S. 1977. *The rise of professionalism: A sociological analysis*. Berkeley: University of California Press.

Lasch, C. 1979. *Haven in a heartless world*. New York: Basic Books.

Mills, C. W. 1951. *White collar*. New York: Oxford University Press.

The organization man, cont'd. 1980. *Newsweek*, October 27, 96.

Poulantzas, N. 1975. *Classes in contemporary capitalism*. London: New Left Books.

Scoville, J. G. 1965. The development and relevance of U.S. occupational data. *Industrial and Labor Relations* 19 (October): 77–78.

U.S. Department of Labor. Bureau of Labor Statistics. 1978. *Occupational outlook handbook, 1978–79*. Bulletin 1955. Washington, D.C.: Government Printing Office.

Veysey, L. R. 1975. Who's a professional? Who cares? *Reviews in American History* (December): 419–23.

Wright, E. O., D. Hachen, C. Costello, and J. Sprague. 1982. The American class structure. *American Sociological Review* 47 (December): 709–26.

Chapter Four

Establishing Professional Positions: The Credential System

Credentialism can take many forms and cannot be dealt with sensibly in global terms. In its most general form credentialism creates market signals (Spence 1974), conventionalized bits of information about the capacity and skill of a worker offering labor in the marketplace. This form embraces informal letters of reference and similar personal testimonials based on patronage and sponsorship as well as formal diplomas, certificates, degrees, and licenses. Some credentials are advisory to the potential consumer of labor—the employer or the client—and some are binding. Some can be ignored while others cannot. Obviously it is the latter that, in a large, complex society, represent the greater amount of potential economic power and presuppose greater political advantage if not power. All forms bear on the central question I ask here—what it is that aids members of professions in gaining a living.

The most impressive form of credentialism works to produce an occupational cartel, which gains and preserves monopolistic control over the supply of a good or service in order to enhance the income of its members by protecting them from competition by others. In order to be fully effective, such a cartel must be able to control the number of people who enter the field so as to maintain relative scarcity and to control as well the competitive behavior of its own members so as to preserve a common price and output policy (cf., e.g., Barron 1966, 644). No modern profession has been able to fulfill all the requirements of a fully effective cartel, and recent court decisions have seriously weakened the capacity of professions to control competition among members by restricting price competition and advertising. Nonetheless, those that have the exclusive right to offer specific services, a right sustained by the state, have some significant attributes of a cartel. They have a monopoly of practice that, in conjunction with their control of the licensing and accreditation boards sustaining them, provides the opportunity to limit entry into the occupation. The calculated use of that opportunity can control the number of people available and keep the cost of the service high, though whether the professions have actually used that opportunity over the past few decades is an empirical question about which there is considerable debate (for limiting entry, cf. Hall and Lindsay 1980; and for questions of economic advantage, cf. Leffler 1978; both examine the medical profession).

In this chapter it is not my intent to dwell on the details of credentialing, something that would in any case be impossible to do in such a small compass. Nor is it my concern to point out the impropriety or the defective functioning of the system, topics on which there is already a large, though mostly ideologically deformed, literature. Rather my concern is to present only enough detail to uncover the overall patterns of formal credentialing in the United States. That pattern is one in which two distinct methods of credentialing intermesh to form a larger system. One of the methods may be called occupational credentialing, whereby credentials are issued to individual members of occupations performing particular kinds of work. Licenses constitute the most conspicuous example of this method, though degrees, diplomas, and certificates of completion of a course of training are more ubiquitous. The second method may be called institutional credentialing, whereby special credentials are issued to institutions that organize the production of particular kinds of services to the public, including the training or education of prospective members of an occupation. Charters, operating licenses, articles of incorporation, and accreditation are examples of this second method. As we shall see, the two types of credentialing are interdependent in the United States today, though there is no reason to consider them to be necessarily intertwined in other circumstances. And as we shall also see, private sources of credentialing in the United States are much more important than public sources. let me begin with occupational credentialing, focusing first on licensing.

Occupational Licensing

The most visible method of establishing something like an occupational monopoly lies in occupational licensing, a process by which a government agency grants exclusive official permission, sustained by law, to eligible individuals to work in a particular occupation. (For a sophisticated discussion of the legal and social background of early twentieth-century occupational licensing, see Friedman 1965, 487–534; for a recent summary of knowledge about occupational licensing and the public policy issues, see Shimberg 1982.) Air traffic controllers, airline pilots, and maritime deck and engineering officers are licensed by the federal government, but many more occupations are not. With only a few exceptions, occupational licensing in the United States is in the hands of the various states and territories. The fact of state jurisdiction over licensing makes it difficult to make generalizations about the United States as a whole, for the states do not have a uniform licensing policy. Some states license occupations that other states do not. Furthermore, some occupational licensing is carried out by town or city governments independently of the state government. To make generalization even more difficult, there is no systematic and up-to-date information available about all the licensing practices of all jurisdictions. Employing a survey of state-regulated occupations in the United States published in 1980 by the U.S. Department of Labor, however (and see also Greene and Gay 1980), it is possible to make a few summary remarks about national policy.

First, it seems clear that professions do not compose a majority of the eighty-four occupations that are regulated by the states. More than twice as many nonprofessional occupations are regulated: among these are abstractors, auctioneers, barbers, beauticians/cosmetologists, boiler inspectors, collection agency operators, contractors, driver training instructors, electricians, insurance agents, moving picture projectionists, pest controllers, plumbers, private detectives and security guards, real estate brokers and salesmen, watchmakers, weather modifiers, and weighmasters. Indeed, the variety of regulated occupations is so great that we must assume that a great number of local, state circumstances come into play in the initiation of some regulation.

When we try to gain some picture of national regulation policy by examining those occupations regulated by all states, we see that the vast majority of those are indeed either professions or occupations that, like practical nursing, work in association with professions. Barbers, beauticians/cosmetologists, insurance brokers and agents, and real estate brokers and salesmen are among the few nonprofessional occupations regulated in all states, while accountants, architects, attorneys, chiropractors, physicians, and many more groups of professionals are regulated. Furthermore, a majority of all the regulated professions are connected in one way or another with the provision of health services rather than being evenly distributed throughout the entire range of professions. But as prominent as the professions are among those groups regulated by the states, less than a quarter of all professions are so singled out. Neither the vast majority of engineers and technicians nor scientists, college teachers, writers, artists, and entertainers are regulated as groups by the states. In spite of the fact that most professions are not regulated by the states, however, those that are regulated make up almost half of the entire professional-technical labor force, for schoolteachers alone, among those regulated, are counted in the millions.

Not only do the states vary in many of the occupations they single out for regulation, but they vary as well in the way their regulatory systems are organized (for details, see Roederer and Shimberg 1980). The states also vary in the exact manner by which they credential occupations (cf. Shimberg 1982, 15–18). In all states, physicians and dentists are among those licensed for exclusive practice. That is to say, anyone who performs without a license activities defined by law as constituting the practice of medicine or dentistry can be prosecuted for illegal practice. (I would suspect, though, that prosecutions are exceedingly rare.) However, that is not the only form of credentialing employed for professions by the states. Statutory certification or registration is employed for some of the professions, creating exclusive right to use a particular title but not establishing an exclusive right to practice. Thus one can be prosecuted for representing oneself to potential customers as one who possesses a controlled title, but one cannot be prosecuted merely for performing the activities connected with the title. Obviously, statutory certification is a much weaker method of controlling the market than is licensing because it controls only the use of a particular market signal.

The scope of state licensing practices is perhaps best seen by examining those of a single state. Let me sketch the system of New York State. It is an atypical state in that its licensing is controlled by a central agency rather than by autonomous professional boards (see the sketch of its organization in Shimberg 1982, 28–30, 114–16, and passim). But it is fairly typical in the occupations it has chosen to license and in the use of both practice licensing and title licensing (for what follows, I rely on New York Consolidated Laws Service 1979, pars. 3501ff.).

In New York State Education Law, Title VIII provides "for the regulation of the admission to and the practice of certain professions" (New York Consolidated Laws Service 1979, art. 130, subart. 1, par. 6500, p. 383)—namely, medicine, physical therapy, physician's assistant and specialists' assistant, chiropractic, dentistry and dental hygiene, veterinary medicine and animal health technology, pharmacy, nursing, podiatry, optometry, ophthalmic dispensing, engineering and land surveying, architecture, landscape architecture, public accountancy, shorthand reporting, psychology, social work, and massage. However, such regulation does not always restrict practice; that is, it does not always control who may offer a particular kind of service. A psychologist, for example, must be licensed in New York State, but by Title VIII that license only provides exclusive use of the title *psychologist* and exclusive right "to describe his services by use of the words 'psychologist,' 'psychology' or 'psychological' in connection with his practice." Similarly, under Title VIII only a licensed person may use the title *certified social worker*, but a nonlicensed person is not prevented from offering the same services to the public. (For a comprehensive review of issues concerning the licensing of psychotherapists, see Hogan 1979; and Fretz and Mills 1980. For a recent comparison of state laws regulating social work, see National Association of Social Workers 1981a.) Legal monopoly of a title is best compared to legal control by copyright of a trademark or a brand name for a product. To the extent that labor consumers are as faithful to occupational titles in seeking services as commodity consumers are loyal to brand names, an exclusive title provides something of an advantage in the marketplace. But the advantage is hardly of the sort for which one might employ strictly the notion of a cartel.

Education Law is not the only body of law in New York State that licenses occupations. The licensing and registration of nursing home administrators is established in Public Health Law (art. 28-D), as is that of funeral directors or undertakers, X-ray technicians, physician's assistants, and specialists' assistants (New York Consolidated Laws Service 1976b, pars. 1–3399). And as in every state, lawyers have a special position, being licensed and ostensibly supervised and disciplined by the judiciary and subject to Judiciary Law (id. 1976a). Furthermore, municipalities may assume responsibility for licensing other occupations, though when state law licenses an occupation, it preempts local jurisdiction. New York City has an extensive body of law governing business and trade.

A few points might be made about New York State licensing law that seem to be applicable to many other states of the Union as well. First, a fairly small proportion of all occupations are singled out for licensing, and most, though not all, are engaged in the sale of services rather than goods. Where goods are sold, as is the case with pharmacists and ophthalmic dispensers, for example, the assumption is that the seller must either exercise the skilled judgment of the quality of the goods that cannot be expected of the buyer or exercise skilled judgment in carrying out the recommendations of another professional. Second, the majority of licensed occupations are connected with medicine and dentistry, that is, with health care. Third, licensing laws tend to be more elaborate and demanding in dealing with occupations related to health care than they are in dealing with others. Fourth, a significant minority of occupations are not licensed in such a way as to be able to monopolize practice: they are licensed for exclusive use of an occupational title, allowing others to perform the same work so long as they do not claim the title. For example, in New York State law, so long as one does not call oneself a masseur or a masseuse or one's business a massage parlor, one can legally operate a "body rub parlor." Finally, many but not all licensed occupations tend to control the criteria for entry, examination, licensing, and discipline by virtue of having their representatives dominate the composition of the professional boards set up to regulate them. The New York State requirement that one board member (two in the cases of medicine, pharmacy, nursing, and accounting) must represent the lay public cannot be expected to do much to temper professionally interested recommendations. And while, in the case of New York, those professional boards are merely advisory to the Board of Regents and so can be subject to a degree of external control that is uncommon in most other states, their influence on policy cannot fail to be enormous.

CERTIFICATION: PRIVATE OCCUPATIONAL CREDENTIALING

Apart from state-controlled credentialing of occupations through licensing, there is an even larger system of privately controlled credentialing. Under the auspices of the professions themselves, through their associations, a certificate or diploma is given to a qualified candidate, usually after having successfully completed a specified course of study and practice at an accredited professional school and sometimes after having passed an examination. The credential testifies to the official acknowledgment of that candidate's qualifications to perform a particular kind of work competently and reliably and therefore to be admitted to membership in that special association. It is often called certification (for a legal review, see Wallace 1972; for a more up-to-date review, though one focusing on health-related occupations, see Havighurst and King 1983). Thus even though a state may not have laws establishing licenses for a certified social worker, for example, social workers can qualify for certification through their own profession, become members of the Academy of Certified Social Workers, and display that credential in their places of work as testimony to their special qualifications.

Such private credentialing is particularly common among the health occupations in general, and in light of the very broad scope of practice encompassed by state licensing provisions, it is particularly well developed in areas of specialization within medicine. Every middle-class consumer is familiar with some of the more common "specialty boards" to which a well-qualified medical specialist is expected to have gained admittance. For the field of health alone, there are more than one hundred certifying agencies: the number of agencies has swollen well past the number of occupations involved because of the separate credentialing done by specialty associations within the profession at large (Falk, Weisfeld, and Tochen 1979, 9).

All forms of occupational credentialing, public or private, have a critical weakness: they may be able to restrict or narrow the supply of qualified professionals, but they cannot, in and of themselves, control demand. What good is it to be a licensed psychologist in New York—to take one vulnerable example—when consumers seeking "therapy" or "counseling" are free to go to others who forgo the title but offer what appear to be the same services?

Obviously, taken by itself without implicitly assuming a larger structure of supports, occupational credentialing constitutes only a limited advantage in the mythical marketplace in which individual sellers freely seek individual buyers and vice versa. In any real marketplace there are a number of institutions that organize economic relations and prejudice them systematically, as institutional economists have noted. It is not occupational licensing in and of itself that can effectively explain what economic advantages actually accrue to the licensed today. For an adequate explanation we must look to the tissue of supportive laws and institutions that control demand.

Some of those controls are fairly obvious: they require the use of a licensed professional as a prerequisite to some other benefit. For example, in many states, anyone who is party to a real estate transaction is required by law to employ a lawyer. Furthermore, in New York State law, with some exceptions, no public official may accept any plans or specifications bearing on the construction or alteration of buildings that do not have the seal of a licensed architect, professional engineer, or land surveyor (New York Consolidated Laws Service 1979, art. 145, par. 7209, p. 569). If we think of the lawyer or land surveyor as a gatekeeper (cf. Freidson 1970, 115–18) of the desired benefit of buying, selling, or building a house, then we can see how the law functions to create demand for professional services independently of the desire of the consumer for those services.

The examples of gatekeeping I have given thus far rely on the single economic image that unfortunately dominates our view of the professions, the image of an individual entrepreneur selling services to individual consumers. While we are comfortable with this image, it is a gross distortion of the market situation of the vast majority of professions and professionals. It does not come close to fitting the situations of schoolteachers, engineers, scientists, professors, social workers, nurses, and many other professionals. As we shall see in chapter 8, many of these professionals do serve as gatekeepers, but they do so on behalf of the resources provided by the organizations that employ them. It is the organizations that attract the clientele, attempt to control both supply and demand, and provide resources, not the professionals as individuals. Even if they have occupational credentials controlled by the state, as do, for example, schoolteachers, few of them can survive economically by offering their services as entrepreneurs to individuals in the external labor market: we should recall that the self-employed governess and tutor of times past were hardly known for successful and secure teaching careers. In order to gain a secure living, what such professionals need are jobs in the internal labor markets of organizations that attract individual clients in large batches. In such circumstances, professions must exercise some control over the employment policies of organizations, gaining assurance that organizations are obliged to employ only their members in particular jobs. Such control is accomplished by a system of institutional credentialing, a system that is, on balance, much more important than occupational licensing in the narrow legal sense.

INSTITUTIONAL CREDENTIALING

In occupational credentialing a system is set up whereby individuals can be given formal credentials testifying to their right to practice a profession or to use a professional title. In institutional credentialing it is an organization that receives a credential that provides it with the legal right to operate or to represent itself as providing a service to consumers that is acceptable to some authoritative agency. A hospital receives an operating license from the state, a school a charter. An engineering firm receives approval from the state to operate as a corporation under its laws of incorporation, while a law or an accounting firm receives official recognition as a legal partnership. Apart from state recognition that provides organizations with the legal credential that permits them to carry on their affairs with the full protection of law, there are forms of recognition that attest to the organization's acceptability to some authoritative private agency. Organizations are licensed, chartered, or incorporated by state law and accredited by private associations. Thus a hospital may obtain an operating license from the state and accreditation from the Joint Commission for the Accreditation of Hospitals, while a college may be chartered by the state and accredited by the Western College Association.

The importance of institutional credentialing to the professions does not lie in the mere fact of the licensed operation, accreditation, or legal recognition of the organizations in which they work. Rather it lies in the terms of the institutional credentials. Insofar as a prerequisite for institutional credentials is conformity to some set of standards, and insofar as those standards bear on the composition and disposition of the internal division of labor and management of the organization, to that extent institutional credentialing mandates that certain positions or jobs be provided by the organization for members of particular kinds of occupations. Thus state laws of incorporation require that all members of the boards of directors of professional corporations be practicing members of the organization with professional credentials. To take another example, the Joint Commission for the Accreditation of Hospitals requires that at least one registered nurse be on duty in a hospital emergency room at all times. So it is that, through institutional credentialing, shelters are provided for professionals in particular positions in organizations.

Finally, as an introduction to a more detailed analysis, it is important to be clear about the way the organizations subject to institutional credentialing are interlinked with the larger credential system. The credential system's most elementary component is the personal credential constituted by the individual degree, diploma, or certificate of training. This is the prime evidence required for both licensing and certification, though separate examinations may also be required. That personal credential is produced by the successful completion of a course of study in an educational organization. It is in a sense the product of that organization and the instructional activities of the members of its staff who are themselves professionals. In order for that organization to offer its clientele a personal credential that is useful to them for obtaining a license or a certificate, it must itself obtain an institutional credential that both allows it to operate as a legal entity and establishes the acceptability of the credentials it offers to its clients and their prospective employers. At the foundation of the credential system, both generating it and being generated by it, are institutions of higher education. Let us look at them more closely from this perspective.

ACCREDITATION IN HIGHER EDUCATION

Both public and private methods of professional credentialing assert as a prerequisite for qualification successful completion of some formal training program associated with higher education. But what is a bona fide program, and what is a bona fide institution of higher education (cf. Selden 1960)? Can one accept the diploma that any program may issue just because it holds itself out as a relevant to training for a particular profession? Can one accept a letter of testimony from a self-employed teacher that a student has successfully completed a proper course of training? Can one accept any degree when it is printed impressively on parchment? Obviously, here is a problem of market signaling.

The most casual reading of the history of professional education in the nineteenth century, with its proprietary diploma mills, informal clerkships, preceptorships, and apprenticeships, cannot fail to persuade us that there was a very real problem of discriminating market claims. (See the following for conventional histories: for medicine, O'Malley 1970; and Norwood 1941; for mechanical engineering, Calvert 1967; for law, Johnson 1978; and Stevens 1983; and for a number of professions more briefly, Blauch 1955; and Haber 1974.) The formalization of professional education in the early part of this century was based on much more than the desire to raise the professions' prestige and restrict the supply of practitioners, as the crude conspiracy theories of recent revisionist histories of the Progressive Era imply. The reorganization of professional education was also an attempt to satisfy a very real need to create a more reliable system of market signals than that which existed earlier.

The need for some degree of predictability and uniformity also existed in the case of the degrees provided by liberal arts colleges and universities, for their variety was perhaps even more staggering than that of professional programs. (For a recent history of higher education, see Brubacher and Rudy 1968.) For example, in 1910 the U.S. Bureau of Education created a list of 602 "colleges" in the United States. When, in 1915, it decided to include on its list only those colleges that actually gave a degree, employed distinct admissions requirements, required from its students at least two years of work of "standard college grade," and had at least twenty students in regular attendance, thirty-nine colleges had to be dropped from the original list (Dickey and Miller 1972, 6).

Formal accreditation of four-year liberal arts colleges by private associations began, like that of professional schools, in the early part of this century (for brief histories, see ibid., 5–24; Wiley and Zald 1968, 36–43; Orlans 1975, 1–34). Private regional associations of educational institutions were established as early as 1885, but not until 1915 were formal accreditation programs begun by the pioneering North Central Association of Colleges and Universities. Other regional associations followed suit, though it was not until 1952 that the last of them, the New England Association, finally undertook such a program, albeit reluctantly.

What is the nature of this accreditation? It consists in the formal knowledgment that an institution conforms with standards established by an association, as indicated by including it in an official list of approved institutions. Insofar as an accrediting association has established its authoritative status, its approval becomes an important market signal: the course credits of one accredited institution will be recognized by similarly accredited institutions and will therefore be transferable; the degree, certificate, or diploma received by a graduate from one accredited institution will be recognized by other accredited institutions and can be taken to fulfill educational requirements that are prerequisite to admission to study for a higher degree. Insofar as it has come to believe in the authority of accrediting associations, the outside world itself may grant respect to the individual credentials that the approved institutions grant. Employers may hire only those job seekers with credentials from accredited institutions and turn away applicants whose degrees were issued by unaccredited institutions.

In fact, private accrediting bodies have gained wide recognition and significant legal support (Orlans 1975). The American regional college and university accrediting associations have become so well recognized that if an institution should lose its accreditation, as did Parsons College almost twenty years ago, it would quickly lose a large proportion of its students and even find it difficult to have its representatives gain access to high schools for the purpose of recruiting new students (Koerner 1970, 220). The state itself routinely relies on private accrediting associations for the determination of the validity and reliability of the credentials of the occupations it regulates. (For the important legal issue of nondelegation of state powers, see Gellhorn 1956; and Liebmann 1975.) For example, in New York State the regulations governing the issuance of certificates for such school personnel as district principals and teachers require a four-year baccalaureat "from a regionally accredited higher institution" and then go on to specify the additional training required (New York Department of State 1983, title 8, vol. A, chap. 2 subchap. C. 80.4–80.6). Furthermore, the regulations allow out-of-state colleges to advertise their degree programs within the state only so long as they are candidates for accreditation by regional accrediting associations.

The same reliance by New York State on private accrediting bodies may be seen in the case of such specialized national associations as the American Council on Pharmaceutical Education, the Engineers' Council for Professional Development, and the National League for Nursing. In regulations governing license-oriented, professional education programs, there is explicit authorization for the Education Department to employ the standards of "nationally recognized accrediting associations" in laying down requirements. And while the licensing laws I discussed earlier are not explicit, leaving the authority to establish educational qualifications to the judgment of the commissioner, in virtually every case explicitly discussed in the *Official Compilation of Codes, Rules and Regulations of New York State* (New York Department of State 1983) there is provision for honoring examinations given outside the state so long as they are given by such private national examining bodies as the National Council of Engineering Examiners, the National Board of Medical Examiners, and the National Association of Boards of Pharmacy. Similarly, degrees given by schools outside the state are honored if they are earned at nationally accredited professional schools—for example, degrees from library schools accredited by the American Library Association.

Finally, I might mention what is in fact the most important example of reliance on the deliberations of private accrediting bodies, the reliance on them by the federal government itself (for a legislative history of federal reliance on private accrediting, see Finkin 1973, 1979). In essence, accrediting associations become gatekeepers of extensive federal economic benefits for institutions and their clients (for the details of the development of benefits, see Dickey and Miller 1972, 11–24; and esp. Orlans 1975, 1–101). Private accreditation bodies have been used by many federal agencies. The National Science Foundation is allowed to give fellowships for study only at accredited schools, and the Immigration and Naturalization Service is allowed to give foreign students visas for entry into the United States to study only at accredited schools. As the welfare state expanded the distribution of federal funds by such measures as the Higher Education Facilities Act of 1963, the Nurse Training Act of 1964, the Higher Education Act of 1965, the Guaranteed Student Loan Program, and many more, federal approval of accrediting institutions became even more important to the economic survival of educational institutions. And while the then Office of Education attempted to exercise some influence over the evaluation procedures and standards of private accreditation associations (Orlans 1975, 35–101; Finkin 1979), those associations seem, by and large, to have remained quite free to serve as the arbiters of which institutions will receive extensive federal benefits and which will not.

It should be clear how important accreditation is for the survival of both general and professional institutions of higher education in the United States and how intermeshed it is with the state systems of occupational licensing and institutional chartering and licensing and with the distribution of federal funds. While the states are ultimately sovereign in the licensing and chartering of educational institutions, at bottom they rely nonetheless on private associations, as does the federal government.

ACCREDITATION AS JOB SPECIFICATION

It should be obvious by now that accreditation establishes a system of market signals that forms the basis for credentialing both institutions of higher education and the individual credentials they issue to their graduates. Less obvious is the fact that, in the course of credentialing institutions, the system also produces a mandatory framework of credentialed jobs for the professionals working in them. This becomes clear once we realize that the approval of an educational program entails approval not merely of the subjects covered in a course of study and training—the curriculum—but also of the capacity of the instructors of those subjects to teach them competently. Since occupational credentials serve as the arbiter of the competence of the teachers in those institutions, part of the accrediting process requires evaluation of the credentials of the teaching staff, and part of the price of gaining accreditation is that the institution must fill at least some of its jobs with credentialed professionals. The employment policies of the accredited institution are therefore determined in part by external accrediting associations.

Under such circumstances the possession of a license for exclusive practice is not necessary to assure work for most properly credentialed professionals when market conditions are reasonably good. A license may be necessary for monopolizing individual clients but unnecessary for a job in an organization that monopolizes the clients. Indeed, as we shall see, when we add to the credentialing of training institutions the credentialing of practice institutions like hospitals through, for example, the Joint Commission for the Accreditation of Hospitals, we can begin to understand why it is that employed professionals without exclusive licenses to practice can have a sheltered position in the marketplace nonetheless. Furthermore, when we turn to examine the empirical details of accreditation, we shall see that it not only shelters those professionals who do the everyday work of teaching, doctoring, or whatever but also reserves for members of the professions supervisory and managerial positions. To see this concretely, let us examine the personnel standards employed by accrediting bodies in higher education, relying primarily on Petersen's useful compilation (1979).

It is typical of the nine regional associations that provide accreditation to colleges and universities that their standards are not precisely stated. In earlier years the standards were quantitative and concrete, including easily measurable criteria like the "size of endowment, number of faculty, number of years of high school required for admission, and length of the educational program" (Petersen 1979, 21). In time, however, probably as much for improving relations with a skittish constituency as for substantive reasons, most regional associations abandoned reliance on explicit quantitative criteria and produced instead very general, qualitative guidelines that were employed as a loose framework for more concrete evaluation of individual cases.

According to Petersen, most agree on their interest in the composition of the governing boards of the institution and on the importance of preserving a "sharp distinction between the policy-making function of the governing board and the operational authority of the administrative staff" (ibid., 28), emphasizing the leadership role of the president or chief executive officer. There is concern therefore for protecting the institution's relative autonomy of operation from the legal authority of public or private governing boards. In the case of personnel, "all agree that the quality of faculty is a major determinant of faculty effectiveness" (ibid., 31), and many exhort that salaries and benefits should be "adequate," tenure "available," and teaching loads and schedules "reasonable." But concrete criteria of quality are missing, as are guidelines for what is "adequate" or "reasonable." Only the Southern Association of Colleges and Schools' Commission on Colleges still boldly asserts what the others must certainly keep in mind, even though they do not state it officially, that is, that one measure of the quality of the faculty lies in the credentials testifying to its formal education. (For a brief history comparing the Southern Association of Colleges and Schools with the North Central Association of Colleges and Universities, see Wiley and Zald 1968, 36–56.) The Southern Association states that about 40 percent of the faculty of community or junior colleges should have a year of graduate study past the master's degree and that "some" should have two years past the master's or the doctorate. It states further that in senior colleges about half the faculty should have that minimum graduate training of one year past the master's degree, that at least 30 percent should have the Ph.D., and that in departments offering a "major" about 25 percent should have the doctorate. In the case of graduate work, "each graduate faculty member should hold the highest earned degree in his discipline" (Southern Association of Colleges and Schools 1977, 40).

I have already noted that all the other regional accrediting associations will not be pinned down on their occupational credentialing requirements for professors. But it is difficult to believe that they do not attend to them. To pose an extreme test, one cannot imagine accrediting a four-year liberal arts college with a faculty on which there is no one with the credential of a B.A. or on which less than a tenth has an M.A. or an M.S. Granting that, we can recognize degrees as credentials that provide the essential economic foundation for the professoriate. They assure minimum qualification for some jobs open solely to those possessing it, and accreditation assures that some minimal proportion of all jobs available in institutions of higher education will be so reserved.

Similar constraints on employment policies in institutions of higher education can be imposed by the states. Indeed, in the *Official Compilation of Codes, Rules and Regulations of New York State* (New York Department of State 1983, title 8, vol. A, chap. 2, subchap. A, 52.2, p. 46), standards for the registration of undergraduate and graduate curricula assert that all faculty must have earned degrees, that at least a "sufficient number" of the faculty must be full-time, that at least one person in each curriculum leading to the baccalaureate must hold an earned doctorate and that all faculty must be allowed adequate time to "broaden professional knowledge," among other things. Some states, in fact, seem to have "higher" and more detailed minimal standards than do the accrediting associations.

Turning to national accrediting bodies concerned with specialized vocational or professional training, we find that, while some remain as vague and "qualitative" as the regional bodies, others are much more explicit and impose many more constraints on the employment policies of the institutions involved. Let me summarize Petersen's (1979) compilation of the personnel standards of the thirty-nine national accrediting associations that accredit schools or programs for specialized professional study and that are recognized by the Council for Post-Secondary Accreditation. The thirty-nine associations accredit programs in law, pharmacy, dentistry, optometry, theology, medicine, chemistry, journalism, librarianship, psychology, social work, architecture, nursing, art, and the twenty-four different technical and paraprofessional health-related occupations approved by the American Medical Association's Committee on Allied Health Education and Accreditation.

Insofar as these accrediting agencies are concerned with the status of professional schools associated with universities, such as law schools (Fossum 1978), or of specialized professional programs within universities or colleges, such as a program in library science, they tend to be concerned that those schools and programs be given the freedom to develop their own standards and practices independently of the host institution and that they have as much status and as plentiful resources as other schools and programs (Petersen 1979, 77–79, 115–16). In short, they seek to assure equity for (and give bargaining strength to) the programs and schools they accredit and to protect them from pressures from the overall system in which they exist. All require the faculty to be "competent," and while not many actually specify the credentials the faculty must have, it is difficult to imagine most professional schools and programs staffed by people who do not hold professional degrees. But while staffing is not specified concretely, a fair proportion of these accrediting associations lay down explicit standards for both the maximum teaching load and the faculty-student ratio in the classroom and laboratory (cf. American Assembly of Collegiate Schools of Business 1981–82). And a great many emphasize the importance of a full-time faculty, using outside practitioners on a part-time basis only for supplementary "enrichment" purposes. Many are explicitly concerned that the faculty has adequate rank, salary, and security.

What is the import of these accrediting standards? First of all, they create the institutional credentials of colleges, universities, professional schools, and professional programs, which in turn assign market value to the occupational credentials they provide their graduates. Second, they also qualify those institutions for recognition and chartering by the states and make them and their students eligible to receive both state and federal benefits, financial and otherwise. Third, in the course of credentialing those institutions they specify standards that, while most often stated abstractly and qualitatively on paper, nonetheless in practice establish the minimum standards to be followed in employing at least some portion of the professional teaching staff. This is not done as rigidly as in licensing laws since no form of accreditation that I am aware of explicitly requires that all faculty must possess a particular degree or credential, but it does establish a floor of credentials below which no institution can fall without threat of loss of accreditation. Fourth, though most written standards are vague on the point, there are reasonable grounds for believing that in practice the process of accreditation establishes some core of faculty positions as full-time jobs on the basis of which professional careers and identities as professors in professional schools or programs can be established. Finally, accreditation standards also attempt to protect those jobs from undue economic or political pressure by taking into account such issues as the degree of autonomy allowed programs and schools; the faculty's academic freedom (cf. Hofstadter and Metzger 1955); the required work load, including sufficient time for scholarship and research; and the adequacy of salaries. Taken together, accreditation standards make a significant contribution to the maintenance and sheltering of the modern profession of college, university, and professional school teaching, even though the minimal standards are modest and do not shelter everyone. They compose one element of a system that produces within the professions themselves both a "knowledge class" and an "administrative class," both of which may be distinguished from the "working class" of everyday professional practitioners.

ACCREDITATION AND THE "KNOWLEDGE CLASS"

I shall have more to say in later chapters about the complex issue of stratification and differentiation within the professions and about the nature and role of professional elites, but here it is useful to show how the scope of institutional credentialing figures in the foundation of what might, for want of a better term, be called *classes* within the professions. Taking the knowledge class first, one might note that, insofar as professions are tied to institutions of higher education for their training, it follows that those who do the training are the authoritative custodians of the knowledge and skill claimed by the professions in constituting their credentials. The authority of those custodians is reinforced even further when, as has been the case in American institutions of higher education for some time, the role of teaching present-day knowledge is combined with the role of creating new knowledge by innovative research and scholarship. Credentialed graduates are expected to absorb the knowledge and skill of their professions and then go out into the world to practice them, keeping up-to-date as best they can as they pursue their practical careers. It is the staff—particularly the full-time staff—of professional schools and programs that produces the bulk of the new knowledge in journals that the practitioners must keep up with in the academic disciplines, medicine, and most other health, education, and welfare professions. In law, engineering, and architecture academics contribute to but do not necessarily dominate the production of new knowledge. Qualification notwithstanding, one can say that the division between academics and practitioners in the professions is hierarchical in nature and one around which there has been a good deal of tension and resentment throughout history (see, e.g., Auerbach 1971; Kendall 1965; Johnson 1978; Calvert 1967).

Thus the accrediting process in higher education supports circumstances in which full-time careers of teaching can be created that in turn sustain a group within the profession that is in a position to serve as the authoritative repository of the basic stock of formal knowledge over which the profession claims jurisdiction: authoritative knowledge remains the preserve of the profession. Those teaching careers also provide the resources for research careers sheltered from the demands of the marketplace, allowing efforts at refining and sorting accepted knowledge or at creating new, especially formal and theoretical rather than applied and practical knowledge. Though there are important variations among the professions in their dependence on academics as their knowledge class, it can be asserted that by creating a shelter for full-time teaching and research in professional schools, which is one of the consequences of accreditation, professions create one important mechanism by means of which they can maintain control over innovations to the body of knowledge they claim as their own by keeping it within the professional family.

INSTITUTIONAL CREDENTIALING AND THE "ADMINISTRATIVE CLASS"

Accreditation and other forms of institutional credentialing also provide support for an administrative class within the professions. Within institutions of higher education, including professional schools and programs, positions of administrative responsibility for professional or academic affairs are reserved for individuals who have professional credentials. In conventional firms, hierarchy is occupationally differentiated. If one moves from a lower to a higher rank, one generally changes one's occupation. And it is not usually a prerequisite that those in a higher rank must have the same basic training and credentials as those in the lower rank—that, for example, a production manager must have had the on-the-job training of a production worker or that a bank manager must have had the training of a bank teller. But this is what is often required of some of those with administrative authority in institutions of higher education and in other firms engaged in providing professional services—that they possess the same professional credentials as those over whom they exercise authority.

In universities and professional schools, the general practice, even if not always the specifically stated requirement, is that key administrative and executive jobs be reserved for those with at least nominal professional credentials. The dean of a school of social work—the chief executive officer—is almost always a member of the profession with professional credentials. So, too, are deans of law and medical schools, directors of professional programs, departmental chairpersons, and, in colleges and universities, "academic" deans, provosts, vice-presidents for academic affairs, and the like. Furthermore, it is my impression that the chief executive officers of colleges and universities—that is, the presidents— usually have some sort of earned academic credential.

Institutions of higher education thus have a hierarchy of jobs with administrative authority and responsibility that are filled by credentialed members of the appropriate profession— qualified engineers in the case of an engineering school and qualified professors (the exact discipline varying) in the case of liberal arts colleges and universities. These professional officials, like their counterparts in such professional practice organizations as law firms, accounting firms, and hospitals, form a "class" within their professions that has interests and powers that are often quite different than those of the practicing professionals—the faculty or staff. They tend to form their own specialized associations, and they tend to be the ones active in the affairs of accrediting institutions, including the creation and maintenance of accrediting standards. Their role in accreditation may explain the special concern accreditation bodies have for the autonomy of the unit—protecting the administration from the interference of the board of trustees, the state, or, in the case of universities and liberal arts colleges, specialized accrediting bodies and protecting the administration of professional programs or schools from the interference of the universities of which they are part. It may also explain the lack of specificity of most accreditation standards themselves, for that leaves much room for the discretionary exercise of their own professional judgment. The judgment of managers is based on their special commitment to the administrative unit as a whole and on its relationship to the environment surrounding it rather than on the commitment of those they administer to their own problems of daily work. (For a revealing statement from the managerial perspective regarding the university as a whole, including good background material and reference to general and specialized accrediting bodies, see Carnegie Foundation for the Advancement of Teaching 1982.)

A professional school or a university may be seen as a firm or an organization devoted to the provision of the professional service of teaching or training. An analogous administrative class of the professions is established in other kinds of professional service firms. Anathema to professions is supervision and control by nonprofessionals. In an effort to avoid this they attempt to establish the custom of filling supervisory and executive positions with people who possess professional credentials. Weak professions can only use moral suasion and the issuance of official standards that have none of the force of organized institutional credentialing. An example of this is the series of "professional standards" for social work in various settings issued as "policy statements" by the National Association of Social Workers (e.g., National Association of Social Workers 1981b). They all have the same characteristic: the credentials for rank-and-file jobs, as well as for supervisors and directors of programs, are established. And where the program is a specialized part of a larger organization like a hospital, the wish is that its social work director be directly responsible to the chief executive officer, without supervision by either a lay supervisor or one from another profession. The association has had some success in getting those standards partially adopted by the Health Care Financing Administration so as to determine the level of Medicare and Medicaid reimbursement to be given to both hospitals and nursing homes. (For a discussion of the ways the Health Care Financing Administration influences staffing, see Weisfeld et al. 1982.)

In the case of stronger professions, we find not mere recommendations but the establishment of a legal requirement that the chief executive officer of an organization offering professional services must be a member of the profession. For example, in the case notes on article 15 of New York State Judiciary Law, it is said that "a corporation which is to practice law must be *controlled and supervised by lawyers* summarily responsible to the court for the maintenance of . . . professional standards . . . , and in any legal assistance corporation supported by federal anti-poverty funds, *the executive staff and those with the responsibility to hire and discharge staff* from the very top to the lowest lay echelon, *must be lawyers.* . . . Corporations where lawyer operations would be subject to ultimate lay control would not be permitted to engage in the practice of law" (New York Consolidated Laws Service 1976, par. 495, p. 358; italics added). Similarly, under New York State law, organizations practicing architecture, professional engineering, and land surveying must have chief executive officers who are licensed members of the appropriate profession. And in the case of the professional service corporation, under article 15 of Business Corporation Law, professional service corporations are established that require that all shareholders be licensed to practice the profession involved and that "no individual may be a director or officer of a professional service corporation unless he is authorized by law to practice in this state a profession which such corporation is authorized to practice and is either a shareholder of such corporation or engaged in the practice of his profession in such corporation" (New York Consolidated Laws Service 1982, par. 1508, p. 179).

These staffing requirements extend even further when we examine the details of state regulations governing public facilities. The *Official Compilation of Codes, Rules and Regulations* states for libraries, "There shall be employed by each approved system of libraries a director, who holds or is eligible to receive a public librarian's professional certificate. . . . In addition to such director, each approved system shall employ at least three full-time . . . certified public librarians" (New York Department of State 1983, title 8, vol. A, chap. 2, subchap. D, 90.3[d], p. 141). For the State University of New York, it is specified that the chancellor must be appointed to the faculty with an academic rank with tenure (and thus must have the credentials to qualify for such appointment) (ibid., title 8, vol. B, chap. 5, subchap. B, 328.1 [c], p. 333). It is also specified that the chief administrative officer (i.e., the president) of a State University of New York college must also have a tenured faculty appointment, though, significantly, the requirement is not imposed on other administrative officers (ibid., title 8, vol. B, chap. 5, subchap. B, 331.1 [c], p. 341).

And it is specified that departmental chairpersons must be members of the academic staff, which also presupposes an academic degree (ibid., title 8, vol. B, chap. 5, subchap. B, 333.10, p. 342.1).

These examples give some insight into the way institutional credentialing establishes administrative positions in professional service organizations that must be filled by people with the same professional credentials as those over whom they exercise supervisory, managerial, or executive authority. Some professions use other devices. Certified public accountants are allowed to establish firms only on the basis of a partnership among the credentialed so that, as in the case of the professional corporation, even the legally responsible governing board is professional in composition. There is a great deal of variation among the professions, but for all of them it is possible to say that, by fairly strong and usually binding custom in some cases and by private and legal institutional credentialing in others, there is created within each profession an administrative class of members that exercises administrative authority over working professionals and that so preserves for members of the profession, albeit a special group, that function of command over everyday work.

THE LIMITATIONS OF THE CREDENTIAL SYSTEM

In conclusion, it is necessary to redress the balance of this attempt to sketch the essentials of an extremely complex system, the details of which are beyond the range of a single book, let alone a single chapter. Since my concern is not with the credential system itself so much as its effect on the position of professionals in the marketplace, I have emphasized the way in which it organizes the creation of formal credentials and mandates both the maintenance of jobs in organizations to be filled by those with formal credentials and, in a minority of cases, the exclusive practice of particular kinds of work by those with formal credentials. But for simplicity I have had to draw a picture that overemphasizes the formal.

In order to understand how the formal credential system works for individual professionals one must understand that it merely establishes the possibility of gaining a living. Formal, impersonal credentials in the form of degrees or licenses constitute the minimal criteria, establish the boundaries of the pool of those who are allowed to be candidates. Choice by clients and employers from that pool is as often as not made on the basis of a variety of informal credentials or credentialing criteria, among the most important of which are personal testimonials from former teachers, employers, supervisors, patrons, clients, colleagues, and friends. While all lawyers' licenses to practice before the bar are equal, as are all physicians' licenses to practice medicine, the prestige of the institution from which they received their training and the influence of informal testimonials from key sponsors play a large role in determining career success. The formal system merely sets the boundaries of the competition, within which an informal credential system, frequently employing discriminatory criteria like gender, race, religion, ethnicity, and class culture, then operates to structure the course of work careers and create the profession's internal system of stratification.

References

American Assembly of Collegiate Schools of Business. 1981–82. *Accreditation council policies, procedures, and standards.* St. Louis, Mo.

Auerbach, J. S. 1971. Emnity and amity: Law teachers and practitioners, 1900–22. *Perspectives in American History* 5:551–601.

Barron, J. F. 1966. Business and professional licensing—California, a representative example. *Stanford Law Review* 18:640–65.

Blauch, L. E., ed. 1955. *Education for the professions.* Washington, D.C.: Government Printing Office.

Brubacher, J. S., and W. Rudy. 1968. *Higher education in transition: A history of American colleges and universities, 1636–1968.* New York: Harper & Row.

Calvert, M. 1967. *The mechanical engineer in America, 1830–1910: Professional cultures in conflict.* Baltimore: Johns Hopkins University Press.

Carnegie Foundation for the Advancement of Teaching. 1982. *The control of the campus.* Washington, D.C.: Carnegie Foundation.

Dickey, F. G., and J. W. Miller. 1972. *A current perspective on accreditation.* Washington, D.C.: American Association for Higher Education.

Falk, D. S., N. Weisfeld, and D. Tochen. 1979. *Perspectives on health occupational credentialing.* DHHS Publication no. [HRA]81-4. Washington, D.C.: Government Printing Office.

Finkin, M. W. 1973. Federal reliance on voluntary accreditation: The power to recognize as the power to regulate. *Journal of Law and Education* 2 (July): 339–67.

————. 1979. Reforming the federal relationship to educational accreditation. *North Carolina Law Review* 57 (March): 379–413.

Fossum, D. 1978. Law school accreditation standards and the structure of American legal education. *American Bar Foundation Research Journal* 1978:515–43.

Freidson, E. 1970. *Professional dominance.* New York: Atherton Press.

Fretz, B. R., and D. H. Mills. 1980. *Licensing and certification of psychologists and counselors: A guide to current policies.* San Francisco: Jossey-Bass, Inc.

Friedman, L. M. 1965. Freedom of contract and occupational licensing, 1890–1910: A legal and social study. *California Law Review* 53 (May): 487–534.

Gellhorn, W. 1956. *Individual freedom and governmental restraints.* Baton Rouge: Louisiana State University Press.

Greene, K., and R. Gay. 1980. *Occupational regulation in the United States.* Washington, D.C.: U.S. Department of labor, Employment and Training Administration.

Haber, S. 1974. The professions and higher education in America: A historical view. In *Higher education and the labor market,* edited by M. S. Hill. New York: McGraw-Hill Book Co.

Hall, T. D., and C. M. Lindsay. 1980. Medical schools: Producers of What? Sellers of Whom? *Journal of Law and Economics* 23 (April): 55–80.

Havighurst, C. C., and N. M. P. King. 1983. Private credentialing of health care personnel: An antitrust perspective. *American Journal of Law and Medicine* 9, nos. 2–3:131–334.

Hofstadter, R., and W. P. Metzger. 1955. *The development of academic freedom in the United States.* New York: Columbia University Press.

Hogan, D. B. 1979. *The regulation of psychotherapists.* Vol. 1, *A study in the philosophy and practice of professional regulation.* Cambridge, Mass.: Ballinger Publishing Co.

Johnson, W. P. 1978. *Schooled lawyers: A study in the clash of professional cultures.* New York: New York University Press.

Kendall, P. L. 1965. The relationship between medical educators and medical practitioners. In Medical education and practices: Relationships and responsibilities in a changing society, edited by S. G.

Wolf, Jr. and W. Darley. Part 2 of *Journal of Medical Education* 40 (January): 137–245.

Koerner, J. D. 1970. *The Parsons College bubble.* New York: Basic Books.

Leffler, K. 1978. Physicians' licenses: Competition and monopoly in American medicine. *Journal of law and Economics* 22 (April): 165–86.

Liebmann, G. W. 1975. Delegation to private parties in American constitutional law. *Indiana Law Journal* 50:650–719.

National Association of Social Workers. 1981a. *State comparison of laws regulating social work.* Washington, D.C.: National Association of Social Workers.

———. 1981b. *Policy statement 6—NASW standards for social work in health care settings, professional standards.* Washington, D.C.: National Association of Social Workers.

New York Consolidated Laws Service. 1976a. *New York Consolidated Laws Service annotated statutes with forms.* Vol. 19, Judiciary law. Rochester, N.Y.: Lawyers Co-operative Publishing Co.

———. 1976b. *New York Consolidated Laws Service annotated statutes with forms.* Vol. 25, Public buildings law to public health law. Rochester, N.Y.: Lawyers Co-operative Publishing Co.

———. 1979. *New York Consolidated Laws Service annotated statutes with forms.* Vol. 10A, Education law. Rochester, N.Y.: Lawyers Co-operative Publishing Co.

———. 1982. *New York Consolidated Laws Service annotated statutes with forms: Cumulative supplement.* Vol. 3, Benevolent orders law to canal law: Professional service corporation. Rochester, N.Y.: Lawyer's Co-operative Publishing Co.

New York Department of State. 1983. *Official Compilation of Codes, Rules and Regulations of New York.* Albany, N.Y.: New York Department of State.

Norwood, W. F. 1941. *Medical education in the United States before the Civil War.* Philadelphia: University of Pennsylvania Press.

O'Malley, C. D., ed. 1970. *The history of medical education.* Berkeley: University of California Press.

Orlans, H. 1975. *Private accreditation and public eligibility.* Lexington, Mass.: D. C. Heath & Co.

Petersen, D. G. 1979. *Accrediting standards and guidelines.* Washington, D.C.: Council on Postsecondary Accreditation.

Roederer, D., and B. Shimberg. 1980. *Occupational licensing: Centralizing state licensure functions.* Lexington, Ky.: Council of State Governments.

Selden, W. K. 1960. *Accreditation: A struggle over standards in higher education.* New York: Harper & Brothers.

Shimberg, B. 1982. *Occupational licensing: A public perspective.* Princeton, N.J.: Educational Testing Service.

Southern Association of Colleges and Schools. Commission on Colleges. 1977. *Standards of the college delegate assembly.* Atlanta, Ga.: Southern Association of Colleges and Schools.

Spence, A. M. 1974. *Market signaling: Informational transfer in hiring and related screening processes.* Cambridge, Mass.: Harvard University Press.

Stevens, R. 1983. *Law school: Legal education in America from the 1850s to the 1980s.* Chapel Hill: University of North Carolina Press.

U.S. Department of Labor. Office of Research and Development. Employment and Training Administration. 1980. *Directory of state-regulated occupations.* Washington, D.C.: U.S. Government Printing Office.

Wallace, D. A. 1972. Occupational licensing and certification: Remedies for denial. *William and Mary Law Review* 14 (Fall): 46–127.

Weisfeld, N., J. Glanz, T. Schlecht, and R. M. Jackson. 1982. *Federal regulation of health occupations.* Washington, D.C.: National Commission for Health Certifying Agencies.

Wiley, M. G., and M. N. Zald. 1968. The growth and transformation of educational accrediting agencies: An exploratory study in social control of institutions. *Sociology of Education* 14 (Winter): 36–56.

Chapter Five

The Position of Professionals in the Courts

In the last chapter I delineated the outlines of the system that creates professional credentials and that reserves at least a small number of positions in work organizations for those who possess those credentials. In the course of following out some of the characteristics of the system I also showed that positions reserved for credentialed members of the professions are not solely those in which everyday work is performed. Positions are also reserved for teachers and researchers in professional schools and for those who supervise the everyday work of credentialed professionals and manage the organizations in which they work. This internal role differentiation aids professions in their efforts to maintain control over both their claimed knowledge and skill and the conditions under which they work. It represents a critical element of the social organization of professions, one without which their characteristics in the United States would be considerably more like other occupations than they are now.

I shall return to the social organization of professions in a later chapter, but here it seems appropriate to continue to pursue the significance of the credential system by examining its consequences for the status of professionals in the legal system. The legal system, after all, represents the framework within which all activities must be fitted whenever they become problematic. The credential system is in part created and in part supported by the legal system. The question is, What is the status of credentials in the legal system? What is the status of professionals? Apart from the right to use a particular title or to perform a particular kind of work, does the possession of professional credentials provide special privileges in the legal system? In this chapter I shall discuss issues that bear on professionals as individuals involved in litigation, exploring the extent to which they, in their roles as credentialed professionals, are granted special status by the courts both in the role of a witness in the conduct of legal inquiry and in the role of a defendant in the law of torts. In the next chapter I shall have occasion to examine other bodies of law bearing on professions as corporate bodies and on the formal organizations in which they work.

On the whole, it seems possible to say that, while professions do have some privilege in their standing, the courts insistently claim to be the ultimate arbiter of entitlement to it. By and large, the deciding criterion for privilege seems to be recognition by the courts of some form of knowledge, skill, or experience sufficiently specialized that the ordinary person— the "reasonable man" in legal tradition—cannot be expected to know, possess, or be able to practice it adequately. It is expertise that is recognized, however, not credentials, for credentials do not provide automatic qualification for privilege. Members of professions are recognized as experts, but so are members of other, uncredentialed occupations. Furthermore, anyone who appears as an expert witness must risk unrestrained attack on his or her learning or qualifications by counsel to the opposing party before being permitted to testify. And what privilege there is is in any case asserted or claimed by the client and justified by reference to the client's good. Privilege cannot be asserted by professionals on their own behalf, and it can be waived by their clients if they so choose. Let us explore the nature of this special status first in testimonial privilege—that is, the right to refuse to provide testimony to a legal inquiry—and second in the privileges connected with being an expert rather than an ordinary witness. For the sake of simplicity, I shall rely on the most authoritative legal commentaries and focus on federal rather than state law.

Testimonial Privilege—the Silent Witness

The matter of testimonial privilege can be addressed fairly quickly if only because of the small number of circumstances in which it is permitted. In the trying of a case in court, the dominant notion is that all facts bearing on the case should be made available to the court and that all relevant witnesses are obliged to testify to the court on pain of a charge of contempt. One exception to this rule that is consistent and forceful, however, bears on the preparation of a litigant's case itself—the lawyer-client privilege. It is "the oldest of the privileges for confidential communications" (Weinstein and Berger 1981, 2:503-15), and it is likely to be an irreducible privilege when all others have vanished. It is the only privilege recognized in common law. Originally, its rationale was in part functional and in part related to the gentlemanly status of the lawyer—the privilege belonged to the attorney for the purpose of "permitting him to keep the secrets confided in him by his client and thus preserve his honor" (Wigmore 1979, par. 2290). It now has a secular and functional rationale and is based on the grounds "that encouraging clients to make the fullest disclosure to their attorneys enables the latter to act more effectively, justly and expeditiously, and that these benefits outweigh the risks posed by barring full revelation in the courts" (Weinstein and Berger 1981, 2:503-15; see also an alternative justification based on the right of privacy discussed in Shuman and Weiner 1982, 906).

The general rule of privilege of Federal Rule of Evidence 503 reads as follows:

A client has a privilege to refuse to disclose and to prevent any other person from disclosing confidential communications made for the purpose of facilitating the rendition of professional [*sic*] legal services to the client, (1) between himself or his representative and his lawyer or his lawyer's representative, or (2) between his lawyer and the lawyer's representative, or (3) by him or his lawyer to a lawyer representing another in a matter of common interest, or (4) between representatives of the client or between the client and a representative of the client, or (5) between lawyers representing the client.

Lawyer is defined by the rule as "a person authorized or reasonably believed by a client to be authorized, to practice law in any state or nation," while his representative is defined as "one employed to assist the lawyer in the rendition of professional legal services." As one might expect, there are many difficulties surrounding the notions of lawyer and of lawyer's representative, not to speak of those of client and of client representative, and there are exceptions to privilege when crime or fraud is involved (cf. the commentary on Rule 503 in Weinstein and Berger 1981, vol. 2).

While the lawyer-client privilege is justified by its protection of a relationship that would allow the most vigorous and informed presentation of a case in the adversarial setting of the court, other privileges granted to other professionals are justified by reference to extrajudicial values. Supreme Court Standard 504 asserts a psychotherapist-patient privilege as follows: "A patient has a privilege to refuse to disclose and to prevent any other person from disclosing confidential communications, made for the purpose of diagnosis or treatment of his mental or emotional condition, including drug addiction, among himself, his psychotherapist, or persons who are participating in the diagnosis or treatment under the direction of a psychotherapist, including members of the patient's family." This privilege is at once narrower and wider than the physician-patient privilege that many states have established since New York first did so in 1828 (for a recent collation of state laws, see Shuman and Weiner 1982, 907–12). It is in fact designed to narrow a general medical privilege for which legal commentators could find little justification (ibid., 894) and to restrict protection solely to consultations that might not occur if the patient could not be assured of confidentiality—namely, consultation for behavioral or emotional disorders (Weinstein and Berger 1981, 2:504-15–16).

But while the psychotherapist-patient privilege does not recognize any absolute physician-patient privilege, its ultimate definition of *psychotherapist* brought a broad form of physician-patient privilege in through the back door while adopting a very narrow view of who, beyond a physician, could be considered to be a bona fide therapist. Witness the definition of *psychotherapist* in Standard 504: "A 'psychotherapist' is (A) a person authorized to practice medicine in any state or nation, or reasonably believed by the patient so to be, while engaged in the diagnosis or treatment of a mental or emotional condition, including drug addiction, or (B) a person licensed or certified as a psychologist under the laws of any state or nation, while similarly engaged." Any physician, not solely those trained in psychiatry, has such privilege when dealing with a patient's mental or emotional conditions, while only a psychologist, among nonmedical psychotherapists, may employ the privilege. Social workers and others may claim privilege only if they work "under the direction of the psychotherapist," not if they work independently. Of the various states, some preserve the general physician-patient privilege without limiting it to a psychotherapeutic relationship, and some recognize the privilege of social workers under some circumstances (cf. Weinstein and Berger 1981, 2:504-31–44).

The final professional privilege recognized by the rules of evidence for U.S. courts is that of the clergyman. Supreme Court Standard 506 asserts that "a person has a privilege to refuse to disclose and to prevent another from disclosing a confidential communication by the person to a clergyman in his professional [*sic*] character as a spiritual advisor." The notion of religious liberty (cf. Weinstein and Berger 1981, 2:506-6–7), in the United States, has permitted the growth of an enormous variety of practices labeled *religious*, so it follows that there would be problems in determining who is a bona fide clergyman. Standard 506 defines the word as follows: "A 'clergyman' is a minister, priest, rabbi, or other similar functionary of a religious organization, or an individual reasonably believed to be so by the person consulting him." This standard represents, as Weinstein and Berger note, "one of the few instances in the federal rules of evidence where the privilege adopted is broader than that generally found in American [state] jurisdictions" (1981, 2:506-10). In some states, a communication must be made as part of a doctrinally required confession in order to be privileged, thereby limiting the privilege to only a few religions and sects. No doubt the broadness of the federal rule rests on a conception of the constitutional obligation of the courts to avoid discriminating among religions in assigning privilege. The consequence of its broadness is an intrinsic ambiguity in determining qualifications because many religions have no formal credentialing procedure analogous to that of medicine or psychology. As Weinstein and Berger note, "self-designated ministers and ministers of fringe cults will probably not qualify. More troublesome is the question of sects such as Jehovah's Witnesses, where each member is designated a minister" (1981, 2:506-7).

Thus we see that, under some circumstances, even the overriding sovereignty of the courts to collect all relevant evidence for a case in order that justice may be done can be opposed by the value imputed to the functions of the work of particular professions. Above all, and least qualified, is the lawyer's privilege, which, paradoxically, is considered essential to collecting all relevant evidence and presenting it most effectively to the court on behalf of the client. The more circumscribed privileges of the psychotherapist-physician and the clergyman, on the other hand, testify to the important functions they are thought to serve for society in general rather than the courts in particular, functions thought sufficiently important to overweigh the value of requiring them to reveal their secrets to the court.

Evidentiary Privilege: The Expert Witness

In another body of testimonial privilege, the role of professionals lies in assisting rather than resisting the court's determination of the facts of a case. All witnesses are presumed to assist the court by their testimony, of course, but the kind of testimony they are permitted to give is limited by the rules of evidence. One special type of witness, however, has the privilege of giving testimony of a different character than that allowed ordinary witnesses—the expert witness.

The common law and trial by a jury of one's peers both rely on the notion that ordinary people are capable of understanding and evaluating the facts of cases set before them. When all the facts are advanced vigorously and properly by counsel for both parties, such a jury is thought able to arrive at a just decision. At least implicit as well is the assumption that, when the ordinary people of the jury sometimes find it difficult to make sense of the facts put forward in testimony as such, the more sophisticated ordinary knowledge or wisdom of the judge, along with the didactic function of counsels' examination of witnesses, can assist them in understanding and evaluating. However, in any society with a complex division of labor, there are areas of highly specialized knowledge, skill, and experience that are not familiar or even comprehensible to ordinary people or even to counsel and the court. When such elaborate expertise is relevant to a case, an expert witness may be called to appraise the facts for the court—on behalf of either or both parties or even on behalf of the court itself.

Wigmore asserts a general theory of experiential capacity within which he places "expertness": "Since upon some matters accurate understanding can never be attained without special preparation or familiarity, the rules of evidence must recognize this, and must see to it that the testimonial statements offered as representing knowledge are not offered by persons who are not fitted to acquire knowledge on the subject at hand. Such fitness or skill to acquire accurate impressions comes from circumstances which may broadly be summed up in the term 'experience'" (Wigmore 1979, par. 555). However, he asserts, such experience is particular and specialized, rather than general, and so must be relative and limited to the topic in question. Since it is particular fitness for a particular topic, it cannot be assumed to exist for any witness in the same way as the general fitness of any ordinary, adult member of society may be assumed. The possession of "some *special and peculiar experience*, more than is the common possession . . . , cannot be assumed for an individual witness, but *must be expressly shown beforehand*," in advance of testimony (ibid., par. 556). Expert qualification can be demonstrated by showing that one has gained specialized "occupational experience" in the course of a steady career in some livelihood and/or by showing "scientific experience" by virtue of systematic training "involving the study of a body of knowledge forming a branch of some science or art" (ibid.). The emphasis is thus on general expertise, not on the more limited institutional notion of credentialed professional expertise. Credentials are necessary for qualification, but they are not in themselves enough: when they exist, they must be plausibly connected to the particular topic at hand. In any case, "the *trial court must be left to determine*, absolutely and without review, the fact of possession of the required qualification by a particular witness" (ibid., par. 561).

Once expert testimony is admitted, certain rules of evidence that hold for ordinary witnesses are qualified if not suspended. One is the "opinion rule" (cf. ibid., pars. 557, 1918), which holds that the opinions of ordinary witnesses—that is, their judgments, inferences, and evaluations—are superfluous.

Since a jury composed of people with ordinary, everyday experience is as fit to arrive at an opinion about the facts of a case as is an ordinary witness, the latter should restrict testimony to the facts themselves. If the topic is highly esoteric, however, then the judgment or opinion of an expert witness can be of value to the jury in helping it to arrive at its own opinion about the facts of the case.

For the expert witness the "hearsay rule" is suspended for similar reasons. Wigmore notes that the courts have often emphasized the critical importance of firsthand observation in establishing knowledge of the facts, "the first corollary from [which] is that what the witness represents as his knowledge must be an impression derived from the *exercise of his own senses*, not from the reports of others" (ibid., par. 657). Thus hearsay, which is not founded on personal observation, is inadmissible as evidence for most ordinary witnesses. However, exception is made for some kinds of evidence and testimony—the records of a public bureau, for example, which may not be personally known by an official to be authentic, and the recorded outcome of "scientific instruments, apparatus, formulas and calculating tables." Furthermore, the expert can testify to the reported data of fellow experts, "learned by perusing their reports in books and journals," without his testimony being rejected as hearsay (ibid., par. 665a).

As Wigmore notes,

The data of every science are enormous in scope and variety. No one professional man can know from personal observation more than a minute fraction of the data which he must every day treat as working truths. . . . The law must and does accept this kind of knowledge from scientific men. On the one hand, a mere layman who comes to court and alleges a fact which he has learned only by reading a medical or a mathematical book, cannot be heard. But, on the other hand, to reject a professional physician or mathematician because the fact or some facts to which he testifies are known to him only upon the authority of others would be to ignore the accepted methods of professional work and to insist on finical and impossible standards. [Ibid., par. 665b]

He admits the difficulty of distinguishing between what constitutes the credibility of the lay witness and what constitutes that of the professional witness. He tries to resolve the problem by suggesting that what should be taken into account is the capacity, based on experience and training, to choose trustworthy authorities, to find the proper source of information, and to have experience allowing some personal observation that will provide a foundation for assessing the plausibility and soundness of textual sources. Such testimony is all the more necessary in a circumstance in which nothing other than reported data is available on the topic.

The Federal Rules of Evidence do not stray very far from Wigmore's doctrines. Rule 701 limits testimony in the form of opinions or inferences when a witness is not testifying as an expert, but it permits the admission of opinion when it may be helpful to the court. This position, according to Weinstein and Berger, recognizes the ambiguous epistemological foundation of a strict distinction between fact and opinion by offering a discretionary rule of admission (1981, 3:701-3–9). As they note, the rule blurs any really rigid distinction between the admissible testimony of lay and of expert witnesses, allowing the court to take a flexible approach, one tailored to the facts of the case.

Rule 702 specifically permits expert testimony in the form of opinion, provided it is helpful to the court: "If the scientific, technical, or other specialized knowledge will assist the trier of fact to understand the evidence or to determine a fact in issue, a witness qualified as an expert by knowledge, skill, experience, training or education may testify thereto in the form of an opinion or otherwise." In commentary, Weinstein and Berger make a number of points of interest to our concern for the status of experts in general and professionals in particular (1981, 3:702-6–31). They note that the helpfulness of expert testimony now emerges as the central test, not, as Wigmore implied, whether the average juror can assess the facts at issue. By that criterion the trial judge has broad discretion in admitting or rejecting expert testimony. Furthermore, by its silence on the *Frye* test (*Frye v. United States*, 239 Fed. 1013 [D.C. Cir. 1923]), which evaluates a novel form of expertise by determining whether it has gained acceptance in the scientific community, Weinstein and Berger conclude that the rule does not require the court to be guided by the consensus of scientific or professional experts. In the words of one opinion (*United States v. Williams*, 583 F.2d 1194, 1198 [2d Cir. 1978]), "the courts cannot in any event surrender to scientists responsibility for determining the reliability of . . . evidence" (1981, 3:702-17). Legal or judicial hegemony is affirmed over the organized scientific community in the Federal Rules of Evidence even if it is not sustained in many federal and state courts, where the *Frye* test is still applied.

Judicial hegemony is similarly affirmed over the institution of credentialism, for the very loose definition of the qualification of the expert is in accord with Rule 104(a), which makes the matter one for the judge to determine. Weinstein and Berger quote with approval, as being in accord with the definition, appellate court's statement that "an expert need not have certificates of training, nor membership in professional organizations. . . . Nor need he be, as the trial court apparently required, an outstanding practitioner in the field in which he professes expertise" (1981, 3:702-23, n. 6). And they emphasize that "Rule 702 recognizes that it is the actual qualifications of the witness that count, rather than his title. . . . Just as the wrong title may mean that the witness is nevertheless qualified, the right title will not suffice if the witness does not have the qualifications required by the facts of the case" (ibid., 702-25). Their review, and Wigmore's, for that matter, makes it clear that members of a large variety of occupations extending well beyond those conventionally called professions have been admitted to give expert testimony and that the courts have often refused to rely on formal criteria alone.

Rules 703 and 704 are addressed to the sources or bases of opinion testimony by experts and the admissibility of expert testimony that bears on the "ultimate facts." They have the net effect of liberalizing the substance of what is admissible as expert testimony, including records and public opinion poll evidence that previously might have been ruled out as hearsay or as bearing too closely on matters that were held to be the sole province of the jury. Rules 705 and 706 bear on the procedure of examining the expert witness and on court appointment of experts.

Thus we see that the rules of evidence recognize the necessity of paying special attention to witnesses who can offer the benefit of specialized knowledge and judgment to the court and of making special provisions for the employment of that benefit. However, the present-day tendency is to set very narrow limits to such special provision, leaving loopholes in every case that are finally adjudicated by the court and not by experts or their peers. Those loopholes extend even to the qualifications of experts themselves, with no consistent reliance on the credential as an unequivocal qualification and no restriction of expert status to professionalized occupations alone. An expert witness can as well be a steamfitter or a farmer as a physician or a dentist.

This assessment would be seriously misleading if left to stand unqualified. There is little doubt that the role of expert testimony is becoming more and more important in the courts. The most visible circumstance is in malpractice suits, when legal action is undertaken against such an expert as a physician, and expert testimony is required to establish negligence wherever the facts cannot speak for themselves. Less obvious and in fact hidden from easy view is what is perhaps the far more pervasive role that expert testimony plays in administrative law. A number of governmental agencies, both federal and state, administer and enforce legislation addressed to the control of environmental pollution, to the safety of construction, aircraft, food and drugs, and nuclear energy plants, and to labor disputes, to name but a few instances. In the event of appeal for enforcement by the relevant agency or appeal from enforcement agency directives by the firm or person affected, hearings are held in which, given the often highly technical nature of the issues, expert testimony must play a central role.

In general, administrative proceedings are governed by the Federal Administrative Procedure Act and the statutes of the agency in question. It is not typical for there to be an insistence on tight adherence to the formal rules of evidence during the course of hearings, though one might suspect that, in cases of doubt or challenge, the administrative law judge or hearing officer will refer to them. Given the issues involved in those various areas of administrative law, one might suspect that there, more than in the civil and criminal law cases emphasized by the conventional textbooks and commentaries I have cited here, the reliance on expert testimony is extensive. And indeed it is possible that a doctrine of deference to professional judgment is developing. So while it is essential to note that the sovereignty of the courts is continuously asserted in principle against claims for autonomy on the basis of professional expertise, the influence of specialized formal knowledge on both the procedures and the substance of legal affairs today should not be underestimated and deserves much closer study than has been possible here.

NEGLIGENCE AND THE LAW OF TORTS

The testimony of an expert is helpful to the court when it involves issues of such a specialized or "advanced" nature that the ordinary person of the jury cannot be expected to evaluate them on the basis of everyday knowledge and experience. As one might expect, with the advance of the industrial revolution and the proliferation of highly technical, specialized knowledge and skill, issues of litigation that are beyond the everyday experience of the average, even the well-educated, person have also proliferated, and the courts have also been obliged to admit testimony on increasingly varied areas by experts of an expanding number of disciplines. Those well publicized by the mass media—the ballistics experts in murder trials, hematologists in paternity suits, and pharmacologists and pathologists in drug-related deaths—constitute only a small number of the variety of experts now employed, something that should be immediately evident when we think of the law of torts and of such issues as product liability on the part of manufacturers and suits for negligence.

Since the essential function of expert testimony is to provide information and evaluation of issues that the ordinary person cannot be expected to possess, it follows that expert testimony is an intrinsic necessity in those cases in which experts are themselves the object of suit—when professionals, for example, are sued for negligence or malpractice. *Negligence*, however, is a very special concept. "Negligent conduct involves unintentional harm resulting from a lack of care. Since intent is not being determined to establish fault, some standard of carefulness must be established against which individual conduct may be measured" (Curran 1960, 1). John Wade has loosely delineated a body of law addressed to professional negligence that is distinct from that connected with product liability on the part of manufacturers and suppliers, land owner's liability, the liability of "masters" or employers for the actions of their "servants," and the like (1960, v–vi). His usage, however, like that of Prosser (1971, 161–62), is so broad as to be clearly addressed not merely to professions but to any kind of full-time, specialized occupation, for he includes both the traditional professions and also barbers, carpenters, launderers, electricians, and plumbers. Indeed, he characterizes the grouping as including negligent conduct on the part of "all those who follow a vocation in which they render a service to others" (Wade 1960, vi)—in short, all service occupations (cf. Moore 1960, 309–11; Winfield 1926, 187; Arterburn 1927).

However, Wade appears to have defined the grouping too broadly, for his definition does not distinguish between a common service and an esoteric service. As he points out, "the first reported negligence cases in the common law [in England] were suits against persons who held themselves out as following a 'public calling'—a surgeon, an attorney or a blacksmith" (1960, v). However, other vocations were equally liable as, perhaps even more strictly liable than, surgeons. I refer to innkeepers, ferrymen, and other common carriers who, if not now then at least in earlier times, did not employ any complex or esoteric skill in their trade but who were held by the courts to a stricter standard of care than was the general run of mankind because of the indispensable and virtual monopolistic character of their services (Wallace 1972, 117). Occupations offering a specialized or relatively esoteric service as well as those offering a "common service" are held liable for negligence by a standard more strict than that applied to the actions of other, ordinary people. They are held liable, furthermore, even though they have not specifically promised to accomplish a particular result—even though, in other words, they have not made a contract. In the absence of a contract they cannot be held liable for breach of contract, but they can nonetheless be held liable in tort for negligence (Prosser 1971, 162).

Merely to offer a service incurs a legal obligation to provide it with reasonable care and competence. Thus both specialized and common service trades are singled out and, rather than being privileged, are liable to charges of negligence. But when it comes to demonstrating negligence in court, it is my impression that the former, the specialized service occupations and perhaps especially the established professions, are judged by the standards of the occupations themselves, while the common service occupations are not. Both are disadvantaged by being held to a stricter standard than the ordinary tradesperson is, but the former have the advantage and privilege of being judged by what are in a sense their own standards, while the latter do not have that privilege.

The specialist, or expert, poses a serious problem to the law. On the one hand, as Prosser puts it, "professional men in general, and those who undertake any work calling for special skill, are required not only to exercise reasonable care in what they do, but also to possess a standard minimum of special knowledge and ability" (ibid., 161). As Curran put it, "a professional service is made up of learning and skill. If a man offers a certain service, he must apply to it his special education, experience and skill" (1960, 4). The problem for the court is, How does one establish the standard of care—that is, the standard of application—when the work involves special skill or knowledge that the ordinary person lacks? In essence, the practice has been to establish the standard of care by calling on expert testimony from members of the same occupation as the defendant. As Prosser puts it, "since juries composed of laymen are normally incompetent to pass judgment on questions of . . . science or technique . . . there can be no finding of negligence in the absence of expert testimony to support it" (1971, 164). Thus was established "the privilege, which is usually emphatically denied to other groups, of setting their own legal standards of conduct, merely by adopting their own practices" (ibid., 165). While this presumably functionally necessary privilege is discussed most often in the case of medicine, the profession that has received the most attention in negligence or malpractice suits, it also holds for more humble crafts. Moore provides examples of one case in which a plumber gave expert testimony on customary methods of cutting soil pipe and of another in which there was an exploration of the customs of "the barbering trade" in the course of determining a barber's negligence (1960, 312–13).

No doubt, as Moore notes (ibid., 309), many jobs previously performed by identifiable artisans like electricians and mechanics are now being performed by employees of large corporations, making the defendant corporate rather than individual; but I would also suspect that the general invisibility of occupations not generally considered professions in discussions of tort action for negligence stems from their more modest economic means (which would tend to discourage suit) and that, related to that, the likelihood that action against them stays mostly in the jurisdiction of lower, local courts, only a small proportion of whose decisions are likely to be appealed and thus come to the attention of legal scholars. Whatever the case, it seems clear that here, too, there is no generic "professional" status in the law of torts or in legal practice. The professional is merely a conspicuous example of a more general class of expert or practitioner of a specialized occupation. And while that class is held to a higher standard of care merely by virtue of offering specialized services to the public, determination of that standard and, on occasion, of whether a defendant has met that standard must rely in large part on testimony from members of that specialized occupation itself.

But reliance on expert testimony is not absolute either. Again, there is the issue of what the ordinary member of a jury can be expected to know and evaluate without the aid of expert testimony. That is a matter for the court to determine, as we have seen from the Federal Rules of Evidence. And there, conceptions of what is self-evident to any ordinary person obviously depend on the level of information and sophistication of a particular population in a particular historical period. Some facts speak for themselves to the ordinary person of a given time, in which case expert testimony is not necessary and the doctrine of *res ipsa loquitur* (the fact speaks for itself) applies. Prosser gives as examples of this instances "where the surgeon saws off the wrong leg, or there is injury to a part of the body not within the operative field" (1971, 164), citing other cases in which a tongue was cut off in the course of removing adenoids, a dentist pulled the wrong tooth, a shoulder was injured during an appendectomy, and the like.

If the rising level of formal education in our society has decreased the knowledge gap between layperson and expert, then we should expect less reliance on expert testimony and more on the doctrine of *res ipsa loquitur*. This is a difficult matter to determine empirically, but one might guess that expert testimony is relied on less in negligence cases involving artisans like carpenters or plumbers because the ordinary person is likely to be believed to be able to evaluate their practice far more readily than that of technicians, scientists, and the major professions. But even here there remains the loophole out of which an absolute privilege drains. The court insists on its ultimate sovereignty: "The factual situation [may be ruled by the courts to be] simple enough for an ordinary layman to pass on it. . . . [Expert] evidence may be desirable, but it is not required" (Wade 1960, vii).

Here, as in the other areas of law I have reviewed in this chapter, the essential dilemma embedded in the expert's role in our society is reflected. On the one hand, specialized knowledge and skill are very often quite esoteric and well beyond the capacity of ordinary people to comprehend and evaluate during the brief course of time they are confronted with it in encounters in court or elsewhere. Furthermore, that formal knowledge and skill is frequently regarded with deference and believed to be of value. But if the court is to be sovereign and rules are to be followed that preserve that sovereignty, neither professional credentials nor the substance of professional opinion can be allowed consistently superior authority. The outcome of that dilemma is refusal to employ professional credentials as an authoritative qualification for granting deference and to attempt to secularize professional knowledge by treating it as merely expertise connected with a particular trade. Nonetheless, because it is expertise, it must have special standing. After it survives the corrosive challenges of adversarial proceedings, it must be relied on by the court to some degree and given some weight. Sovereign though the courts may be, they must temper their powers in the face of expertise, trying to minimize the influence of the forms by which expertise is institutionalized into professionalism while recognizing the need for significant areas of privilege in the position of expertise itself. Surely such privilege reflects some of the intrinsic power accruing to the formal knowledge represented by the professions.

References

Arterburn, N. F. 1927. The origin and first test of public calling. *University of Pennsylvania Law Review* 75:411–28.

Curran, W. J. 1960. Professional negligence—some general comments. In *Professional negligence*, edited by T. G. Roady, Jr., and W. R. Andersen, 1–12. Nashville, Tenn.: Vanderbilt University Press.

Moore, J. L. 1960. Liability of artisans and tradesmen for negligence. In *Professional negligence*, edited by T. G. Roady, Jr., and W. R. Andersen, 309–21. Nashville, Tenn.: Vanderbilt University Press.

Prosser, W. L. 1971. *Handbook of the law of torts*. 4th ed. St. Paul, Minn.: West Publishing Co.

Shuman, D. W., and M. S. Weiner. 1982. The privilege study: An empirical examination of the psychotherapist-patient privilege. *North Carolina Law Review* 60 (June): 893–942.

Wade, J. R. 1960. Foreword. In *Professional negligence*, edited by T. G. Roady, Jr., and W. R. Andersen, v–ix. Nashville, Tenn.: Vanderbilt University Press.

Wallace, D. A. 1972. Occupational licensing and certification: Remedies for denial. *William and Mary Law Review* 14 (Fall): 46–127.

Weinstein, J. B., and M. A. Berger. 1981. *Weinstein's evidence: Commentary on the rules of evidence for the United States courts and state courts*. 3 vols. New York: Matthew Bender.

Wigmore, J. H. 1979. *Evidence in trials at common law*. Vol. 2. Rev. by J. H. Chadbourn. Boston: Little, Brown.

Winfield, P. H. 1926. The history of negligence in the law of torts. *Law Quarterly Review* 166 (April): 184–201.

Chapter Six

The Question of Professional Decline

At this point it is essential to take stock. I initiated my analysis by noting that formal knowledge has grown enormously in complexity, quantity, and sophistication over the past century and that a number of observers have raised important questions about its power over our lives. I then argued that the professions can be seen as the agents of that formal knowledge and that the possibility of their exercising power can be appraised by analyzing their political, economic, and other institutions. After identifying the professions as typically credentialed on the basis of higher education and as relying for their living on labor-market shelters built around those credentials, I went on to sketch the institutions and practices that create both those credentials and their sheltered positions in the political economy. And I attempted to appraise the legal status of professional credentials in such fundamental areas as the rules of evidence and the law of torts.

By now enough information has been presented to allow us to return momentarily to the issue of power and to note that a number of observers have argued that professions did have significant power in the past but are now sufficiently along the way to losing it that one can assert they are in decline. If this is true, of course, the tenor of analysis should lie more in documenting those shifts in history and their consequences and less in following through the details of the interconnected circumstances in which professional powers are organized and exercised today—the balance, if not the general substance, of the analysis would be different. Before continuing my analysis of the present day, therefore, I must discuss in this chapter the varied writings that assert the professions to be losing their privileged position, discuss the evidence for it, and in the course of doing so identify further some of the characteristics of that position in the United States today.

IDEAS OF PROFESSIONAL DECLINE

There is a fairly large amount of writing on the theme of professional decline, but much of it is in the form of either ephemeral and exaggerated feature articles in the mass media or musings by elderly professionals about how the times have changed since the good old days of their youth. In the literature more worthy of sustained attention there is some consensus about the issues, with two broadly different sets of preoccupations.

One broad group arguing professional decline marks the professions of the past with characteristic high prestige and public trust or confidence and sees them to be losing those characteristics because of changes in the attitudes and behavior of the public and in the character of their knowledge. In essence, the claim is that the professions are being deprofessionalized (Toren 1975; Haug 1973, 1975, 1977; Rothman 1984; cf. Yarmolinsky 1978, 159; for medicine, see Burnham 1982; and Betz and O'Connell 1983, 84; for attacks on the major professions, see Barber 1983). Where there is an attempt to explain that loss, a number of other changes are invoked. For one, there is reference to a trend toward greater egalitarianism, which means that clients are more inclined to question authority today than they were in the past. More often, reference is made to the rising educational level of the public, which narrows the gap between the professional's knowledge and the client's and thus erodes the professional's authority. Furthermore, the public is said to have become more active and aggressive as consumers, which, in conjunction with the narrowed "knowledge gap," also makes them inclined to question the professions. In the case of major professions like medicine (e.g., McKinlay 1982, 50–55) and law (Rothman 1984, 190–91), reference is made both to the standardization and routinization of knowledge (Toren 1975, 329–31) and to the importance of computer technology in removing control over practice from the hands of the practitioner. Finally, some claim that other occupations are taking over the traditional areas served by the professions, thereby destroying their monopolies.

Another broad group of writers is inspired by Marxist theory, including its theory of history, and pays less attention to the relations between consumers and professionals and more to the place of professionals in the capitalist political economy and their relations to the owners of capital. Consonant with the broader theory, the emphasis is on professionals as workers and on how their changing position over this century parallels that of manual labor in industry over the course of the nineteenth century, when independence and the ability to control their own work was lost (for general statements, see Oppenheimer 1973; Larson 1977, 1979, 1980; and Derber 1982; for medicine, see McKinlay 1982; and Coburn, Torrance, and Kanfert, 1983; for nursing, see Wagner 1980). While writers in this tradition vary in the degree to which they discuss the issues that those in the other broad group do, it seems accurate to say that all of them emphasize two factors central to the process of proletarianization—first, that the trend over this century has been for professionals to become employed and, second, that they are employed in bureaucracies. On becoming employed, the professional cannot be independent, free to choose what work to do and how to do it. And when employed in a bureaucracy, the professional becomes subject to strict controls that routinize and, according to some writers, deskill professional work. The trend toward proletarianization is thus predicated on the postulation of a trend from self-employment in an individual "free" practice to employment in large bureaucracies.

SORTING THE ISSUES

It is possible to sort out the serious issues raised by these writers fairly easily, for many of the assertions made to support the idea of professional decline will not stand up to close inspection. Central to many arguments is the matter of professional prestige and trust, both of which are difficult to establish unequivocally. If we rely on what is at least an effort at systematic comparison, however, we find that the relative prestige of the various professions has been quite stable over the past fifty years in the United States. There is no evidence that the prestige of medicine, law, schoolteaching, or the ministry has changed in relation to other occupations. Similarly, a recent collation of public opinion surveys between 1966 and 1981 shows that confidence in such professions as medicine, education, and science has indeed declined, but not in relation to confidence in other American occupations and institutions. The professions received the highest degree of confidence compared to that received by corporate executives, politicians, bureaucrats, and labor leaders. Thus the public continues to have a relatively high degree of confidence in the professions, with medicine retaining its preeminence in spite of the heavy criticism it has received (Lipset and Schneider 1983). There is no evidence of a sufficiently massive shift in public trust and confidence to motivate most clients to act much differently than they have in the past, consumerism notwithstanding.

Furthermore, while at least that minority of middle-class, well-educated consumers may have become more sophisticated over the past few decades (see Nelson and McGough 1983 for a study of their "illusion of autonomy"), the major professions continue to produce new, more esoteric specializations at the same time as the consumer's knowledge increases, so it is difficult to see any "knowledge gap" closing. Nor does the computer help so long as its programs and the evaluation of its printouts remain in the hands of the professions involved, as they do. And finally, there is no evidence that either encroachment by competing occupations or consumer self-help (do-it-yourself) movements have seriously threatened more than the margins of the licensed professions. The success of occupations like midwifery and real estate sales in infringing on the prior jurisdictions of medicine and law means little for the future of those professions if it is contained at the fringes while new areas of work are being invented.

These elements of public opinion, knowledge, and attitudes advanced by some of those who assert professional decline are not very persuasive when looked at closely (for a detailed appraisal of medicine in the light of assertions of decline, see Freidson 1985; for law, see Powell 1985). That there have been expressions of distrust and disrespect over the past two decades cannot be denied. What would make them consequential for the position of the professions today would be their effect on the stable institutional practices sustaining the position of the professions. It is precisely those institutional arrangements that have been ignored by those who assert professional decline. More important than the factors they cite have been governmental efforts at regulating some of the professions that could seriously alter some of the professions' institutional arrangements. Antitrust actions might be examined as an example. They are affecting primarily that minority of self-employed professions.

Antitrust Law and Limiting Professional Autonomy

In the course of analyzing the credential system I pointed out that in its most binding form, namely, licensing, it creates a monopoly over the performance of particular kinds of work. Licensing, like the rest of the credential system, is established by political activities, usually by professional associations in the individual states. Not all methods by which professions attempt to protect their collective interests are embodied in concrete laws, however. Some of the most important methods of controlling relationships with occupational competitors and of restricting divisive and potentially destructive competition among colleagues within the profession have been advanced as part of the professions' private codes of ethics rather than as a body of law. The violation of those codes, if enforced, could lead to expulsion from the professional association—a penalty that could have serious effects on the individual's livelihood in some of the more tightly organized professions. Let me examine some of them here.

Many of the better organized self-employed professions have traditionally had a number of proscriptions in their codes of ethics, some having to do with relations with other occupations and others dealing with relations between colleagues. In the former case, it is sometimes forbidden to split fees with laypersons and to refer clients to or otherwise collaborate with members of competing and disapproved occupations. In the latter case, such economic activity as competitive price bidding is forbidden, as are competitive advertising in general and advertising prices for specific services in particular. There is also a strong tendency to establish fixed, or at least minimum, fee schedules. All such bans, in addition to exclusive licensing itself, are nominally restraints of trade and in violation of antitrust law in the United States. But until recently the major professions were not considered to be "trade or commerce" and hence were not subject to governmental antitrust action (cf. Coleman 1967; and Herndon 1979). Their position was surrounded with the mystique of the old "status professions." This privileged exclusion is now on the way to being lost, leaving the professions with more limited economic and substantive privilege and a secularized set of privileges based on their presumed possession of a special kind of expertise. (For a sophisticated discussion, see Pollard and Leibenluft 1981; and Kissam 1983).

The first paragraph of the Sherman Act reads as follows: "Every contract, combination in the form of trust or otherwise, or conspiracy, in restraint of trade or commerce among the several States, or with foreign nations, is declared to be illegal" (15 U.S.C., § 1 [1970], quoted in Bauer 1975). A well-organized profession like medicine obviously constitutes one such combination. Its members have, through their exclusive license to practice, a monopoly over the provision of certain services. The profession's organization is technically a cartel of sellers of certain services whose policy is to regulate the behavior of its members in such a way that the freedom of individuals is maximized while at the same time limited so as to "not clearly affect other cartel members adversely" (Horowitz 1980, 11). Licensing itself is in restraint of trade or commerce in that those who are not licensed are not free to offer goods or services on the market.

"Fifty years ago, the Supreme Court would have invalidated much of the present licensing regulations on substantive due process grounds" (Wallace 1972, 51), for the Fourteenth Amendment to the Constitution refers to the right to due process and had been held to embrace both liberty from incarceration without due process and freedom to earn one's livelihood however one wishes. Nonetheless, the substantive due process doctrine has not been employed in the federal courts to attack licensing, though some state courts have invoked it to invalidate licensing of the manual trades (ibid., 52–53, nn. 32, 33). The traditional professions were protected by their special standing. Furthermore, the fact that licensing is largely a state rather than a federal activity gives it some measure of protection from federal action in the United States, though, as I shall note, that protection has been reduced. Nonetheless, "the possibility of anti-trust liability is inherent in self-regulatory . . . plans due to the common practices of excluding professions from the employment market and limiting competition in spheres of professional activity" (ibid., 89).

A number of issues bearing on the nature of professional work hindered efforts to consider the professions to be subject to the proscriptions of the Sherman Act, and these proscriptions reveal some of the foci of changes now taking place in the standing of the traditional professions. There is first the question of whether selling any service constitutes "trade or commerce"—whether antitrust law as written refers solely to the manufacture and sale of goods or material commodities, and whether selling a service is intrisically different from selling goods. (I rely on Wallace 1972, 89–91; Bauer 1975, 571–78.) The issue first arose in 1922, when Justice Holmes, in his opinion in *Federal Baseball Club v. National League* (259 U.S. 200 [1922]), stated that baseball was not trade or commerce in the usual sense even though it is "professional" in being played for money. By 1932, the issue was partially resolved when the Supreme Court ruled that Atlantic Cleaners and Dryers, Incorporated, while rendering services rather than selling goods, nonetheless did engage in trade or commerce. That decision relied on the definition of *trade* by Justice Story written in 1834, which appears to exclude those "in the liberal arts or in the learned professions" (*The Schooner Nymph*, 18F. Cas 506 [No. 10, 388] [C.C.D. Me. 1834], cited in Bauer 1975, 575). The definition was re-cited with approval in a 1949 case involving price-fixing by real estate boards and realtors. By then, services as a class were no longer exempt from antitrust action, though the special status of professional services continued to exist.

Aside from the issue of whether professional services constitute "trade or commerce," there is the issue of "state's rights." Professional licensing and a number of restrictive regulations formulated by state legislation may be seen to constitute supervision and regulation on the part of the state itself, which displaces federal law. In *Parker v. Brown* (317 U.S. 341 [1943]), which involved a California state program that set quotas on the amount of raisins to be produced by growers, the Supreme Court held that actions of a state or of state officials were exempt from the Sherman Act. Subsequent application of the doctrine has been inconsistent and its scope reduced, but Bauer suggests that two principles underlying its application are agreed on. In order to be exempted, "a state . . . must in some undefined fashion purport to act for the public good of its citizens. Furthermore, the state must act in its governmental or regulatory as opposed to a private or proprietary capacity" (Bauer 1975, 599). Licensing, of course, as justified by reference to the public good.

The third issue involved in the applicability of antitrust law to the professions lies in the professions themselves—whether they, among all those occupations selling services rather than goods, are distinct and special by virtue of the kind of services they sell, and if so, whether they therefore should be exempt from antitrust regulations. Recalling that they were excluded from the definition of *trade* by Justice Story, we may note their exemption in a number of other instances. In *Semler v. Oregon State Board of Medical Examiners* (249 U.S. 608 [1935]), the Court upheld a state ban on advertising by dentists because it asserted that dentistry was "a professional treating bodily ills and demanding different standards of conduct from those which are traditional in the competition of the market place" (p. 612). In its 1949 decision on real estate boards that rejected claim for exemption because personal services were being sold, the Supreme Court specifically asserted that, while it held real estate to be a trade, it was not ruling on whether the professions were trades as well.

All three issues have come together recently. In its 1976 opinion, the Supreme Court struck down the ban on price advertising imposed by the Virginia Pharmacy Board on First Amendment grounds of "freedom of commercial speech." It noted, citing *Parker*, that the state is free to regulate pharmacists, subsidizing them or protecting them from competition in order to protect the public interest, but that it is not free to keep the public in ignorance of competitive price differences. In a significant footnote, however, it restricted its opinion to the case at hand and expressly stated that "other professions . . . may require consideration of quite different factors" (Virginia State Board of Pharmacy v. Virginia Citizens Consumer Council, Inc., 425 U.S. 748 [1976] [p. 773]). In a concurring opinion, Chief Justice Burger noted that the decision deals with advertising the retail price of prepackaged drugs, which is a very different matter from the services offered by lawyers and doctors, services he considers not to be so routinized as to be prepackaged.

This unwillingness to make sweeping determinations about the exceptional legal status of professions in general has continued in subsequent decisions. In *Goldfarb v. Virginia State Bar* (421 U.S. 773 [1975]), which struck down minimum fee schedules for certain legal services, the Court was careful to note that "it would be unrealistic to view the practice of professions as interchangeable with other business activities, and automatically to apply to the professions anti-trust concepts which originated in other areas. The public service aspect, and other features of the professions may require that a particular practice, which could properly be viewed as a violation of the Sherman Act in another context, be treated differently. We intimate no view on any other situation than the one with which we are confronted today" (p. 787, n. 17). And in *Bates v. State Bar of Arizona* (433 U.S. 350 [1976]), which struck down a ban on advertising the price of such routine legal services as uncontested adoptions and changes of name on First Amendment grounds of free commercial speech, the Court quoted its own qualifying and limiting footnote in *Virginia Pharmacy Board* and restricted its opinion to the narrow issue of advertising routine (i.e., prepackaged) services while agreeing that some kinds of advertising might warrant restriction in the public interest. Chief Justice Burger's separate opinion in *Bates* is diagnostically interesting because he expresses doubt that advertising the price of legal services can really inform the public "because legal services can rarely, if ever, be 'standardized' and because potential clients rarely know in advance what services they do in fact need" (p. 386). Justice Powell also expressed doubt about equating legal services with prepackaged prescription drugs and about effective enforcement of any norms established to regulate the character of legal advertising.

In all, it is clear that certain heretofore privileged "anticompetitive" practices of professions have recently been reduced by the invocation of antitrust laws or, where commercial information is involved, First Amendment rights. The Justice Department and the Federal Trade Commission have also been responsible for pressing some professional associations to eliminate such practices. All this bears on competitive practices within professions, however, and bears only rarely and in a small way on competition between professions and potentially competitive occupations. Internal economic relations among the members of single professions have been modified, but professional control over its formal technical knowledge and the institutions protecting its control remain unchallenged. Kissam put the matter clearly: "Two contrapuntal themes . . . suggest limits to the courts' willingness to question closely those professionalism claims that relate directly to issues of technical quality. One is the continuing respect anti-trust courts have shown for the 'public service' goal and 'professional expertise' of professional self-regulation in a technical-quality context. The second is that most professionalism cases, including all Supreme Court decisions, have involved attempts to regulate the organization of professional work rather than its technical nature" (1980, 146).

As I have noted elsewhere (Freidson 1983, 1984), these events, in conjunction with others that have required greater accountability on the part of some of the professions, are in some sense reorganizing those professions internally but not seriously influencing their relations with competing occupations. In spite of the potential that some (e.g., Dolan 1980) see in antitrust law to break the control of medicine over other health-related occupations, state "sunset laws" that were meant to provide an opportunity to reorganize licensing practices have not succeeded in making any significant changes (cf. Lippincott and Begun 1982, 477). The legally sustained institutional forms of credentialism, which virtually none of those asserting professional decline take the trouble to understand, seem still able today to contain any serious change in the position of at least those professions with strong credential systems. There is no doubt that the premodern mystique connected with that minority of "learned professions" is disappearing, but their privileged position remains very strong nonetheless.

THE TREND TOWARD EMPLOYMENT

The invocation of antitrust law is addressed primarily to professions whose members can themselves, as individuals, offer services to the public—the nominally self-employed professional. Professional engineers, physicians, lawyers, and pharmacists have been the targets of antitrust actions, not social workers, schoolteachers, or professors. The proponents of proletarianization have asserted that there is a trend toward employment among the professions, and it is employment status that leads them to equate professionals with the working-class proletariat. As Braverman put it, "the formal definition of the working class is that class which, possessing nothing but its power to labor, sells that labor to capital in return for its subsistence" (1974, 378). But there is more to it than that. Employment is an important issue because it implies the loss of the capacity to control work. Beyond loss of control over the economic terms of work there is also loss of control over what work is to be done, how the work is to be done, and what is to be the aim or goal of work. The thesis is that, as professionals become employees, they lose their independence and so become proletarianized, like the artisans before them. Employment in a bureaucracy then so constrains their discretion that they become mere cogs in a machine of production (cf. Aronowitz 1973, 305; Oppenheimer 1973, 214).

I shall discuss in more detail the matter of bureaucracy in chapter 8, but here it seems appropriate to address the prerequisite to working in a bureaucracy, namely, employment. What evidence there is provides little support for the statement that there is a long trend among professionals away from self-employment toward being employed. Those who advance the thesis have failed to distinguish between number and proportion or percentage in citing census statistics. The gross statistics do show that the proportion of self-employed work-

ers in the labor force as a whole has declined from 25 percent in
1900 to only 9 percent in 1975. However, that statistic reflects
primarily shifts from the agricultural to the nonagricultural
sector: between 1900 and 1975 the proportion of the total
labor force in agriculture went from 38 percent to 4 percent.
Since a large proportion of workers in agriculture were
self-employed, whereas in nonagricultural pursuits most were
and are employed, those who move from agricultural to
nonagricultural pursuits move largely from self-employment
to employment. A massive shift of the agricultural labor force
into nonagricultural activities would thus create a large down-
ward shift in the proportion of self-employed in the total labor
force even when there is no decline in the number of self-
employed in the nonagricultural labor force.

If, however, one examines the agricultural and nonagricultural sectors independently, without merging them, one
finds that self-employment has been extraordinarily stable
over this century. The proportion of those self-employed in
agriculture in 1900 was 53 percent, compared to 51 percent in
1975 (a figure based on a considerably reduced number of
people in agriculture). The proportion of those who were
self-employed in nonagricultural work was 8 percent in 1900
and 7 percent in 1975 (Tausky 1978, 2). Given the increase in
size of that nonagricultural labor force that occurred over that
period, there had to be an increase in the number of self-
employed in order for the proportion to remain steady. Indeed, over this century there has been a "pronounced rise in the
number of [self-employed] professionals" (Bregger 1963, 37).
The question is whether the number has risen enough to
increase the proportion of self-employed professionals over
this century.

I have already discussed in chapters 2 and 3 the difficulties of
working with the census, for the occupations included in its
categories do change in sometimes consequential ways. Similarly, there are changes in its methods of determining employment status. Furthermore, employment status itself fluctuates
a great deal with economic cycles, people moving back and
forth between employment and self-employment as jobs increase or decrease in availability. (Compare ibid., 38; for an
illuminating study of movement into self-employment, see

Peterson, Schmidman, and Elifson, 1982). These matters make determination of trends rather difficult.

Turning to the specific issue of self-employment among professionals, one must note that a change in both state laws and Internal Revenue Service regulations relating to the incorporation of professional practices has contributed to a marked reduction in the number of self-employed represented by official statistics. In January 1967, the number of self-employed in the labor force was reduced at one stroke by some 850,000 when operators of incorporated businesses or practices, regardless of size, were counted as wage and salary workers (Ray 1975, 49; DiCesare 1975, 23–24). Among those reclassified were professionals: once the tax advantages of incorporation were permitted professions by the Internal Revenue Service—a matter I shall explore shortly—an unknown number of physicians, lawyers, dentists, and other traditionally self-employed professionals incorporated their practices. Thus any decline in the number of self-employed professionals recorded in official statistics between 1960 and 1970 must be partly artifactual in character. The fact is, however, that the number increased. The most recent appraisal, which focuses on the period between 1972 and 1979, pointed to an increase of over a million in the number of self-employed in the labor force as a whole, an increase of self-employed workers (12.4 percent) that surpassed the increase of wage and salary workers (10.8 percent) (Fain 1980, 3). This increase is reinforced even more when we note that the number of owners of incorporated businesses, technically classified as employed since 1967, has also increased since that time by some 1.15 million. Thus even though during that period there was only a slight increase (.7 percent) in the proportion of professional and technical workers who were self-employed, surely it is the professionals who were more likely to have escaped the self-employment classification.

The decade of the 1970s thus shows an increase in professional self-employment, not a decline: the only issue is whether the official statistics underestimate that increase. Taking the century as a whole, it is possible to say that, while there can be no doubt about a gross decline in self-employment in the total labor force, the decline must be assigned primarily to the agricultural sector, in which we do not find professionals. Among professional workers themselves, there is considerable ground for doubting that a decline in de facto self-employment has occurred and at least some ground for arguing that there has been an increase. In the case of professionals we might note that, while members of traditionally self-employed professions like medicine and law have been entering employment, members of traditionally employed professions like social work have found new opportunities for self-employment.

But while there is good statistical ground for rejecting the assertion of a historic trend over this century from self-employment toward employment among professionals, there can be no doubt that the overwhelming majority of all nonagricultural workers, including professionals, has been in the past and is at present employed. To say this, however, is to refer to a constant tradition rather than to a historic trend and to forsake the dramatic vision of some pitiless millstone of history grinding away at self-employed professionals so as ultimately to reduce them to the abject state of the proletariat. Most professions were employed from the moment of their invention. Looking at the component occupations of the traditional professions—medicine, law, the military, the clergy, and (connected with the clergy historically) university teaching—we see that three of the five were always typically employed, though not necessarily by a wage contract or for more than a token wage made attractive by the understanding of additional income from opportunities to collect bribes, loot, tithes, rents, student fees, or whatever (cf. Halliday 1983, 330).

When we examine the component occupations assigned to the modern professional category, we see that the vast majority of new professions have also always been typically employed rather than self-employed. Reconsider the list in chapter 3. In 1970 there were roughly eleven million members of the professional, technical, and kindred workers category. Forty-two percent of those eleven million compose five occupations that developed before this century and that were, with minor exceptions, always employed—nurses, religious workers, social workers, and college, university, and schoolteachers. Another nineteenth-century profession, engineering, which composes 9 percent of the census category, is predominantly employed and had its origins in employed work in large organizations (cf. Layton 1971, 2).

The truth in the thesis of a trend toward employment lies solely in the slow trend toward greater employment on the part of the members of those traditional professions that were mostly self-employed in the past—lawyers (but not judges), physicians, dentists, and architects. But taken together those occupations constitute only 6 percent of the entire professional-technical labor force. That 6 percent is a very small tail of a rather large dog. It is entirely inaccurate and inappropriate to use it to represent professions in general, for it is the exception rather than the rule.

The Dubious Significance of Employment Status

Taking them as members of a category characterized by gaining a living by virtue of possessing credentials based on higher education, then, we must say that professions are typically employed rather than self-employed, the majority having been employed from the moment of their constitution as professions. Does that fact of employment have any consequences for their independence, their capacity to control their work, and the "labor process"? Can it be said that when one is self-employed one has such control and that when one is employed one does not?

When we examine the conditions surrounding self-employment for real people in real historical circumstances, it becomes impossible to argue that the mere fact of self-employment allows greater control over one's work. First, self-employment may not even offer a living. We might remember that Tobias Smollett twice attempted to support himself by the practice of medicine and, failing that, had to settle on the indignity of supporting himself by writing novels. As for lawyers, Adam Smith estimated that in England in the late eighteenth century only about one in twenty could actually gain a living. No one familiar with the history of the self-employed professions can claim consistent capacity to gain a living, without which one cannot be independent and free.

Indeed, in his contemporary study of self-employed lawyers, Carlin (1962, 184–200) referred to "the illusion of independence."

Under circumstances in which the self-employed are economically insecure, it is difficult to claim that they are autonomous in their work, that they are truly free to make their own decisions and be their own bosses while surviving as well. In the case of medicine, history is littered with circumstances in which physicians had to fit their diagnoses and their remedies to the prejudices of their patrons, sometimes even on pain of death (cf. Freidson 1980, 171–207). And in the case of law it is not difficult to find circumstances in which the self-employed were dominated and controlled by their clients, as were eighteenth-century barristers, who served primarily as the instrument of their patrons (Duman 1979, 101), and as are even elite law firm lawyers serving powerful clients today (Heinz and Laumann 1982, 379–85). If we think of the "free" artisan and shopkeeper in the same terms, we cannot fail to observe how penury, long hours, panicky fear of losing essential customers, and bankruptcy are commonly associated with the condition of self-employment (cf. Bridenbaugh 1961 for data on the increase of self-employed artisans in debtors' jails in eighteenth-century America). Indeed, it might be argued that such oppressive conditions are typical of self-employment, success being the exception. Beggars and ragpickers, after all, are self-employed.

Owning property, whether a professional practice or a shop, owning the means of production, can hardly be important in and of itself in assuring one control over one's economic fate and one's work. Surely the more critical matter is the relationship one has to the market, capitalist or otherwise. When one's goods or services are so valuable on the market as to make consumers supplicants, then one can exercise considerable control over the terms, conditions, content, and goals of one's work. But when one's goods or services are not in heavy demand, then one can only be a desperate supplicant of indifferent consumers or employers. If one concedes the critical significance of position in the market, then whether one is employed or self-employed ceases to be a serious issue. As Zussman (1985, 158–59) notes for engineers, the job one holds can be seen as part of one's "career capital," as part of the experience and reputation that cannot be alienated from the worker. Given a strong position in the market, one can be employed and nonetheless "write one's own ticket." There was a time when the sons of the British gentry avoided the self-employed bar in favor of more secure, lucrative, and equally gentlemanly employment in the church, the military, and the civil service (Duman 1979, 93–94).

When all is said and done, the very concept of self-employment is misleading in a market economy. In a market economy one's labor is a commodity whether one sells it to an employer or to a customer. All in all, it might be well to make the routine assumption that, when one is self-employed, one is not independent but rather operating a franchised trade, the terms of the franchise varying with the institutions that structure one's place in the market. The task is then to trace out the direct and indirect set of dependencies created by the franchise. It makes a real difference to one's independence when one's labor or goods are scarce and desired by virtue of a shelter or other market conditions. It also makes a difference when one's franchise to offer one's labor or goods comes from a feudal lord rather than Howard Johnson's, from Exxon rather than venal tax collectors, or from licensing officials rather than bands of armed marauders. Both self-employment and employment have terms that are variable, and it would be ignorance of both the past and the present to assume that the terms of self-employment are necessarily more advantageous than those of employment.

The Sheltered Professional Corporation

Not very long ago, professions gained a special form of incorporation that has important consequences for self-employment as well as employment. In my discussion of the elements of the credential system I indicated how a number of laws and strong private customs have established shelters for professionals in the marketplace, assuring in some cases and strongly encouraging in others that the credentialed are used to fill jobs. This obviously influences the position of professionals in the market for employees. There are other institutional supports for the professional's position in the market, however, one of which might be noted here because of its obvious contradiction of what is a characteristic institution of capitalism—the modern business corporation. Taken as an aggregate, most professionals are not employed in conventional corporations, engineers being the major exception. Rather most are employed in nonprofit corporations, public agencies, and firms organized as partnerships, all of which deviate from the business corporation in one way or another. There is still another form that requires mention because of its special "worker-controlled" character, one that can be used by individual practitioners and by groups of professionals. It is, furthermore, a form in which professionals who are "owners" can employ other professionals.

One of the virtues of a corporation is that it can be treated as a legal person so that liability can be limited to the assets of the corporation as a legal person without touching the personal assets of shareholders or of the officers and employees of the corporation itself. This, of course, is an advantage that was of some importance to the capacity for modern capitalist enterprises to attract investment capital. Other advantages are that the corporation can remain an entity that is quite independent of the loss of any of its members, that there can be free transfer of ownership interests, and that management can be centralized by vesting it in a board of directors that is ultimately responsible for organizational policy and the designation of the executives who administer day-to-day affairs. Furthermore, under present laws there are tax advantages to corporate status that facilitate pension and profit-sharing plans and other fringe benefits for its employees, including managers.

For such traditionally entrepreneurial professions as law and medicine, which are born and bred with notions of personal responsibility and autonomy, a corporate form of practice was problematic. First, for a conventional corporation that raises capital by selling shares, incorporation raises the specter of being controlled by lay shareholders and the board of directors they select, though it is true that the close corporation form can restrict the class of shareholders. The corporation also suggests by its characteristic of limited liability that personal responsibility to individual clients will be diminished, and this raises ethical questions for professionals (cf. Starr 1982, 198–232).

Whatever the reason, before World War II most states had laws that "prevented corporations from engaging in the practice of medicine" (Hannaford 1969, 24), and doubt was expressed within organized medicine and the bar whether practice in the form of a corporation was ethical (see the discussion in Note 1962). Partnerships were the preferred mode of association among professionals, and they remain so for law and accounting. But the financial advantages and flexibility of corporate status were very seductive. After World War II various states passed legislation creating "professional service organizations" that were designed to avoid the threatening characteristics of conventional corporations while gaining their advantages. Those "organizations" then sought to gain from the Internal Revenue Service the advantages of being treated as corporations for federal tax purposes.

The officials of the Internal Revenue Service resisted and, in fact, wrote an amendment to the Internal Revenue Code in 1965 to exclude the professional service organization from treatment as a corporation. Essentially, the amendment took note of the fact that, where they were permitted by state law, professional associations or organizations were defined in such a way that all shareholders, or owners, had to be licensed members of the profession, practicing their trade, and that their shares could not be sold to or inherited by a layperson or sold to any fellow professional without first being offered to the other members of the organization. As such, they fail the test of "free transferability of interests," which is regarded as one essential characteristic of a genuine corporation. However, the courts struck down the 1965 regulations as invalid, ruling that such associations were enough like corporations to be so treated for income tax purposes. By 1969, the Internal Revenue Service conceded its defeat and announced that "organizations of doctors, lawyers and other professional people organized under state professional association acts will, generally, be treated as corporations" (Jones 1969, 245).

The professional corporation could thus have its cake and eat it too. It could have the substantial tax shelter benefits that corporate status provides, gain the efficiencies of centralized management and continuity of organization that partnerships make difficult, and facilitate the transfer of interests that is difficult in a partnership while assuring that those interests will not fall into the hands of laypeople. They were thus sheltered from the power of impersonal capital. And, finally, they gained the benefits of a more limited liability than is the case with partnerships, "substantially the same as that which obtains in the case of any other closely held corporation. [Solely] the assets of the corporation are subject to the liability, as are the assets of the individual who performed the wrongful act" (Ray 1978, 25).

It is difficult to determine how widespread the professional corporation is in comparison with partnerships and other forms. It may very well be that it has been more popular with individual practitioners or very small partnerships since large law and accounting firms as well as large medical groups or health maintenance organizations do not appear to assume that form often. Furthermore, recent changes in the federal tax laws have made it less attractive for individual professionals to incorporate (Quinn 1984), and whatever can exist depends, in any case, on the laws of each state, which can vary (for state variation in engineering corporate practice acts, see National Society of Professional Engineers 1983). In New York State the "professional service corporation" conforms to my general description, requiring that no shareholder or officer be anyone other than a licensed professional. Accountants, architects, chiropractors, lawyers, physicians, podiatrists, psychologists, and architectural, electrical, industrial, mechanical, and structural engineers are among those who have formed professional service corporations.

THE PROFESSIONAL MARKET POSITION

In this chapter I have attempted to assess a number of elements in the position of the professions in contemporary American society that have led some writers to believe that they are in decline. I argued that there is not very persuasive evidence to support most of the assertions underlying that belief, though I do not mean to imply that some professions are not undergoing important changes that affect the working lives of individual professionals. Many professionals who were traditionally self-employed are now moving into employment, and the working conditions of all are now being affected by severe, though not necessarily permanent, budgetary pressures.

However, the position of individual professionals has no necessary bearing on the position of their professions as corporate bodies. As I have noted elsewhere (Freidson 1983, 1984, 1985), the internal organization of some professions is changing under the impact of the court decisions discussed in this chapter, of government regulatory policies, and of newly developed commercial enterprises selling professional services. Those changes are affecting the interrelations of members of those professions and developing new relations between the professions and the state, but they have not made any significant change in the institutional supports for the professions. Antitrust actions have not threatened licensing or other elements of the credential system, and special forms of law provide professions with forms of organizing their enterprises that make large-scale practice enterprises possible without lay control. And as I noted in chapter 4, other laws and customs mandate supervisory and even executive positions to those with professional credentials in organizations devoted to providing professional services. Taken together, we can see institutional devices that shelter the self-employed from some potentially threatening market forces and other devices that shelter the employed from organizational forces.

Virtually all those who write of the decline of the professions ignore the institutions that support the position of the professions in the political economy. By and large, the professions are represented as mere collections of individuals who negotiate with individual customers if self-employed or with individual employers if employed. But professions are more than that, as I have shown. They are organizations or corporate bodies with institutions that shelter them in the political economy to a degree and kind that vary from one to another but that in a broad way distinguish all professions from other ocupations. It is their organization as professions and their sheltering institutions that make a significant contribution to the market position of their members, whether or not they are employed.

I have argued that it is typical of the vast majority of professions for their members to be employed, that employment is characteristic of professions. That fact in itself has no intrinsic significance for appraising the powers professionals can exercise, however: the critical issue lies in the characteristics of the employment position itself, whether it is closely analogous to the position of the blue-collar worker, as many proletarianization theorists claim, or whether it is in some sense distinct and special. That is what I shall examine in the next chapter.

References

Aronowitz, S. 1973. *False promises: The shaping of American working class consciousness.* New York: McGraw-Hill Book Co.

Barber B. 1983. *The logic and limits of trust.* new Brunswick, N.J.: Rutgers University Press.

Bauer, J. P. 1975. Professional activities and the antitrust laws. *Notre Dame Lawyer* 50 (April): 570–602.

Betz, M., and L. O'Connell. 1983. Changing doctor-patient relationships and the rise of concern for accountability. *Social Problems* 31 (October): 84–95.

Braverman, H. 1974. *Labor and monopoly capital.* New York: Monthly Review Press.

Bregger, J. E. 1963. Self-employment in the U.S., 1948–1962. *Monthly Labor Review* 76 (January): 37–43.

Bridenbaugh, C. 1961. *The colonial craftsman.* Chicago: University of Chicago Press.

Burnham, J. C. 1982. American medicine's golden age: What happened to it? *Science* 215 (19 March): 1474–79.

Carlin, J. 1962. *Lawyers on their own.* New Brunswick, N.J.: Rutgers University Press.

Coburn, D., G. M. Torrance, and J. M. Kanfert. 1983. Medical dominance in Canada in historical perspective: The rise and fall of medicine? *International Journal of Health Services* 13:407–32.

Coleman, J. E. 1967. Antitrust exemptions—the learned professions. *Antitrust Law Journal* 33:48–55.

Derber, C. 1982. The proletarianization of the professional: A review essay. In *Professionals as workers: Mental labor in advanced capitalism,* edited by C. Derber, 13–33. Boston: G. K. Hall & Co.

DiCesare, C. B. 1975. Changes in the occupational structure of U.S. jobs. *Monthly Labor Review* 98 (March): 23–34.

Dolan, A. K. 1980. Antitrust law and physician dominance of other health practitioners. *Journal of Health Politics, Policy and Law* 4 (Winter): 675–91.

Duman, D. 1979. The English bar in the Georgian era. In *Lawyers in early modern Europe and America*, edited by W. Prest, 86–107. London: Croom Helm.

Fain, T. S. 1980. Self-employed Americans: Their number has increased. *Monthly Labor Review* 103 (November): 3–8.

Freidson, E. 1980. *Patients' view of medical practice*. Chicago: University of Chicago Press.

————. 1983. The reorganization of the professions by regulation. *Law and Human Behavior* 7, nos. 2/3:279–90.

————. 1984. The changing nature of professional control. *Annual Review of Sociology* 10:1–20.

————. 1985. The reorganization of the medical profession. *Medical Care Review*. 42 (Spring): 11–35.

Halliday, T. C. 1983. Professions, class and capitalism. *European Journal of Sociology* 24:321–46.

Hannaford, J. M. 1969. Risks and rewards of professional corporations. In *Professional corporations*, vol. 2, edited by H. B. Jones, 23–24. New York: Practising Law Institute.

Haug, M. B. 1973. Deprofessionalization: An alternative hypothesis for the future. *Sociological Review Monograph*, no. 20:195–211.

————. 1975. The deprofessionalization of everyone? *Sociological Focus* (August): 197–213.

————. 1977. Computer technology and the obsolescence of the concept of profession. In *Work and Technology*, edited by M. R. Haug and J. Dofny, 215–28. Beverly Hills, Calif.: Sage Publications.

Heinz, J. P., and E. O. Laumann. 1982. *Chicago lawyers: The social structure of the bar*. New York and Chicago: Russell Sage Foundation; American Bar Foundation.

Herndon, W. W. 1979. Competition policy and the professions. *Antitrust Law Journal* 48:1533–49.

Horowitz, I. 1980. The economic foundations of self-regulation in professions. In *Regulating the professions*, edited by R. D. Blair and S. Rubin, 3–28. Lexington, Mass.: Lexington Books.

Jones, H. B., ed. 1969. *Professional corporations*. New York: Practising Law Institute.

Kissam, P. C. 1980. Antitrust law, the First Amendment, and professional self-regulation. In *Regulating the professions*, edited by R. D. Blair and S. Rubin, 143–83. Lexington, Mass.: Lexington Books.

———. 1983. Antitrust law and professional behavior. *Texas Law Review* 62 (August): 1–66.

Larson, M. S. 1977. *The rise of professionalism*. Berkeley: University of California Press.

———. 1979. Professionalism: Rise and fall. *International Journal of Health Services* 9:607–27.

———. 1980. Proletarianization and educated labor. *Theory and Society* 9 (January): 131–75.

Layton, E. T., Jr. 1971. *The revolt of the engineers*. Cleveland: Press of Case Western Reserve University.

Lippincott, R. C., and J. W. Begun. 1982. Competition in the health sector: A historical perspective. *Journal of Health Politics, Policy and Law* 7:460–87.

Lipset, S. M., and W. Schneider. 1983. *The confidence gap*. New York: Free Press.

McKinlay, J. B. 1982. Toward the proletarianization of physicians. In *Professionals as workers: Mental labor in advanced capitalism*, edited by C. Derber, 37–62. Boston: G. K. Hall & Co.

National Society of Professional Engineers. 1983. *State-by-state summary of the engineering corporate practice laws*. National Society of Professional Engineers Publication, no. 2217. Washington, D.C.: National Society of Professional Engineers.

Nelson, M. K., and H. L. McGough. 1983. The informed client: A case study in the illusion of autonomy. *Symbolic Interaction* 6 (Spring): 35–49.

Note. 1962. Professional corporations and associations. *Harvard Law Review* 75:776–94.

Oppenheimer, M. 1973. The proletarianization of the professional. *Sociological Review Monographs*, no. 20:213–27.

Peterson, R. A., J. T. Schmidman, and K. W. Elifson. 1982. Entrepreneurship or autonomy? Truckers and cabbies. In *Varieties of work*, edited by P. L. Stewart and M. G. Cantor, 181–98. Beverly Hills, Calif.: Sage Publications.

Pollard, M. R., and R. F. Leibenluft. 1981. *Anti-trust and the health professions*. Policy Planning Issues Paper. Washington, D.C.: Federal Trade Commission, Office of Policy Planning, July.

Powell, M. 1985. Developments in the regulation of lawyers. *Social Forces* 64 (December): 281–305.

Quinn, J. B. 1984. To "Inc." or not to "Inc." *Newsweek*, January 9, 10A–10D.

Ray, G. 1978. *Incorporating the professional practice.* 2d ed. Englewood Cliffs, N.J.: Prentice-Hall, Inc.

Ray, R. N. 1975. A report on self-employed Americans in 1973. *Monthly Labor Review* 98 (January): 49–54.

Rothman, R. A. 1984. Deprofessionalization: The case of law in America. *Work and Occupations* 11 (May): 183–206.

Starr, P. 1982. *The social transformation of American medicine.* New York: Basic Books.

Tausky, C. 1978. *Work organizations.* 2d ed. Itasca, Ill.: F. E. Peacock.

Toren, N. 1975. Deprofessionalization and its sources. *Sociology of Work and Occupations* 2:323–37.

Wagner, D. 1980. The proletarianization of nursing in the United States, 1932–1946. *International Journal of Health Services* 10:271–90.

Wallace, D. A. 1972. Occupational licensing and certification: Remedies for denial. *William and Mary Law Review* 14 (Fall): 46–127.

Yarmolinsky, A. 1978. What future for the professional in American society? *Deadalus* 107, no. 2:159–74.

Zussman, R. 1985. *Mechanics of the middle class: Work and politics among American engineers.* Berkeley: University of California Press.

Chapter Seven

The Special Position of
Professional Employees

I have established the fact that employment is typical
of the market status of professionals. Therefore the serious
issue for theorizing and descriptive analysis is not some trend
toward the loss of independence through entrance into employment but rather the conditions for employment themselves and whether they are changing sufficiently to be worth
comment. Obviously, in capitalist societies the market cycle is
a variable of some importance, as are changes in state policy,
but one must be cautious to avoid seeing a linear trend in what
might be a cycle or an oscillation. Taking the present day for
analysis, is it possible to say that, as an employee, the professional is in the same position as the semiskilled industrial or
white-collar worker? At least some proponents of both the
deprofessionalization and the proletarianization theses have
emphasized the significance of the conditions of employment
of professionals in large organizations with a complex division
of labor and with goals and policies over which they are said to
have little control. The conditions of employment for professionals are said to have become so bad today that the description of them as "proletarians in a factory setting is more than a
metaphor, but corresponds at least in a great measure to their
actual position" (Aronowitz 1973, 312). Is it possible to characterize the position of employed professionals that way, or do
they have a special and distinct position? Do they lack any
significant control over their work? Those are the questions
that I shall try to address in this chapter.

Obviously, such questions are difficult to answer because of
the heterogeneity of the professional aggregate and the variety
of public and private agencies, firms, and industries in which
they work. The professions themselves vary in the strength of
their credential systems and in their relative scarcity in the

labor market. The organizations in which they work vary in the kind of corporate charter they have and in the degree to which institutional credentialing influences their staffing policies. Divisions of labor vary, as do hierarchical structures. Such variety makes sweeping generalization treacherous, particularly in light of the fact that there is very little concrete, empirical information available about the vast majority of work organizations in the United States.

I shall attempt, in this chapter, to establish the least common denominator of the position of professional workers by examining their position in labor law and then analyzing the characteristics of that position by discussing some of the controversies surrounding it in contested cases before the National Labor Relations Board (NLRB) and the courts. The virtues of such an approach lie, first, in the fact that the law establishes what is empirically official and consequential, even if from a critical point of view it is mistaken, and, second, in the fact that adjudication, whatever its other failings, rests at least on building up a record of "fact" on the basis of documents and sworn testimony. In the case of labor law, the record is composed of documents and testimony related to what people actually do at work: surely that is a useful basis for an analysis of control over work and the labor process.

Types of Employees in the NLRA

The U.S. National Labor Relations Act (NRLA) is designed to govern the process of collective bargaining between employees and and employers: it protects the right of eligible comployees to choose representation by a union or bargaining agent, creates a system by which employees vote on whether to be represented by a bargaining agent and choose the agent or union, and sustains a system for adjudication of conflicts during collective bargaining. However, all nominal employees are not considered equally entitled to the protections provided by the act. Among those excluded from coverage by the act are "independent contractors" and employees who are "supervisors," "managerial employees," and, unimportant for our present purpose, "confidential employees."

The exclusion of independent contractors is based on the notion that they are self-employed and therefore not employees entitled to protection. Gorman (1976, 28) notes in his commentary that "a person completing a job by his own methods and without being subject to the control of the employer as to the means of doing the work was an independent contractor; a person performing work subject to the employer's control or right to control as to both the end result and the manner of achieving it was an employee within section 2(3)." Among the criteria currently used to discriminate employee from independent contractor in such circumstances is the common law "right of control" test, which refers to control over the manner of performing the job, and the test of dependence on profit after expense rather than on a salary or wage. However, as I have suggested in my discussion of self-employment in the last chapter, when consumers are few, well organized, and powerful, the self-employed person's "right of control" is at best academic. This was the case for the street-corner newsdealers at issue in *NLRB v. Hearst Publications, Inc.* (U.S. 1944) and in later cases discussed briefly in Gorman (1976, 28–31), in which a single "client" in the shape of a large metropolitan newspaper can dictate the terms of the contractual relationship.

The exclusion of actual employees from the protection of the act is based on the principle that the focus of collective bargaining is on a basic cleavage of interests between labor and management and that conflict of interest within each great cleavage should be minimized. Thus while managers and supervisors are as much employees as unskilled operatives are, they are nonetheless "employers" in that, in the language of section 2(2) of the act, they are "acting as an agent of an employer." A supervisor in section 2(11) of the act is defined in part by the authority to act as an employer—that is, "to hire, transfer, suspend, lay off, recall, promote, discharge, assign, reward, or discipline other employees." This is, in Gorman's (1976, 36) judgment, the most important single criterion of the act, though hiring and firing seem to be the most persuasive actions of all those mentioned. Another criterion invoked by the act is that the authority of such a supervisor must be "not of a merely routine or clerical nature, but requires the use of independent judgment." A true supervisor has sufficient autonomy to be free to exercise discretion.

In the case of "managerial employees" there is rather more ambiguity since the act does not define or explicitly exclude them. However, Gorman notes that there is evidence to support the belief that it was Congress's intention to exclude managers from coverage by the act and quotes the definition of managerial employees in the Bell Aerospace decision as "those who formulate and effectuate management policies by expressing and making operative the decisions of their employers, and those who have *discretion in the performance of their jobs independent of their employer's established policy.* . . . [M]anagerial status is not conferred upon rank-and-file workers, or upon those who perform routinely, but rather it is reserved for those in executive-type positions, those who are closely aligned with management as true representatives of management" (1976, 38; italics added).

These distinctions revolving around policy-making authority and supervisory authority become central in evaluating the position of professional employees, for in the 1980 Supreme Court decision concerning Yeshiva University, professors were classified as part of management because it was decided that they actually possessed policy-making authority. They were therefore excluded from the group of employees who are protected by collective-bargaining rights under the terms of the act. It was not denied that the Yeshiva faculty were professionals but rather asserted that the substance of the authority they exercised was such as to ally them with management. This is not true of all professional employees, however, for the act explicitly recognizes professionals as a special category of employee ordinarily entitled to collective-bargaining rights.

In essence, professional employees share with members of the crafts a special status as workers in the act because it is assumed that they have special interests that make it desirable for them to be able, if they so choose, to be represented in collective bargaining by agents who are separate from those of other employees in the same firm. This special status of professional employees is predicated on the assumption that they have a community of interest that distinguishes them from other employees, a community of interest created by different scales of compensation, employment benefits, hours, and other terms and conditions of work and by similarity in the kind of work performed, qualifications, skills, training, and the like (cf. Cox, Bok, and Gorman, 1977, 274–75). The assumption may be arguable, but the fact of the special status is objective and official.

NLRA Criteria for the Professional Employee

Simple as these criteria may be in the abstract, the problem, as it is with all abstractions, is to apply them in reality. How does one decide whether a given group of employees in a given firm is in fact professional and therefore entitled to choose to be represented separately from other employees? How, in short, does the NLRB define *professional* so as to discriminate among claims for the purpose of administering the act? The act does have a definition and a set of criteria for determining what a professional employee is. It reads as follows:

The term "professional employee" means—(a) any employee engaged in work (i) predominantly intellectual and varied in character as opposed to routine mental, manual, mechanical or physical work; (ii) involving the consistent exercise of discretion and judgment in its performance; (iii) of such a character that the output produced or the result accomplished cannot be standardized in relation to a given period of time; (iv) requiring knowledge of an advanced type in a field of science or learning customarily acquired by a prolonged course of specialized intellectual instruction or study in an institution of higher learning or a hospital, as distinguished from a general academic education or from an apprenticeship or from training in the performance of routine, mental, manual, or physical processes; or (b) any employee, who (i) has completed the courses of specialized intellectual instruction and study described in clause (iv) of paragraph (a), and (ii) is performing related work under the supervision of a professional person to qualify himself to become a professional employee as defined in paragraph (a). [Sec. 2(12) of 29 U.S.C. par. 152 (12) (1970)]

In controversies surrounding the classification of a group of employees as professional, NLRB hearings designed to make a determination have typically paid close attention to the facts of the particular activities of the particular group of workers in the particular firm, attempting to make a determination on pragmatic rather than abstract grounds. In the course of attempting to make a determination, the board not only seeks to employ the criteria advanced by the act but may employ others as well. It may choose to rely on rulings by the Wage and Hours Division of the U.S. Department of Labor as to whether a particular occupation is professional in character (cf. 29 U.S.C. par. 541.3). It may take into account the fact that the persons possess state licenses. It assesses the salary and terms of employment, whether or not the employee is actually using his or her training on the job, whether work duties are interchangeable with those of other employees, and the like. And since the particular work of an occupation and the conditions of employment surrounding it can vary from situation to situation, it is no wonder that, in board rulings, we find that the same occupational or job title has been found to be filled by professional employees in one instance and not in another.

Detailed collation and analysis of the criteria the board has used and how it has used them is available in Gillespie's invaluable legal annotation (Gillespie 1978, 25–234). Suffice it to note here that the board's determinations have not been guided by merely formal and mechanical criteria like licenses and education. The actual character of the work performed as revealed in testimony, and not mere credentials, is said to be determinative, so that when "unqualified" individuals are found to be performing work that other professionals perform, their lack of formal training cannot prevent their classification as professionals. Similarly, the mere fact that a person has the "credential" of a general college education does not lead to classification as a professional employee.

Obviously a collation of NLRB determinations cannot tell us everything. Rulings are made on contested issues of unit determination, so we do not know how often uncontested assignment of professional employee status was made for particular job titles. Furthermore, we cannot know how many people are involved in each contested case without returning to the record of each. Nor can we assume each case to be subject to the same pressures on the part of the contestants and biasses on the part of the board. The composition and political sym-

pathies of the NLRB itself change with each presidential administration, as occurred, for example, with Eisenhower's
appointees to the board, who "swung over to a position far
more favorable to craft unions" (Cox et al. 1977, 290). Thus
we cannot assume a consistent pattern of interpretation over
time, though the constraints of the law and of formalism
prevent wild variation in decisions. Gerrymandering is common in establishing bargaining units: sometimes it is the firms
who may argue for professional status for some of their employees in order to break them off into a bargaining unit
separate from the rank and file; in other cases rival unions may
be involved in arguing against each other; in still other cases
firms may argue against professional employee status entirely,
preferring to deal with a single bargaining unit or to avoid
bargaining at all with professionals (cf. the discussion of the
issue of unit size in Gorman 1976, 67–70). Different "facts" are
likely to be produced for different issues and by different
contestants. The financial resources available to each side are
rarely equal, so that equal quality of evidence and argument
may not be available. Furthermore, given the small and declin-
ing proportion of the American work force that is unionized or
engaged in unionization, with credentialed professionals
(rather than the aggregate of those in the entire census category) very weakly represented in even that small proportion,
the activities of the NLRB can hardly be taken to be a fair
sample of all the conditions of professional employment (for
data on professional unionization, see Brint and Dodd 1984).

Nonetheless, examination of NLRB eligibility and bargain-
ing-unit determination does tell us that there is a clear assertion
in labor law of a difference between professional employees
and other employees that parallels the difference between craft
workers and others. That difference is predicated not on mere
prestige or status but rather on the idea that professional employees have a community of interest that sets them apart from
other workers. Their work being by definition discretionary,
requiring judgment, it is considered to be sufficiently different
from the routine work of ordinary blue- or white-collar employees to merit special treatment. Implicitly, then, it recognizes that ordinary employees have little technical control over

their work and distinguishes professionals by determining from their actual work activity what they do. Thus the truly professional employee is explicitly distinguished from the proletariat on grounds of technical autonomy. That they are distinguished this way is all I can show. Whether they really have a significant amount of discretion on grounds independent of the quasi-legal process that attempts to review the detailed facts of each contested case is a question no one can answer in the face of the absence of reliable evidence. If it is conceded that many members of many professions, even though employees, do exercise a significant amount of discretion in their work and that enough of their work is sufficiently unpredictable to preclude characterizing it as predominantly routine, then it is not possible to consider them to be in substantially the same position as the factory or the white-collar proletariat. They have greater control over their work. The problem is to characterize that control in more detail.

PROFESSIONAL EMPLOYEES AS SUPERVISORS

The minimal characteristic of the professional employee, then, is technical autonomy, the freedom to employ discretion in performing work in the light of personal, presumably schooled judgment that is not available to those without the same qualifications. At least one proletarianization theorist (Derber 1982) has agreed that professional workers do have this form of autonomy. What is not self-evident, however, is that the very exercise of technical autonomy has complex consequences for the nature of control over work that spill over into areas of control that are conventionally conceived of as supervisory and even policy-making in character. These empirical consequences have created a problem of interpretation in labor law and in some cases have led to legal controversy over whether some professional employees are "really" supervisors or managers.

The problem of determining when professional employees are statutory supervisors under the act and therefore not eligible for protection has not been very serious since the adoption of the "50 percent rule," which defines a professional employee as a supervisor when he or she spends more than 50 percent of his or her working time supervising nonprofessionals. The issue is worth examining here for theoretical purposes, however, because what it shows is that mere technical autonomy sometimes contains within it the necessity to perform supervisory functions that in conventional work contexts are performed by foremen, unit heads, managers, and others. Finkin's (1977, 805–34) discussion summarizes the issues for the professional employee and discusses how the board dealt with them to the date of his paper. (See also Finkin 1974.)

Finkin first analyzes the legislative history of the 1947 Taft-Hartley amendments to the NLRB, which on the one hand excluded foremen and other supervisory employees from coverage but on the other included professional employees and gave them the right to have separate bargaining units because of what was deemed their special community of interest. In formulating the amendments, he notes, Congress recognized two rather different issues in the organization of work. On the one hand, "the supervisory exemption is founded upon the assumption of bureaucratic managerial structures widely followed in industry [where] . . . the legitimacy of a decision rests ultimately upon the decisionmaker's position in the hierarchy" (1977, 808). Supervisors are declared to be agents of management by virtue of their position in the hierarchy. On the other hand, citing such writers as Marcson (1960) and Kornhauser (1962), Finkin notes that, by recognizing them as a special class of rank-and-file worker, Congress recognized a situation in which "professional employees consistently lay claim to authority independent of the hierarchy derived from their professional status" (1977, 809), a status resting on expertise rather than on administrative rank.

Finkin argues that Congress recognized the difference between the two modes of authority by its willingness to separate professionals from other employees and by its explicit inclusion in the professional employee category of both "full-fledged professionals" and those who have completed their academic training but who work under the supervision of the former "in order to qualify for full professional status" (ibid., 809–10)—the salaried physician of a hospital staff and the residents he supervises, for example, or the engineer and associate and assistant engineers. "Thus, the statute assumed that professionals 'supervise' their junior professional assistants; nevertheless it seems quite clear that that supervision was deemed insufficient to exempt those senior professionals under the supervisory exemption inasmuch as they were to be explicitly included with their professional assistants in professional bargaining units" (ibid., 810).

This means that some forms of "supervision" are not managerial in character but rather professional. Similarly, Finkin points out, when professionals supervise nonprofessional assistants who are essential for the successful performance of their work, that too does not necessarily evoke the supervisory exemption. The problem is where and how to draw the line between professional "supervision" and managerial or administrative—that is to say, statutory—supervision. Finkin goes on to discuss the board's decisions on professionals in a number of cases—engineers and scientists serving as project leaders or program managers (some of whom were declared supervisors and some not), architects serving as project captains, and pharmacists, librarians, registered nurses, social workers, and professors.

Finkin's analysis clearly distinguishes between the person whose official position is to supervise others who perform a particular kind of work and the person who, in the normal course of work involving cooperation with others in a division of labor, may, because of experience or specialized knowledge, direct those others. Pursuing the industrial analogy, the latter is a rank-and-file worker who performs the productive tasks of the organization, and the former is the person employed specifically for the purpose of supervising the latter. But that is as far as the industrial analogy goes: once the matter of being a professional employee is introduced, the clarity of the distinction disappears. The industrial-commercial milieu in which labor law was born and the strictly pyramidal structure of authority that it assumes (cf. Angel 1982) are ill fitted to provide the resources for clarifying and adjudicating issues surrounding professional employees because by the definition of the law itself the work and the status of professional employees cannot be treated the same way as that of nonprofessional employees. In the context of professional work one must not consider supervision to be the exclusive task of an official of the firm whose full-time duty is to "hire," "promote," "assign," "reward," and "discipline" others who are subordinates. One must also recognize that it is an intrinsic functional part of the everyday duties of professionals who require the assistance of others for the successful performance of their work and who must therefore have some say in their selection and use. Thus physicians may direct the work of nurses, dieticians, laboratory technicians, and many others in the hospital without having the organizational authority to hire, fire, or promote them. Similarly, the scientist may assign work and direct the efforts of technical personnel in the laboratory. Intrinsic to technical autonomy, when it is practiced in a division of labor and when some forms of expertise set the conditions for the operation of others, are functional supervisory prerogatives that can look very much like administrative or statutory supervisory prerogatives. There is the official position of being a supervisor, and there is the functional activity of supervision.

Once we are outside conventional blue- and white-collar settings and find ourselves in professional settings, then, the conventional distinction between supervisors and employees becomes problematic. Both supervisors and professional employees perform functionally supervisory tasks, though, as Finkin points out, only the former do so virtually exclusively as officials of the organization with the power to fire and hire. Both supervisors and employees use judgment and discretion in their work. And both supervisors and employees can be members of the same occupation, with the same training and credentials. What appears to be necessary for developing both realistic and workable distinctions in dealing with professional employees is the attempt not to force an entirely inappropriate industrial analogy but rather to draw out the implications of the technical autonomy that is the minimal characteristic of the professional worker. Intrinsic to technical autonomy, when it is exercised in a division of labor, when some forms of expertise set the conditions for the operation of others, and when there is peer review, are functional supervisory prerogatives that can look very much like official or administrative supervisory prerogatives. The same may be said for policy-making or managerial prerogatives.

PROFESSIONAL EMPLOYEES AS MANAGERS

It may be remembered that in a great many of the organizations in which professionals work—particularly those in which professionals perform the primary productive tasks—the supervisory, managerial, and executive staff are often also professionals. The dean of a dental school, the executive director of a community legal services or social agency, the chief of staff of a hospital, the principal of an elementary school, all and many more are professionals by training and credentials. So too are the senior partners of architectural, legal, accounting, and engineering firms that have many professional employees. As managers, such professionals have the authority from their governing boards to advance the policies of the organization for which they are responsible and to exercise their own judgment in advancing them. The official positions they hold—as president, dean, managing partner, executive director, and the like—make them unambiguously managerial and give them the power of managers. But in an important decision bearing on the future of unionism among all professionals, the Supreme Court declared (in a 5 to 4 decision that hardly expressed unanimity) that the rank-and-file professional employees of a private university were managerial and therefore not entitled to the protection of the act. I refer to *NLRB v. Yeshiva University* (44 U.S. 672 [1980]). The faculty of a university clearly constitute its rank-and-file teaching employees who perform the basic, presumably productive activities of the organization. We have already seen how it is possible to conceive of such employees as supervisory (and therefore aligned with management). But how is it possible to conceive of them as managerial, as making policy? (For a recent review of the managerial exclusion in the case of professionals, see Krent 1981.) Let us take a closer look at the Yeshiva decision to see how that conception is possible and then go on to analyze the issues embedded in it that bear more generally on the special character of professional employees and their work.

The key point of the majority decision of the Supreme Court in the matter of *Yeshiva* is as follows:

The controlling consideration in this case is that the faculty of Yeshiva University exercise authority which *in any other context* unquestionably would be managerial. Their authority in academic matters is absolute. They decide what courses will be offered, when they will be scheduled, and to whom they will be taught. They debate and determine teaching methods, grading policies, and matriculation standards. They effectively decide which students will be admitted, retained and graduated. On occasion their views have determined the size of the student body, the tuition to be charged, and the location of a school. When one considers the function of a university, it is difficult to imagine decisions more managerial than these. *To the extent the industrial analogy applies*, the faculty determines within each school the product to be produced, the terms upon which it will be offered, and the customers who will be served. [44 U.S. at 686 (1980); italics added]

Presumably the facts on record on which briefs were based and argued supported this characterization. My personal suspicion is that a rather more inquiring and skeptical eye would have put additional facts on record that would have at least seriously qualified such a conclusion about the faculty at Yeshiva, but the Court's conclusion may be taken here as a statement of how a group of professors who are unequivocally employed perform functions that can be considered managerial in character. (There have been many commentaries on *Yeshiva*. One example is Sussman 1981. See also Angel 1982.)

In essence, I believe that the majority decision of the Court rests on the same mistaken assumption that marks the arguments of the Marxist proponents of the proletarianization thesis—namely, that the general criteria by which one can effectively conceptualize employer-employee relations and sort out rank-and-file from supervisory and managerial employees are to be discerned in traditional management-worker relations in industry. Those relations are characterized by both the NLRB and by Marxists as adversarial. The underlying assumption also is of clear hierarchical control: management formulates the work to be done, tells the worker to do it, and supervises to make sure that it is done correctly, by management's criteria. Management is active, and the workers are passive.

It is technical autonomy in their work that creates the ambiguity in the rank-and-file professional employees' positions in the firm, for insofar as they are free to perform their work according to their own judgment, much that would otherwise be done by supervisors and managers must be done by them. Freedom to use discretion presupposes freedom from meticulous supervision and direction by others. It also means the virtual necessity to be involved in setting up and maintaining the framework of tasks performed by others that impinge on their own work. Incidental to their everyday work they must perform from time to time many of the tasks that in an industrial setting are performed exclusively and on a full-time basis by supervisors and managers—functional tasks of "organizing," "coordinating," and "supervising" conventionally ascribed to management by textbooks (e.g., Sprunger and Bergquist 1978, 8). Indeed, insofar as they exercise discretion and judgment in defining and performing their daily tasks, it is not possible for anyone else to organize, coordinate, and supervise for them because their tasks are not laid out in advance in detail. Managers and supervisors in professional organizations, therefore, cannot possibly perform the same tasks they do in industry, nor can they perform their own tasks in the same way. This is especially the case in the university, where the variety of bodies of formal knowledge expressed in the division of labor is so great. While a university cannot serve as an exemplar for all organizations employing professionals, a closer look at its labor process can show us how it is that professionals do in fact make policy of an important sort but do not, in fact, serve as policymakers in an ultimate, truly managerial sense.

It is possible for a doctor or a lawyer to work wholly as an individual in a general office practice, removed from other colleagues, hospitals, and courts, but it is impossible for a professor to do so. In a college, university, or professional school each professor's courses are part of a larger intellectual division of labor called a curriculum. The individual's "product" in the form of course grades is virtually meaningless outside of the context of a larger curriculum and the degree that represents it (for a useful history of the curriculum, see Rudolph 1977). Formal education is a fundamentally collective, highly specialized enterprise requiring the coordination of a number of separate courses and disciplines into an organized curriculum. Each of those disciplines is organized by department in colleges and universities and sustained by national scientific societies or professional associations that give the disciplines lives of their own outside of individual colleges or universities (cf. Higham 1979, 3–18; Rosenberg 1979, 443–44; Veysey 1965). Professors are employed by individual institutions and paid to teach their disciplines to students (cf. Hawkins 1979, 285–301), but their intellectual life is oriented toward their disciplines.

While disciplinary departments thrive more in universities where graduate training and research are possible than in four-year colleges, even the latter—or at least the "better" among them—"have had to adopt the disciplinary reward structure . . . in order to get and hold a staff of competence" (McGee 1971, 35). The various disciplines are organized separately and proliferate into specialties and subdisciplines, all of such complexity as to be penetrable only by their members. In order to develop a curriculum in a single area, only members of the discipline can judge what are the essential qualifications for entering students who will be able to succeed in the courses they teach, how courses must relate to each other, and what group of courses is sufficient for a degree. (For a history of admission policies, with clear indication of how dependent even the powerful entrepreneurial presidents of earlier universities were on faculty judgment, see Wechsler 1977.)

In order to develop a general "liberal arts" curriculum, members of the various disciplines must collaborate in planning, organizing, and coordinating the relations and interrelations of the courses each is competent to teach. The enormous range and depth of formal knowledge represented by the faculty of a university is such that by no stretch of the imagination is it possible to conceive of a lay management that is able literally and figuratively to command it or the substance of the activities of its practitioners. Nor, as could conceivably be the case for one-profession organizations like law firms, can one imagine a management composed of a limited number of professionals capable of commanding the whole range of disciplinary and specialized activities of all its rank-and-file workers. There is no practical alternative to a fair amount of self-management.

It follows from that necessity of relying on the workers' specialized knowledge that during the course of their work they must also engage in selecting the "customers" they are competent to deal with, deciding the exact nature of the "product" they create, "supervising" and "directing" the work of nonprofessional assistants, planning and coordinating the work they do in collaboration with colleagues, and the like. Those functional tasks are an essential part of any discretionary work. They are not intrinsically managerial tasks but rather tasks intrinsic to discretionary work. Such tasks are managerial only when the rank-and-file worker is deskilled and proletarianized, stripped of the capacity to use discretion and judgment in performing work that is part of a complex division of labor.

THE GENERIC FUNCTION OF MANAGEMENT

This is not to say that managers do not direct and control professional work. They do, but in a professional setting they do so in a different way. Management exercises direction by the use of its exclusive power to allocate the resources necessary for the work, indeed, the very existence of the jobs of the rank and file. The faculty may "plan" the curriculum, but "planning without a decision to commit human and fiscal resources is not a plan; it is only a review, a study, or an intellectual exercise" (Sprunger and Bergquist 1978, 9). Reece McGee put the implications of the power to allocate resources for the professor very clearly: "All academic institutions except the most unabashedly tyrannical have some form of faculty government. Such structures are typically charged with determination of curriculum, grading, standards of scholarship, and so on. This is, indeed, a form of power, but . . . real power in academic institutions is the power over budget, for budget decisions determine who is to be hired and who not, and what he will be paid, what programs will be encouraged or shut off from further support, and what lines of endeavor will be rewarded" (1971, 21; cf. Blau 1973, 278).

Faculties may propose, but the administration disposes. Faculties may be the only ones competent to lay out the choices, but it is the administration that chooses. That is where the generic fault line between rank and file and management lies in universities and in other organizations producing professional services.

In most if not all American colleges and universities the faculty does not have the authority to allocate the resources needed to advance its collective activities. Academic administrators, from department head on up, do have such authority: they decide not merely what individual faculty members will be paid and what the standard work load will be but also what faculty positions will be filled, which is to say, what courses can be taught competently, what disciplines will be staffed, what programs will exist, and what the curriculum itself can be. The faculty has the discretionary right to determine how those resources, once granted, will be put to use but not the right to determine how those resources are to be allocated in the first place. Thus while in some sense the functional ramifications of the faculty's technical autonomy leads to a significant measure of what in an industrial context would be interpreted as supervisory and even policy-making authority, the power to allocate resources that remains in the hands of the administration places limits on the work the faculty is able to do and the manner in which it is able to do it.

The fundamental functional divide between managerial employees and mere professional employees, then, lies in the capacity of the former, on behalf of the governing board constituting "management," to allocate on the basis of its own discretion and judgment the resources of the organization. That divide is more than functional, however, for it also represents formal or official power to advance particular interests and aims that may be different from those of the faculty. Committed to its disciplinary interests, a university department may wish to hire new staff in order to develop a new specialty that is, in its judgment, essential for an up-to-date program. Believing that other programs have a higher priority, the administration may refuse the resources necessary for hiring that new person and thus prevent an up-to-date program. A faculty may wish to institute a program composed of small discussion groups and tutorials by which each student would receive intensive attention and instruction, but since this would require hiring more staff, the administration may refuse the necessary resources and so preclude the possibility of employing such methods of teaching. In short, the professional staff seeks resources for the advancement of its work as it conceives of it, and management allocates resources according to its own view of priorities. There is a clear division of interests and power between the two quite apart from obvious bread-and-butter matters of salary and work load. And it is quite possible that, from the point of view of overall social policy, management can be on the side of the angels. There is no more reason to think that professors or any other rank and file are always right than there is reason to think management always right.

The conflict within the university between the faculty of departments, programs, and schools seeking the resources they believe are essential for their well-being, on the one hand, and managers attempting to allocate resources with the goals of the entire institution in mind, on the other, is paralleled outside the university by tension between accrediting associations concerned with institutions as whole, such as the regional college associations or the Joint Commission for the Accreditation of Hospitals, and those concerned with disciplines or professions, such as the American Chemical Society or the National League for Nursing. It is that tension that is reflected in efforts by institutional spokesmen to eliminate both specialized accreditation and occupational licensing and to rely instead solely on the accreditation and licensing of the employing organizations as wholes. To the president of a university or the director of a hospital, specialized accrediting associations are "outsiders" seeking to interfere with their discretionary authority to choose among priorities in allocating resources to the various units of their institutions. To the faculty, however, as Dickey and Miller noted (1972, 18–19; and cf. Orlans 1975, 14), those "outside" specialized associations are their representatives who exert leverage on behalf of their discipline in order to press management to provide them with the resources they believe they need to do their job adequately. A trade union of professional employees, of course, is also seen as an "outside" and divisive force that presses for the allocation of more institutional resources for staff salary rather than for other purposes.

THE PROFESSIONAL RANKS

In a public legal services corporation it is the executive director and the supervisors and in a university it is the president and deans who are the true managerial employees. The practicing lawyers and the teaching professors are merely professional employees. The full-time duty of the managerial employee is to decide how to allocate resources to the various units of the organization, some of which are staffed by the rank-and-file professional employees. Since those resources ultimately determine what work can be done and how it can be done, their allocation is of critical importance to the advancement of the aims or goals of the organization as a whole and to the advancement of the aims or goals of the rank and file.

In conventional labor relations the division between managers and rank and file appears both wide and deep. It is also a division of training and of occupational identity. In professional organizations this difference does not hold firmly. Some professional employees are rank and file, using their training in the course of performing their productive tasks. But other professional employees, with the same Ph.D.'s, M.S.W.'s, D.Sc.'s, M.D.'s, or J.D.'s, use their training as a foundation for the exercise of discretion in supervising and deciding how to allocate resources in light of the general policies and aims of the board of directors, governing board, or whatever. The basic difference between the two lies in their aims and interests, for managing professionals are essentially concerned with the preservation of the integrity of the organization (or organizational unit) as a whole in the light of the general policy of its governing board, while the rank and file are concerned with the preservation of the integrity of their specialized pursuit of a discipline or a profession.

This is the fundamental difference in orientation and commitment between managers and rank and file in the professions, which is why there is so much tension between them and why the latter regard those of their number who become managers as another breed, no longer really colleagues in spite of their common training and experience in working as professionals before they undertook administrative responsibilities. And indeed, there is some truth to the idea that managerial professionals are no longer true members of the profession with which the rank and file is identified, for while they may keep their hand in practice by teaching a course, seeing a few clients, or otherwise performing the tasks of the rank and file, the fact is that if they are to be truly managerial employees they cannot spend much time at managing for very long without becoming quite rusty at professional practice. They become specialists in administration with a professional background, which is generically different from being specialists practicing substantive professional tasks on a full-time basis. Becoming different, they tend to lose their rank-and-file identity as practicing teachers, lawyers, nurses, social workers, engineers, or whatever (for physicians, see Goss 1962, 183–91; and Hall 1959, 185–94).

Managerial employees in professional organizations also tend to lose the perspective of the practitioner. After all, insofar as they "formulate and effectuate management policies," to use the words of the Bell Aerospace decision (*NLRB v. Bell Aerospace Co.*, 416 U.S. 267 [1974]), their perspective must be different, directed to the fortunes of the organization or unit as a whole rather than to those of the particular individuals who work in it. The managerial employee's concern with the organization as a whole is shared less with rank-and-file professional employees than with other managers in similar positions in similar organizations. Thus it should come as no surprise that the associational life of managers differs from that of the rank and file, that college deans or hospital administrators, for example, form their own specialized occupational associations. Furthermore, they represent their institutions in associations formed to represent them collectively—the Association of American Medical Colleges, for example, or the Association of Schools of Music. In those organizational associations they attempt to formulate common policies both for the administration of the internal affairs of their institutions and for dealing with the political economy on which the ultimate support of their organization depends.

THE PARADOX OF PROFESSIONAL CONTROL OF WORK

Now that I have sketched out the broad framework of law and definition within which employed professionals work, it is possible to conclude by returning to the issue of control over work that was raised in the last chapter. In this chapter the issue emerged first as a central element of the special position of professional employees in labor law, within the broader framework of the credential system that, to varying degrees, sustains them in the labor market. I attempted to show how technical autonomy contains within itself the right, indeed, the necessity, to perform supervisory and policy-making functions. But when I argued that in a professional setting those functions are not intrinsic to management, as they are in conventional industrial settings in which discretion is denied the rank-and-file worker, I went on to argue not that professional workers were therefore truly part of management, as the Supreme Court majority ruled in the *Yeshiva* case, but rather that the basic distinction lay in other criteria. By the power to allocate the total resources of the organization, management is sharply distinguished from rank-and-file professional workers. And that power to allocate resources determines the particular kind of work that can be done and limits the way work can be done. When the generic power of the manager is specified, the autonomy of the special position of the professional employee seems to vanish. It does and it does not, that is the paradox.

Professional employees possess technical autonomy or the right to use discretion and judgment in the performance of their work. In order actually to exercise that technical autonomy during the course of work they must from time to time be able to exercise some degree of both supervisory and policy-making authority. Furthermore, within certain limits, they must be able to select the work they do and decide how to do it. The limits, however, are set by management's resource allocation decisions. In the former sense they are autonomous, possessing a distinct measure of freedom and independence on the job that conventional workers lack, and it is a measure of freedom and independence that cannot be deprecated as trivial. In the latter sense, however, they are helpless and dependent because they have no control over the "economy" of the organization that employs them.

In one sense, then, professional employees are autonomous, and in another they are not. Both senses are real, however, so while we may believe professional employees who consider themselves truly autonomous to be shortsighted, we cannot accuse them of out-and-out blindness. Their myopic sense of autonomy within unobserved limits is as well grounded in reality as is the self-employed person's sense of being free and independent, though in the latter case, even when the visible franchising limits of taxation and state regulation are missing and only the market reigns, the hand that limits the autonomy of the self-employed is invisible, and so visual acuity may not explain the illusion. Professional employees do have genuine privilege in being able to exercise considerable discretion in their work. They are, furthermore, to a variable degree sheltered by a credential system. But they must do their work in circumstances that are shaped by the structure of the organization in which they work and by the resources made available to them by others. What powers, then, can they exercise? In the next chapter I shall examine the nature of the organizations in which they work and then attempt to assess the powers of the rank-and-file professional employee.

References

Angel, M. 1982. Professionals and unionization. *Minnesota Law Review* 66 (March): 383–457.

Aronowitz, S. 1973. *False promises: The shaping of American working class consciousness.* New York: McGraw-Hill Book Co.

Blau, P. 1973. *The organization of academic work.* New York: John Wiley & Sons.

Brint, S. G., and M. H. Dodd. 1984. *Professional workers and unionization: A data handbook.* Publication no. 81-4. Washington, D.C.:

AFL-CIO, Department for Professional Employees.

Cox, A., D. C. Bok, and R. A. Gorman. 1977. *Labor law: Cases and materials*. 8th ed. Minneapolis: West Publishing Co.

Derber, C. 1982. Managing professionals: Ideological proletarianization and mental labor. In *Professionals as workers*, edited by C. Derber, 167–90. Boston: G. K. Hall & Co.

Dickey, F. G., and J. W. Miller. 1972. *A current perspective on accreditation*. Washington, D.C.: American Association for Higher Education.

Finkin, M. W. 1974. The NLRB in higher education. *University of Toledo Law Review* 5 (Spring): 608–55.

————. 1977. The supervisory status of professional employees. *Fordham Law Review* 45:805–34.

Gillespie, J. F. 1978. Annotation: Who are professional employees within meaning of National Labor Relations Act (29 USCS P152[12]). *American Law Reports, Federal Cases and Annotations*, 40:25–134. Rochester, N.Y.: Lawyers Co-operative Publishing Co.

Gorman, R. A. 1976. *Basic text on labor law: Unionization and collective bargaining*. Minneapolis: West Publishing Co.

Goss, M. E. W. 1962. Administration and the physician. *American Journal of Public Health* 52 (February): 183–91.

Hall, O. 1959. Half medical man, half administrator: A medical dilemma. *Canadian Public Administration* 2 (December): 185–94.

Hawkins, H. 1979. University identity: The teaching and research functions. In *The organization of knowledge in modern America, 1860–1920*, edited by A. Oleson and J. Voss, 285–312. Baltimore: Johns Hopkins University Press.

Higham, J. 1979. The matrix of specialization. In *The organization of knowledge in modern America, 1860–1920*, edited by A. Oleson and J. Voss, 3–18. Baltimore: Johns Hopkins University Press.

Kornhauser, W. 1962. *Scientists in industry*. Berkeley: University of California Press.

Krent, H. J. 1981. Collective authority and technical expertise: Reexamining the managerial employee exclusion. *New York University Law Review* 56 (October): 694–741.

Marcson, S. 1960. *The scientist in American industry*. New York: Harper & Bros.

McGee, R. 1971. *Academic Janus: The private college and its faculty*. San Francisco: Jossey-Bass, Inc.

Orlans, H. 1975. *Private accreditation and public eligibility*. Lexington, Mass.: D. C. Heath & Co.

Rosenberg, C. E. 1979. Toward an ecology of knowledge: On discipline, context and history. In *The organization of knowledge in modern America, 1860–1920*, edited by A. Oleson and J. Voss, 440–55. Baltimore: Johns Hopkins University Press.

Rudolph, F. 1977. *Curriculum: A history of the undergraduate course of study since 1636.* San Francisco: Jossey-Bass, Inc.

Sprunger, B. E., and W. H. Bergquist. 1978. *Handbook for college administration.* Washington, D.C.: Council for the Advancement of Small Colleges.

Sussman, A. M. 1981. University governance through a rose-colored lens: NLRB v. Yeshiva. In *Supreme Court Review: 1980* edited by P. B. Kurland and G. Casper, 27–55. Chicago: University of Chicago Press.

Veysey, L. R. 1965. *The emergence of the American university.* Chicago: University of Chicago Press.

Wechsler, H. S. 1977. *The qualified student: A history of selective college admission in America.* New York: John Wiley & Sons.

Chapter Eight

Professional Powers in Work Organizations

Formalisms, whether legal or logical, always distort. The formal legal status of professional employees as well as the formal legal and quasi-legal characteristics of credentialing give an impression of solidity, of a strong position in the political economy from which professionals can carve out a well-protected shelter in the world of work. The empirical reality is rather different, however. The professional employee's shelter does provide some protection from the chill winds of an entirely free market or a monopsony but it is not sealed off enough to be a true haven. The credential system fails to provide all the privileges and powers that are necessary for the creation of complete professional control of working conditions at their places of employment. This is due in part to the relationship of those organizations to the public or private sources of support on which they depend and in part to the distribution of power within those organizations. The special position of the rank and file is created by its important powers of discretion at work, on the one hand, and its important powerlessness in the determination of the allocation of the resources essential for its work. It is that ambivalent position that I shall analyze in this chapter.

BUREAUCRACY—RHETORICAL AND CONSEQUENTIAL

Before addressing the power and weakness of rank-and-file professionals it is necessary to clarify the nature of the organizations in which they work. A proponent of the proletarianization thesis asserts that "the bureaucratized workplace . . . tend[s] to replace in the professionals' own workplace factory-like conditions—there are fixed jurisdictions, ordered by rules established by others; there is a hierarchical command system; jobs are entered and mobility exists on the basis of performance in uniform tasks, examinations, or the achievement of certification or 'degrees'; work tends to become specialized, hence extensive division of labour develops. . . . The gap between what the worker does, and an end product, increases" (Oppenheimer 1973, 214). Is this in fact an accurate characterization of the position of the rank-and-file professional employed in large organizations? Are those large organizations truly bureaucratized?

As many writers have observed, there is an intrinsic conflict between Weber's concept of rational-legal bureaucracy and the Anglo-American concept of professionalism (cf. Hall 1982, 107–112). It is not a conflict bearing on rationality, which professionalism claims equally with bureaucracy, but rather one revolving around authority. In a bureaucracy officials are expected to be obeyed by subordinates by virtue of their formal positions as officials, not of their personal qualities or even their competence. Professionals, on the other hand, expect to be autonomous and self-directing, subject only to the constraints of competent knowledge and skill related to their task. They can accept advice, perhaps even orders, if it stems from someone of competence, but it is only competence, not official position as an administrative superior, that is accepted as the source of effective authority over work. At bottom, the issue is whether control over work is to be exercised by administrative personnel with management skills but without training to perform the work involved or by the members of the occupation or profession itself (cf. Freidson 1973). The conflict, however, is logical, between concepts of control. The empirical question is how close organizations come to reflecting the elements of the formal concept of Weber's rational-legal bureaucracy and, most particularly, how close organizations employing professionals do so.

By and large, it is possible to state that there are reasonable grounds for arguing that most formal organizations—even civil service agencies (cf. Blau 1963)—deviate sufficiently from the abstract model of rational-legal bureaucracy to call into question its usefulness as a schematic representation of the realities of work in any large, modern organization, including industrial organizations. In the special case of organizations employing professionals as their prime workers, deviation from the model is even greater. In fact, the rational-legal model of bureaucracy differs so much from what was observed that those studying actual organizations employing professionals have almost all had to invent hybrid models in order to take into account both important elements that are not referred to by the model and the absence of some elements of the model. Studying doctors in an outpatient clinic, Goss (1961, 1963) advanced the idea of "advisory bureaucracy" to fit what she found. Studying lawyers in large law firms, Smigel (1964) employed the concept of "professional bureaucracy." Montagna (1968) employed the term *professional organization* for large accounting firms, as did Bucher and Stelling (1969) for hospitals and Scott (1965) for social agencies.

Indeed, in a more general context organizational theorists have found difficulties in the fit between Weber's model and a variety of industrial, commercial, and professional organizations. Recent theories have emphasized the fluid and organic qualities of organizations rather than the fixed and mechanical features of bureaucracy or scientific management (for a recent review, see Scott 1981). It seems no accident that many of those theories owe part of their genesis to the stimulus of studying organizations that employ professionals. For example, the notion of organizations as "organized anarchies" derived in part from the study of universities (Cohen and March 1972), while the most influential elaboration of the idea of organizations as "loosely coupled systems" was addressed to the analysis of public school systems (Weick 1976). Both universities and school systems have bureaucratic characteristics, but they are not enough like bureaucracies in a strict analytic sense to sustain the use of the concept.

THE VARIOUS PROFESSIONS IN "BUREAUCRACIES"

There can be no doubt that, whenever a number of people are brought together to work, some formal organization orders their relationships of authority and specialization. In the case of relatively large organizations in our society the formal structure is likely to be both distinct and a matter of public record, with an assortment of hierarchical titles representing managerial and supervisory authority as well as differentiation of the rank and file by job title, rank, and perhaps seniority. There are also likely to be written rules and regulations and, almost certainly, written records. But these formalisms may not mean *bureaucracy* in any strictly analytic sense of the term. The critical question is how the organization works, how common the routine exercise of discretion by professionals in the organization is, and how extensive that exercise of discretion is.

Let us begin with the schoolteacher, who is often considered to be in a powerless position, rigidly constrained by bureaucratically organized school systems and powerful principals and superintendents. No one can doubt that school systems have many bureaucratic characteristics, not only because they are large, but also because they are public and accountable to the state board of education and its mandated guidelines (cf. Anderson 1968; and Campbell, Cunningham, and McPhee 1975). The chief executive officer of the system is the superintendent, while that of the individual school is the principal. Below them is a variety of personnel, most professional, but some not. The professional personnel are divided by the level at which they teach (i.e., primary or secondary), subject-matter teaching specialization (particularly on the secondary level), and other forms of specialization, such as school psychologists, "special education" teachers (Milofsky 1976), school social workers, and guidance counselors (Cicourel and Kitsuse 1963; Armor 1969). Apart from that hierarchy and division of labor, the state board of education is prone to formulate some kind of curriculum guide that specifies the subjects to be taught at each grade level, and it is common to require that every teacher submit a lesson plan for what will be taught. Clearly, there is some basis for asserting that schools are bureaucracies that impose elaborate restraints on the autonomy of their teachers.

Nonetheless, those who actually study schoolteachers paint a picture of distinct autonomy stemming from the way the teacher's position in the classroom is insulated from systematic observation and control even by peers. Lortie, who describes school bureaucracy as rudimentary (Lortie 1969, 11), notes that, while the school administration may limit options, the teacher is free, like most professionals, to choose among them and that the primary work of instruction "is least controlled by specific and literally enforced rules and regulations" (ibid., 14).

In the classroom, which is the primary locus of their work, schoolteachers have considerable autonomy. Within the overall limits set by the state board of education and the local school system, they expect to be able to perform what Lortie called the managerial tasks of setting the goals of their classrooms, allocating the time and resources made available to them by the system, and the like (Lortie 1975, 166–67). They are in essence brokers between policies established from above and the concrete conduct of the classroom (Schwille et al. 1983, 376–77). There are thus certainly bureaucratic constraints on the work of rank-and-file teachers, but few might be identified with the pathos of the rhetoric invoking bureaucracy as a rigid, discretion-erasing mechanism.

Turning to the professions of law, medicine, and accounting, we find even less evidence of rigid, all-encompassing constraints on the work of professionals in large organizations. It is common among students of professional organizations to note an administrative hierarchy that is parallel to the professional hierarchy but that is insulated from influencing the conduct of what are defined as professional or technical affairs. Baldridge (1971, 114–59) explored the relationship between the two in the university, as did Goss (1961, 1963), Nathanson (1971), and Freidson (1980), among others, in medical clinics. In both cases, autonomy in technical, professional aspects of work was observed, with the professionals accepting some but not all administrative constraints and accepting technical supervision so long as it was carried out by a respected practicing professional. The same pattern was found in large law and accounting firms, which, unlike schools and hospital-based clinics, are organized as partnerships. In both cases there is a distinct hierarchy of rank (cf. Sorensen and Sorensen 1974, 98; Smigel 1964, 228–39; Spangler and Lehman 1982; Nelson 1981, 118–30) and increasing specialization. In the case of accounting firms, there is a non–certified public accountant hierarchy that runs parallel to that of the certified public accountants, its head being not a partner in the firm but a "principal" (Montagna 1974, 103). Hierarchy or no, large accounting firms have emphasized personal autonomy on the part of the full-fledged employee (ibid., 108), and in large law firms "the individual attorney controls his own work process. . . . Departmentalization and specialization primarily affect the scope of an individual's practice rather than the productive process itself" (Nelson 1981, 127).

Little as is known about the conduct of work in law firms that are owned and managed by professionals, even less is known about those public organizations that employ a substantial number of lawyers—public prosecutor or district attorney systems on the one hand (cf. Eisenstein 1978; and Jacoby 1980 for overviews but no details on the work process) and public defender or legal services systems on the other (cf. Katz 1982; and the recent review by Spangler and Lehman 1982). In both cases there is a distinct formal hierarchy delineated by civil service and therefore literally bureaucratic criteria, distinct provision for formal supervisory positions, and legal responsibility for the conduct of prosecution or defense located not in the individual who actually does the work but rather in the supervisor or executive officer of the organization. How far a defense attorney can invoke the sanctity of the attorney-client relation to resist the directives of superiors, as Katz (1982, 111) suggests, is uncertain, but we may assume considerable discretion on the part of attorneys in deciding whether and how to presecute or defend a case.

The same may be said for judges, who, with the exception of "fee judges," are primarily professional employees. Since there is a variety of judicial systems—city (e.g., Wice 1981), state (e.g., Gazell 1975), federal (e.g., Goulden 1974; Heydebrand 1977), and executive or administrative (e.g., Nonet 1969)—it is difficult to generalize. Certainly there has been a strong movement over decades to reorganize court procedures in order to reduce delay in adjudication, if not improve the quality of justice. By and large, it seems that the emphasis has been placed on integrating judges and their courts into a hierarchy presided over by the chief judge of the highest court as well as on using lay court administrators to schedule and otherwise "process" cases efficiently. However, the ultimate authority of the chief judge over the court system remains supported by law, and "by definition the [trial] judge must exercise larger amounts of discretion. Control is achieved through professional norms, peer review, and appellate review" (Henderson, Guynes, and Baar 1981, 46; and cf. Ryan et al. 1980). While Sheskin and Gram (1981, 227) argue that court reform constitutes "a direct assault upon the judicial prerogative of independence," their case study of Ohio shows a judicial rather than a lay administrative hierarchy to which judges are responsible.

Law, of course, is a well-organized, comparatively strong profession, so we should expect its practitioners to be able to hold on to a fairly large area of discretion in their work even when employed. On the other hand, we might expect weaker professions to be in far less free situations. But there is evidence that in a curious way even in heteronomous professional organizations—that is, organizations directly controlled by nonprofessional employers—management may find it convenient to accept occupationally formulated standards for filling its positions and establishing its work procedures rather than to create its own managerially "rational" system. Reeves (1980) shows in some detail how the personnel standards of the American Library Association have been adopted by many large employers and how administrators follow association recommendations of procedure. Reeves points out further that it is the librarian profession and "not the organization [that] promotes bureaucratic control in library work settings" (ibid., 105), for lacking the means available to stronger professions, its standards are more likely to be established and sustained in organizations large enough to desire "rational" procedures.

Social work is difficult to characterize because, like librarianship and unlike nursing and schoolteaching, it has not been able to establish a minimum professional credential for the most common rank-and-file jobs. Well over two-thirds of all "social workers" do not have the M.S.W. (Cohen and Wagner 1982, 162–63), and the fact that the National Association of Social Workers lowered its requirements and accepted the B.S.W. as a professional degree is perhaps unprecedented in American professionalization movements. The most common social work–like job—case worker in public welfare offices—does not require more than a high school diploma in most jurisdictions. What can be said is that, for professionally qualified social workers, supervision of the content of practice is traditional and is considered to have pedagogic as well as administrative functions (cf. Toren 1972, 65–85; Eaton 1980) and that the more professionally qualified social workers are, the more they are likely to resent administrative rules that constrain their discretion (Scott 1969). But given this wide variation of qualification and of the way public welfare offices operate (cf. Goodsell 1984), it is thus difficult to make sweeping characterizations (e.g., Patry 1978; Cohen and Wagner 1982) of social workers as professionals and of their working conditions.

Nursing is in a rather different position than social work, being firmly credentialed. Unlike most other professions, however, nursing is usually conducted in a very elaborate, highly technical division of labor among a number of occupations ordered both by specialization and by authority. There is a hierarchy among occupations performing nursing and ancillary functions, with nurses superordinate to some and themselves subordinate to their own nursing supervisors. There is also a hierarchy in the overall division of labor, with members of the medical profession in the superordinate position. While few would doubt that nurses employ considerable discretion routinely in the course of their work, the elaborateness of the occupational division of labor, especially in some of the special diagnostic and treatment facilities of modern hospitals, creates constraints on individual discretion that are greater than appears to be the case for most other professions that either are superordinate in the division of labor or function in a fairly simple division of labor. But nurses do work in a complex and not a detailed division of labor.

Finally, I might mention the position of rank-and-file engineers and scientists employed in manufacturing and other commercial enterprises. The "scientists" in this context are primarily those with a B.S. degree, like engineers, and not those with advanced degrees, who are usually studied by sociologists of science (cf. Ben-David 1976 for an overview of the latter). Unfortunately, there have been few empirical studies of engineers and industrial scientists (cf. Marcson 1960; Kornhauser 1963; Miller 1968; Glaser 1964; Ritti 1971; Pelz and Andrews 1966). Furthermore, the job title *engineer* has not been based consistently on formal educational credentials (cf. Cain, Freeman, and Hansen 1973, 19). In any case, a recent review concluded that engineers and scientists do have a "relatively high degree of autonomy in their work" (Meiksins 1982, 137). How and why such autonomy exists is shown in a rare empirical study (Zussman 1985, 104–111). A recent study of architects (Blau 1984, 24–45) analyzes some of the factors involved in the autonomy of rank-and-file architects.

In all, it is possible to conclude that, at its best, the concept of bureaucracy provides only a very loose guide to the reality of professional work in organizations. At its worst, the concept applied to professional work settings is debased to mere rhetoric in the service of preconceived ideas. So long as professionals are free to use their own judgment during the course of their work they can be called bureaucrats and their employing organizations bureaucracies only in a special sense. They are distinguished from other workers at the very least by their technical autonomy. The question is, What powers does such freedom from close organizational control give them?

The Power of the Gatekeeper

Paradoxically, the bureaucratic facet of the circumstances of professional work provides some of the power that rank-and-file professionals have in their dealings with the public. That power stems from their position as credentialed professionals, on the one hand, and from their position as officials of formal organizations or systems, on the other. I refer to the power of professionals to act as gatekeepers of desirable goods and services (cf. Freidson 1970, 115–23).

All professions engaged in providing services to individual clients, whether their members are characteristically employed or not, are prone to have some form of official gatekeeping powers attached to their credentials. I have already noted in chapter 4 how in New York State the seal of a licensed land surveyor or professional engineer is needed to make construction plans eligible for official approval and how in some states a lawyer must be involved in real estate closings. Similarly, in default of a civil ceremony, an officially recognized member of the clergy must sign a wedding certificate, just as a licensed physician must sign a birth or a death certificate. Furthermore, professionals are instrumental in distributing resources that a variety of institutions offer. Typically, they do not dispense those resources but instead approve their disbursement by the institution that employs them. Thus neither schoolteachers nor professors have the power as individuals to issue diplomas or degrees; it is the school or the collective faculty that has such power, and the certificate is more likely to bear the signature of the executive officer of the institution than those of the graduate's teachers. But only teachers are authorized to give students officially recognized grades for their performance in the classroom, and adequate grades are prerequisite for a diploma or degree. Ostensibly without the power to provide the concrete, marketable credential that students seek from educational institutions, teachers nonetheless have the exclusive power to give the grades that determine whether that credential can in effect be granted the student by the institution.

Other professions have similar powers to grant or withhold benefits on behalf of the employing institution that possesses and disburses them. Case workers determine eligibility for a variety of economic and other benefits sought by their clientele, for which there is no other place to go (Scott 1969, 127). The physician alone determines whether a person will be admitted to a hospital and when he or she is to be discharged. Lawyers in the public prosecutor's office determine whether to prosecute a case or to dismiss it, while certified public accountants have the power to certify or withhold certification of confidence in the accuracy of a corporation's financial statements, and professional engineers have the power to grant or deny certification that a construction is sound.

The examples I have given are scattered, designed to sample the broad range of personal service professions and the concrete gatekeeping powers that their practitioners exercise during the normal course of their work. Such powers vary considerably from profession to profession and from work setting to work setting. Perhaps the most extensive are exercised by the medical profession, whose members serve as gatekeepers in a far more complex way than merely prescribing, certifying births and deaths, and admitting and discharging from the hospital. Quite apart from being gatekeepers of access to health care, physicians serve as gatekeepers of government disbursements. They do so by certifying illness and disability, thereby making individuals eligible for financial benefits from varying government programs. A series of papers by Stone elaborated in systematic detail the variety of federal and state income-maintenance programs (whose benefits in 1975 amounted to some twenty-three billion dollars) that are disbursed to applicants on the basis of medical certification of illness or disability (Stone 1978–79 1979a, 1979b).

I trust that these examples indicate how extensive the gatekeeping powers of professionals can be. How those powers are exercised, however, can vary quite a lot, depending in part on the organization of professional practice and the relations of professionals to their clientele. When the professional is associated with the agency providing benefits, both personal concern for the allocation of the agency's resources and pressures from the agency to adopt a hard line toward certification may encourage an adversarial relationship with the client (see, e.g., Walters 1982). The agency or organization may try to control the process by issuing an elaborate set of rules and regulations regarding eligibility and review the decisions of its employees on that basis. It is when the professional's own judgment of what resources the client needs contradicts the rules and regulations that we find one facet of "professional-bureaucracy" conflict. This may be a conflict in conceptions of the proper criteria to employ in arriving at a decision or a conflict induced by the way management has decided to allocate the resources of time, money, and personnel needed by the professionals to perform their work as their judgment advises.

RESOURCE ALLOCATION AND
PROFESSIONAL WORK

In chapter 7 I argued that the critical fault line between the professional employee and the management of the employing organization lies in resource allocation. While the professional employee has discretionary power and exercises it either to grant goods or services directly or to give official approval to the provision of goods or services by other members of the institution, he or she has little control over the amount and type of goods and services available. Even in providing their own services rather than benefits, professionals cannot distribute their own finite energies beyond certain limits, and the quality of their services must by necessity be influenced by their work load. It follows from the fact that resource allocation, which influences both what can be done and how it can be done, is everywhere the central power retained by management that it is also the central source of conflict between the rank and file and management, whether management possesses professional qualifications or not. In organizations employing professionals, it is not the rank and file as individuals that decides how many of them are to be employed to cope with the demand for services. Management determines caseload, though with certain limits established by professional definitions of the minimum time and resources necessary for work. The rank and file does not determine the formal rules of eligibility for service—the fees clients pay, for example, or the other characteristics required to establish eligibility for service. While the working hours of virtually all professional employees are restricted and controlled by their terms of employment and a given income is guaranteed by those terms from year to year, the critical variables are the number and type of tasks performed in a working day, the number and type of cases to be handled, and the supportive resources to be made available to aid performance—the rules of eligibility that determine, for example, task flow, equipment, space, and assisting personnel.

These resources, the allocation of which is controlled by management, are the focal point for the tensions of work in organizations. Because discretion is intrinsic to professional task performance, it can in theory be easier for professionals than it is for other workers to cope with what is seen as inadequate resources because more flexible adaptation is possible for them than it is for those whose pace is tied to the speed of an assembly line. The relative freedom to adapt may be no small advantage so long as one cares nothing about the quality of one's work: one can shrug, cut corners, routinize, and soldier (see, e.g., such adaptations on the part of some physicians in Freidson 1980). But because many professionals tend to be committed to their work, such adaptation is problematic. Professionals have notions, formed in part by their training, of how work should be performed and of what work is interesting and worthy of their training. They are also prone to believe that their work is valuable. Such positive commitment to their work leads professionals to deplore, if not actually resist, management's allocation decisions and its efforts to establish greater productivity. It may also create "burnout" in professionals, particularly those newly employed with "unrealistic" conceptions of what their work should be like (Cherniss 1980). The emphasis of the practitioners in discussing their work is on its quality, while, when all is said and done, management's de facto emphasis is on what can be measured readily—cost and quantity (Lipsky 1980, 48–53).

In evaluating this tension between rank and file and management, it would be a mistake to consider it as a conflict between virtue and sin, with the professional worker on the side of the angels and management beyond the pale. The professional's commitment to one discipline and its practice may very well inflate its importance in the larger scheme of things and may very well require reasoned constraint by non-professionals and by professionals serving in administrative positions who may represent their interests. The professional's tendency to perform work in traditional ways and within settled jurisdictional boundaries may have no justifiable foundation and may need to be frustrated. There can be very sound policy reasons bearing on the good of an organization as a whole, of the community in which it exists, and indeed of the nation in general that justify the allocation of finite resources skimpily to one set of professional tasks and generously to another.

Every organization, no matter what the nature of its character and no matter how it is governed and by whom, and every society, no matter what its political economy, must assign differential priorities to the allocation of resources, and there is likely to be no single perspective on the issue that, taken by itself, can be accorded automatic deference. The tension between professional employees and management is paralleled by the tension between professions and society, a tension not only of interests but also of perspectives. Lipsky posed that tension well for professional employees committed to serving their clients:

The organization hoards resources, the advocate seeks their dispersal to clients. The organization imposes tight control over resource dispersal if it can; the advocate seeks to utilize loop-holes and discretional provisions to gain client benefits. The organization seeks to treat all clients equally and to avoid having to respond to claims that others received special treatment; the advocate seeks to secure special treatment for individual clients. The organization acts as if available resource categories had fixed limits (which is often not absolutely true); the advocate acts as if resources were limitless (which is also not true). [Lipsky 1980, 73]

INTERACTIONAL POWER OVER CLIENTS

Within the framework of resources provided by management (or, in the case of the self-employed, by their position in the marketplace), the everyday work of the professional may be seen as coping with a number of contingencies. Some contingencies are imposed by the type and amount of resources available for the time and effort necessary to accomplish various tasks, some by relations with supervisors and managers, and some by relations with other workers, both professional and nonprofessional, and some are created by clients. By and large, one can assume that routine methods of coping are developed for all those contingencies. This is not to say that all is worked out harmoniously, that there are not persistent and patterned tensions that create trouble each time they arise and must be negotiated. Because professional workers are expected to practice discretion during the daily course of their work, their relations with supervisors, managers, and their directives are probably more prone to elicit tension than the relations of nonprofessionals, as are their requests for resources beyond those routinely available. The relatively settled modus vivendi that is worked out between members of various professions in an organization's division of labor is similarly not without its tensions and the necessity to negotiate around particular issues as they arise. These tensions are all among employees of the same organized enterprise—between superordinates and subordinates and between members of different specialties and occupations. Because they are all employees, working together in the organization every day of the week, they have the opportunity and the motivation to work out over time a set of agreements about the way they conduct their relations and a set of strategies by which they deal with recurrent tensions that have not been resolved by agreement.

But the relationship with clients is rather more problematic. Whereas members of the organization are relatively permanent, clientele are relatively transient. Whereas members of the organization work out common understandings about their relationships on the basis of their collaborative efforts within the organization and of their sharing a common perspective that is based on their working in the organization, the client is an outsider seeking what may not be possible or convenient or fair for an organization member to give. Furthermore, members of the organization are familiar with its resources and procedures, while clients, however sophisticated they may be in general, are less likely to be so familiar. These characteristics make the client relationship the most troublesome for professional employees. Indeed, in studies of dentists, teachers, and nurses, clients or patients were listed along with work load as being among the major sources of stress (Cooper 1980, 9; Marshall 1980, 27–31; Phillips and Lee 1980, 98). All professionals use what power they have to control that relationship so as to be able to work in the way they think appropriate.

One need not express approval of efforts to control the client when one observes that they are both inevitable and understandable. However inspired and dedicated to service, the professional is doing a job with its own economy of resources. In the case of most professionals, that job entails serving more than one client, which means that time and effort must be rationed to one in order to have enough left to give to another. Furthermore, standards get worked out that have been useful in past cases and that are likely to be employed in a new case even though the client may not believe that his or her case is like others. Without some such typifications, stereotypes, or precedents to establish a framework that conventionalizes individual cases, it would be impossible to deal with a number of different cases (for a stimulating analysis of some important sources of categorization, see Emerson 1983). A work relationship cannot possibly entail the particularism of an intimate social relationship in which the full-blown uniqueness of an individual is plumbed and responded to freshly and in which time, energy, and cost count for little.

Furthermore, what the client may want as an individual may be in conflict with what the professional worker's job properly requires. Teachers, for example, are supposed to do the best job at teaching all that is possible to their students as well as to evaluate how much each student has learned in comparison with general standards or the standard set by the performance of all the students in the classroom. Thus while all students are likely to want high grades, teachers must give low grades to some in order to reflect their comparatively poor performance. In that instance and in many others there is thus an intrinsic conflict between the desires of individual clients and some basic elements of the professional's job. In order to accomplish that job one must manage those desires while frustrating them. This may be done by persuading clients to lower their expectations on grounds of their being "unrealistic" about themselves, as guidance counselors have been found to do for working-class students (Cicourel and Kitsuse 1963), by persuading them to moderate their complaints and demands so as to be perceived as "reasonable" by other agents important to their case, as did legal aid attorneys in Chicago (Katz 1982, 56–59), by "cutting corners" in the way one does one's work (Rosenthal 1974, 106 ff.), or by outright intimidation of the client (Miller 1983; Lipsky 1980, 93–94, 120–22). The propriety of any of these techniques of control can probably not be judged fairly without attention to the circumstances of individual cases.

The professional worker is not always able to control the client, even when there is a patently asymmetrical situation of expertise on the one hand and ignorance on the other, for there are many instances in history that show how really powerful clients can have their own conceptions of what is to be done to or for them and can force professionals to do what they want done even when that is contrary to the professionals' judgment. In the present day there is fairly good evidence that wealthy or otherwise powerful individual or corporate clients can pretty much dictate the content of their professional service and that affluent, well-educated, upper-middle-class clients can gain a great deal, if not all of what they want, from professionals. In the case of law, Heinz and Laumann (1982, 338) point out the paradox that the lawyers who gain elite status because they have powerful corporations as their clients have little interpersonal power over them, while the scorned lawyers who serve the personal needs of individual clients of lower status have great interpersonal power.

In the vast majority of cases of professional work, however, clients are neither sophisticated nor powerful, so that the professional's position as gatekeeper of desired resources combines with a monopoly of organizationally relevant knowledge about how the system works to create a position of interpersonal power that few are in a position to challenge. As Reeves (1980, 137) points out, even though librarians possess no genuine monopoly of a body of specialized knowledge that might be said to produce a "knowledge gap" between them as a group and consumers as a general class, individual librarians in particular libraries do have a monopoly of organizationally relevant knowledge that provides them with considerable leverage over the transient client. They, like other professional employees, can control clients in part by restricting information on how to work the system and by keeping them dependent (Lipsky 1980, 90–93).

THE RANK AND FILE AND POLICY-MAKING

I have observed that, as professional employees, the rank and file have important areas of discretion in their work and that they also have significant powers as gatekeepers that are exercised over those clients who lack either the information or the power to be able to get their own way. However, they do not have the power to establish the formal policies of their employing organizations, including how available resources for their work are to be allocated. Yet, in a way, they may be said to have the power to make policy after all, for as Lipsky (1980, xii) noted, their implementation decisions at work constitute the actual policies of the organization no matter what the policy stated or desired by legislation, formal organizational aims, and the like. At the very least they are "policy brokers" (Schwille et al. 1983).

The capacity of the rank-and-file professional to make policy in that sense is created by the technical autonomy expressed in the exercise of discretion in work. Technical standards imply goals like any set of standards, so that, when one controls execution, one advances the goals implicit in it. Such autonomy is sustained by barriers to supervisory information posed by the conventions of many kinds of professional work—particularly those in which there is an intangible product and in which a personal service is involved. Even without legal support, concern for the privacy of the client has insulated the work of many professionals from direct observability. The information about performance available to supervisors, then, must be indirect, based on inference from records rather than on observation. And it is the professional worker who creates those records, from the time and appointment records used to determine how clients are to be billed to the case records, notes, or completed forms that are used to represent the key substance of the work performed—the presenting problem, its evaluation, and its disposition by denying or granting service, by referral, or whatever. Rather less is known about engineering than about most other professions, perhaps because the vast majority of engineers work in private-enterprise organizations, but occasional revelations in the newspapers about practices in the automobile, tire, and nuclear power industries indicate that it is the engineers who "construct" the record.

Until recently, when clients in some settings have been conceded the right to see and comment on their own records, or when company records are subpoenaed, this monopoly over "official information" about cases has been an enormously powerful tool by which professional workers could defend their practices against challenge by clients or other outsiders, for beyond the written record there is merely the hearsay of client complaints or claims. Furthermore, written records tend to be institutionally privileged, inaccessible to outsiders but accessible to all others working in the organization. Thus like a privileged credit rating that circulates to those businesses seeking to determine whether to extend credit to a consumer, the record can prejudice all others in an organization dealing with the client, creating a common stance among them toward his or her complaints or requests. The classic illustration of this power to create the record that all others see, and of its consequences for the fate of the client, is to be found in Goffman's discussion of the psychiatric record in mental hospitals of the 1950s (1961, 146–69). In schools, the grade a teacher has given a student similarly prejudices other teachers (and guidance counselors) who are uncertain about their own evaluation.

The physician's assessment and comments (cf. Freidson 1980, 167–85), the caseworker's notes and recommendations, and other records play similar roles in establishing the effective policy of the organization as a whole toward individual clients. (For an ethnography of how records in a nursing home and a residential child-treatment center are selectively created and of how the staff regards that selective creation, see Gubrium and Buckholdt 1979.) In some cases, the record is no doubt deliberately created to protect the professional worker from blame. In others, it is no doubt deliberately created for the worker's advantage. In the case of engineers, as Ritti (1971, 23) notes, specifications are often "fudged" in order to ensure the adoption of a design and requirements inflated in order to make sure it will work. In the case of professionals claiming reimbursement fees, some records are fraudulently constructed so as to maximize income.

Apart from the use of the record to extend control over clients and so to establish the policy toward them of other members of the organization, it might be noted finally that the record is a critical element in influencing policy in a broader context, for the records that the professional rank and file create and maintain are frequently the only source of information on which organizational policy and broader societal policy can be based. They form the foundation for the statistics of the number and type of cases "processed" and the number and type of services provided. Those statistics are both the source of measures of need, on the basis of which funds are solicited, and the measure of accomplishment, on the basis of which programs are evaluated, defended, and justified.

INTERPERSONAL POWER AND ORGANIZATIONAL IMPOTENCE

In this chapter I have been emphasizing the special character of the working conditions of the rank-and-file professional employee, spreading my references broadly enough so as to be able to deal with a variety of professions, including even those that some sociologists would deny the honor of being "true" professions. In doing so, it has been necessary to grapple with the semantic ghosts of the term *bureaucracy*, a task that requires a delicate balancing of the indubitable weight of formal positions and procedures to which professional employees are assigned and expected to conform against the technical autonomy that is the minimal characteristic of their work role and that protects them from the full impact of formalisms. In reaction to the heavy-handed rhetoric on the subject, I may very well have overweighted that limited autonomy, but to underweight it is a greater danger for a balanced appraisal.

The professional employee has discretionary privileges that most other rank-and-file workers do not. Furthermore, the professional employees who provide a service to lay clients use that discretion to wield organizationally provided powers that can have great influence on the lives of those clients. It is the manner in which these interpersonal powers are exercised in the course of dealing with clients that has been the prominent focus of a large number of critical commentaries on the professions. Teachers, doctors, social workers, nurses, lawyers, and others have all been accused of asserting their own conceptions of need or problem without respecting the client's, of being authoritarian, or of categorizing or standardizing individual problems, accused even of rudeness, manipulativeness, and intimidation. Those charges could not be made unless there were considerable freedom on the part of professionals to act as they choose.

Such charges are frequently accurate. And they are entirely appropriate to raise. But focused as they are on interpersonal relations, they pay little attention to some of the organizational sources of the behavior for which the rank and file cannot be held responsible. While some of the outrageous ways in which professional workers have been shown to treat their clients might be ascribed—as some have—to the worker's tendency to reduce human problems to mere technical issues or to middle-class elitism, ethnocentrism, male sexism, or even personal arrogance, some must be ascribed not to professionals as individuals or to their training but rather to the way the professional's work is organized and to the resources available for performing it. The heavier the work load, the less one is likely to be able to expect anything other than such behavior.

The different tasks, conventions, and settings in which the various professions work preclude many generalizations about the work of all professions, but it can be said that the resources available for doing work inevitably shape what work is done and how it can be done. When resources are severely limited in the face of demand, decisions about what work to do carefully, what work to hurry through, and what to delay or avoid entirely are inevitable. Similarly, it is essential to choose methods for performing work that minimize the use of scarce resources. There are, of course, different styles of choosing, as suggested by the various "stances" taken toward their work by overloaded physicians (Freidson 1980), so there can be important variations among professional workers in the choices that are made. But all choices are limited by the resources allocated differentially by management and by the absolute level of resources available to management. The consequence for clients may be marked impersonality, long periods of waiting, lack of information, and unresponsive categorization of their problems—what some might call bureaucracy. Such a consequence stems from the fact that, while the professional rank and file have direct interpersonal power over their clientele, they lack any direct power as individuals over the allocation of the resources they need to do their work the way they wish or the way their professional judgment might dictate. In that sense, they are organizationally impotent even though technically autonomous.

The rank and file are not entirely impotent, however. Apart from their capacity to use the techniques of resistance that all workers have available to them, they are part of a larger, organized profession. That fact is at least partially responsible for the very jobs they have, for their technical autonomy, and for the fact that their supervisors and often their managers are themselves professionally trained. It is also at least partly responsible for preventing the restriction of resources below a certain minimum. Insofar as it has sustained a certain scarcity on the part of its members in circumstances in which management cannot employ cheaper, uncredentialed substitutes, the organized profession also creates a situation in which management may have to provide comparatively generous resources in order to attract and hold professional workers. And as we have already seen, accreditation criteria have some influence on work load (as in the case of maximum teaching loads, e.g.), minimum staffing requirements (as in the case of a variety of health facilities), and the qualifications of supervisors and managers.

Traditional professional strategies to influence the allocation of resources are relatively indirect, addressed to controlling the labor market in which the organization seeks people to employ and the qualifications of those they must employ. A more direct strategy to influence the allocation of resources is also possible, mounted by the professional employees of particular organizations rather than by the professional association to which they and many others belong, the strategy of unionization and collective bargaining that has been adopted primarily by schoolteachers in public employment and by nurses. But whether professional association or union, there must be an organization, and organization involves leadership, which comes to be separated off from the rank and file. It is to such professional elites and their powers that I turn now.

References

Anderson, J. G. 1968. *Bureaucracy in education*. Baltimore: Johns Hopkins University Press.

Armor, D. J. 1969. *The American school counselor*. New York: Russell Sage Foundation.

Baldridge, J. V. 1971. *Power and conflict in the university*. New York: John Wiley & Sons.

Ben-David, J. 1976. Science as a profession and scientific professionalism. In *Explorations in general theory in social sciences: Essays in honor of Talcott Parsons*, vol. 2, edited by J. J. Loubser, R. C. Baum, A. Effrat, and V. M. Lidz, 874–88. New York: Free Press.

Blau, J. R. 1984. *Architects and firms: A sociological perspective on architectural practice*. Cambridge, Mass.: MIT Press.

Blau, P. 1963. *The dynamics of bureaucracy*. Chicago: University of Chicago Press.

Bucher, R., and J. Stelling. 1969. Characteristics of professional organizations. *Journal of Health and Social Behavior* 10 (March): 3–15.

Cain, G. G., R. B. Freeman, and W. L. Hansen. 1973. *Labor market analysis of engineers and technical workers*. Baltimore: Johns Hopkins University Press.

Campbell, R. F., L. L. Cunningham, and R. F. McPhee. 1975. *The organization and growth of American schools*. 3d ed. Columbus, Ohio: Charles E. Merrill Publishing Co.

Cherniss, C. 1980. *Professional burnout in human services organizations*. New York: Praeger Publishers.

Cicourel, A. V., and J. I. Kitsuse. 1963. *The educational decision-makers*. Indianapolis: Bobbs-Merrill Co.

Cohen, M. B., and D. Wagner. 1982. Social work professionalism: Reality and illusion. In *Professionals as workers*, edited by C. Derber, 141–64. Boston: G. K. Hall & Co.

Cohen, M. D., and J. G. March. 1972. *The American college president*. New York: McGraw-Hill Book Co.

Cooper, C. L. 1980. Dentists under pressure. In *White collar and professional stress*, edited by C. L. Cooper and J. Marshall, 3–17. New York: John Wiley & Sons.

Eaton, J. W. 1980. Stress in social work practice. In *White collar and professional stress*, edited by C. L. Cooper and J. Marshall, 167–85. New York: John Wiley & Sons.

Eisenstein, J. 1978. *Counsel for the United States: U.S. attorneys in the political and legal system*. Baltimore: Johns Hopkins University Press.

Emerson, R. M. 1983. Holistic effects in social control decision-making. *Law and Society Review* 17:425–55.

Freidson, E. 1970. *Professional dominance*. New York: Atherton Press.
———. 1973. Professions and the occupational principle. In *The professions and their prospects*, edited by E. Freidson, 19–38. Beverly Hills, Calif.: Sage Publications.

————. 1980. *Doctoring together: A study of professional social control.* Chicago: University of Chicago Press.

Gazell, J. A. 1975. *State trial courts as bureaucracies: A study of judicial management.* New York: Dunellan Publishing Co.

Glaser, B. G. 1964. *Organizational scientists: Their professional careers.* Indianapolis: Bobbs-Merrill Co.

Goffman, E. 1961. *Asylums.* Garden City, N.Y.: Anchor Books.

Goodsell, C. R. 1984. Welfare waiting rooms. *Urban Life* 12 (January): 467–77.

Goss, M. E. W. 1961. Influence and authority among physicians in an out-patient clinic. *American Sociological Review* 26:39–50.

————. 1963. Patterns of bureaucracy among hospital staff physicians. In *The hospital in modern society,* edited by E. Freidson, 170–94. New York: Free Press.

Goulden, J. C. 1974. *The benchwarmers: The private world of the powerful federal judges.* New York: Weybright & Talley.

Gubrium, J. F., and D. R. Buckholdt. 1979. Production of hard data in human service institutions. *Pacific Sociological Review* 22 (January): 115–36.

Hall, R. H. 1982. *Organizations: structure and process.* 3d ed. Englewood Cliffs, N.J.: Prentice-Hall, Inc.

Heinz, J. P., and E. O. Laumann. 1982. *Chicago lawyers: The social structure of the bar.* New York: Russell Sage Foundation; American Bar Foundation.

Henderson, T. A., R. Guynes, and C. Baar. 1981. Organizational design for courts. In *Courts and judges,* edited by J. A. Cramer, 19–58. Beverly Hills, Calif.: Sage Publications.

Heydebrand, W. V. 1977. The context of public bureaucracies: An organizational analysis of federal district courts. *Law and Society Review* 11 (Summer): 759–821.

Jacoby, J. E. 1980. *The American prosecutor: A search for identity.* Lexington, Mass.: Lexington Books.

Katz, J. 1982. *Poor people's lawyers in transition.* New Brunswick, N.J.: Rutgers University Press.

Kornhauser, W. 1963. *Scientists in industry.* Berkeley: University of California Press.

Lipsky, M. 1980. *Street-level bureaucracy: Dilemmas of the individual in public services.* New York: Russell Sage Foundation.

Lortie, D. L. 1969. The balance of control and autonomy in elementary school teaching. In *The semi-professions and their organization,* edited by A. Etzioni, 1–53. New York: Free Press.

————. 1975. *Schoolteacher: A sociological study.* Chicago: University of Chicago Press.

Marcson, S. 1960. *The scientist in American industry*. New York: Harper & Bros.

Marshall, J. 1980. Stress amongst nurses. In *White collar and professional stress*, edited by C. L. Cooper and J. Marshall, 19–59. New York: John Wiley & Sons.

Meiksins, P. F. 1982. Science in the labor process: Engineers as workers. In *Professionals as workers*, edited by C. Derber, 121–40. Boston: G. K. Hall & Co.

Miller, G. 1983. Holding clients accountable: The micropolitics of trouble in a work incentive program. *Social Problems* 31 (December): 139–51.

Miller, G. A. 1968. Professionals in bureaucracy: Alienation among industrial scientists and engineers. *American Sociological Review* 32:755–68.

Milofsky, C. 1976. *Special education: A sociological study of California programs*. New York: Praeger Publishers.

Montagna, P. 1968. Professionalization and bureaucratization in large professional organizations. *American Journal of Sociology* 74:138–45.

———. 1974. *Certified public accounting: A sociological view of a profession in change*. Houston: Scholars Book Co.

Nathanson, C. A. 1971. Peer surveillance and patient orientation in a pediatric out-patient clinic. *Human Organization* 30 (Fall): 255–65.

Nelson, R. L. 1981. Practice and privilege: Social change and the structure of large law firms. *American Bar Foundation Research Journal* 1981:95–140.

Nonet, P. 1969. *Administrative justice*. New York: Russell Sage Foundation.

Oppenheimer, M. 1973. The proletarianization of the professional. *Sociological Review Monograph*, no. 20:213–27.

Patry, B. 1978. Taylorism comes to the social services. *Monthly Review* 30 (October): 30–37.

Pelz, D. C., and F. M. Andrews. 1966. *Scientists in organizations*. New York: John Wiley & Sons.

Phillips, B. N., and M. Lee. 1980. The changing role of the American teacher: Current and future sources of stress. In *White collar and professional stress*, edited by C. L. Cooper and J. Marshall, 93–166. New York: John Wiley & Sons.

Reeves, W. J. 1980. *Librarians as professionals: The occupation's impact on library work arrangements*. Lexington, Mass.: Lexington Books.

Ritti, R. R. 1971. *The engineer in the industrial corporation*. New York: Columbia University Press.

Rosenthal, D. E. 1974. *Lawyer and client: Who's in charge?* New York: Russell Sage Foundation.

Ryan, J. P., A. Ashman, B. D. Sales, and S. Shane-DuBow. 1980. *American trial judges: Their work styles and performance.* New York: Free Press.

Scott, W. R. 1965. Reactions to supervision in a heteronomous professional organizaton. *Administrative Science Quarterly* 10 (June): 65–81.

————. 1969. Professional employees in a bureaucratic structure: Social work. In *The semi-professions and their organization*, edited by A. Etzioni, 82–140. New York: Free Press.

————. 1981. *Organizations, rational, natural and open systems.* Englewood Cliffs, N.J.: Prentice Hall, Inc.

Schwille, J. A. Porter, G. Belli, R. Floden, D. Freeman, L. Knappen, T. Kuhs, and W. Schmidt. 1983. Teachers as policy brokers in the content of elementary school mathematics. In *Handbook of teaching and policy*, edited by L. S. Shulman and G. Sykes, 370–91. New York: Longman Inc.

Sheskin, A., and C. W. Gram. 1981. Judicial responses to technocratic reform. In *Courts and judges*, edited by J. A. Cramer, 225–51. Beverly Hills, Calif.: Sage Publications.

Smigel, E. O. 1964. *The Wall Street lawyer: Professional organization man?* New York: Free Press.

Sorensen, J. E., and T. L. Sorensen. 1974. The conflict of professionals in bureaucratic organizations. *Administrative Science Quarterly* 19 (March): 98–106.

Spangler, E., and P. M. Lehman. 1982. Lawyering as work. In *Professionals as workers*, edited by C. Derber, 63–99. Boston: G. K. Hall & Co.

Stone, D. A. 1978–79. The deserving sick: Income maintenance policy towards the ill and disabled. *Policy Sciences* 10:133–55.

————. 1979a. Diagnosis and the dole: The function of illness in American distributive politics. *Journal of Health Politics, Policy and Law* 4 (Fall): 507–21.

————. 1979b. Physicians as gatekeepers: Illness certification as a rationing device. *Public Policy* 27 (Spring): 227–54.

Toren, N. 1972. *Social work: The case of a semi-profession.* Beverly Hills, Calif.: Sage Publications.

Walters, V. 1982. Company doctors' perceptions and responses to conflicting pressures from labor and management. *Social Problems* 30 (October): 1–12.

Weick, K. 1976. Educational organizations as loosely coupled systems. *Administrative Science Quarterly* 21 (March): 1–19.

Wice, P. B. 1981. Judicial socialization: The Philadelphia experience. In *Courts and judges*, edited by J. A. Cramer, 149–72. Beverly Hills, Calif.: Sage Publications.

Zussman, R. 1985. *Mechanics of the middle class: Work and politics among American engineers*. Berkeley: University of California Press.

Chapter Nine

Professions in the Political Economy

Many of the powers ascribed to professions by critics cannot be discerned in the activities of everyday practitioners. The average professional is likely to be puzzled, if not indignant, when confronted by the charges of such writers as Ivan Illich and is likely to say, Who, me? and go on to complain of the stressful trials of everyday work life, of clients who grant little deference, and of supervisors and employers who have insufficient sympathy for their problems. And there is justification to such puzzlement, for the powers that individual practitioners wield are both highly variable and in most cases considerably less than those ascribed to their professions. Nor are the ostensibly free self-employed protected from stress: a study of dentists, for example, found that "the only variable that consistently appears in each of the health indices as a significant source of pressure is 'the demands of sustaining and building a practice'" (Cooper 1980, 14), while "coping with difficult patients" was described by them as one of the most stressful aspects of their work.

To gain insight into the full range of professional powers, we must move outside the workplace and into the broader political economy. A profession is not merely an aggregate of practitioners or a community of individuals sharing a common occupational identity. Practitioners do not create the credential system, nor do those of their colleagues who exercise administrative authority over them at work or those who teach them their trade in professional school and publish articles in professional journals. All in their own way are rank and file. As recruits to the profession they aspire to positions in the system and conceive of pursuing careers in it. Who, then, creates, sustains, and alters the official framework of professional activities—the credential system that establishes staffing stan-

dards for employers and standards for the content of professional training? And who establishes the standards that define
the substance of what is acceptable professional work? Who
negotiates with the state to secure the official adoption of
professional standards across work settings?

In order to answer such questions, we must examine the
broader political economy and identify those who are in a
position to influence the policies of the state on which the
special position of the professions depends. That is what I turn
to in this chapter. First, I shall identify the major professional
actors in the arena in which legislation and administrative law
are created. Then I shall discuss one critical set of activities in
which they participate—namely, the promulgation of official
standards to govern the production of goods and services.

The Professional Association

The professional association is the most obvious man-
ifestation of formal organization among professions in the
United States. It is one key to understanding how the power of
a profession can be organized and directed into the lay world in
general and the political economy in particular. It is the major
formal means by which the interests of its members are expressed collectively and focused politically, and it is the major
source of the architecture of the shelters provided by the
credential system for its members. As professional association
pure and simple it attempts to protect and advance the fortunes
of its members as its leaders conceive of those fortunes. It
characteristically attempts to work through legislation and
other formal agreements that favorably structure both the
external and the internal labor markets by means of both
occupational and institutional credentialing. Even in the
minimal case of seeking legislation and formal agreements that
sustain the credential system it is clear that those who are
entitled to act on the profession's behalf as its agents are in
positions of potential power in the world outside the profession.

Professional associations look both inward to their membership and outward to the political economy in which they
are embedded. There is greater variation among them in the
degree to which they exercise significant influence over the

activities of their members than there is in their operation as pressure groups in the political world outside. A great many professional associations have a formal code of ethics, but few have any really viable machinery by which to search out violations and undertake effective action to correct them. The small minority of associations representing licensed or legally certified or registered occupations have representatives on the state boards that provide such credentials, as well as on whatever disciplinary boards the state may have, and so may participate in efforts to control some of their members' behavior. Large and conspicuous professions like law and medicine may have both local and state committees designated to hear complaints from consumers or colleagues and very occasionally undertake sanctions against individual members. By and large, however, professional associations tend more to provide services to their members than to exercise control over their ethical or technical work behavior.

PROFESSIONAL ASSOCIATIONS AND THE STATES

Insofar as professions are characterized by credentials based at the very least on postsecondary education and more especially on occupational licensing, it is the state government and its legislation that is most important to them. This is so because there is no centrally controlled educational system in the United States and very little federally controlled licensing. Thus the history of the development of the credential system of the professions is primarily one of campaigns carried out in state capitals that culminate in state laws that establish standards for professional schools and degree requirements for eligibility for state licensing. It is in the various states that licensing boards are established, and it is by state agencies that schools are licensed or chartered and their degrees approved. In the case of state-supported systems of education, public financing of schools becomes an additional matter of some importance to the fate of professions.

These are only the most visible and obvious issues involved in the relation of professions to state government. And they are relatively old issues, having been established and pursued successfully by a number of professions during the Progressive Era and still pursued by other occupations now. For those professions seeking state licensing or some other form of legal recognition, the pattern of activity seems fairly uniform: leaders of a professional association seek a legislative sponsor in the state capital for a bill establishing the credential and work at "educating" members of the legislature so as to gain their support or at least weaken their opposition. As Akers's (1968) study of the Kentucky legislature indicates, it is also necessary to neutralize the potential opposition of other professional associations if they feel threatened.

By and large, it is possible to say that, wherever particular professional practice acts do not infringe on the jurisdiction of established professions, they stand a fair chance of passage by state legislatures so long as key legislators can be interested in their status. Social work has had a difficult time gaining title licensure because both clinical psychologists and psychiatrists are threatened by the possibility of social workers practicing as self-employed psychotherapists and encourage legislative opposition. Nursing has had little difficulty gaining its "registered" status because it fitted itself under the umbrella of medicine, but its attempt to develop independently practicing nurse practitioners has led to considerable resistance. Insofar as no other profession is opposed, however, the matter of licensure is fairly technical and specialized and does not attract very much attention from the lay public. Nor does licensure involve any significant expenditure of public funds that might attract the resistance of either the public or legislators. Perhaps this is why there has been no serious slackening of professional practice acts over the past two decades in spite of criticism by liberal economists and a federal effort to establish a moritorium on licensing of more health-related occupations.

Beyond establishing the fundamental elements of the credential system, the task of establishing and sustaining places in the labor market is considerably more complex and difficult. (For a case study of optometry in four states, see Begun and Lippincott 1980.) For self-employed practitioners the issues are relatively simple once they gain the protection of licensing or registration: they must fend off competitors and also control internal competition by such devices as banning advertising, most particularly advertising prices. Recent Supreme Court decisions have seriously damaged efforts to control internal competition, and there are some signs that efforts to control competition between occupations are being tempered considerably by the courts. (For a recent review, see Kissam 1983.) In addition to controlling competition, the self-employed professions have another task when the state or another mediating agent is involved in paying their clients' bills—to make sure that the services of their members are officially recognized as legitimate and thus eligible for generous reimbursement.

The task of the professional associations of employed professionals, on the other hand, is to press for either legislation or administrative regulations that require jobs in professional institutions to be filled only by their own credentialed members and that minimize the exercise of lay authority over the rank and file. The health professions, which are by all odds the most regulated of all professions in the United States, must keep a virtually continuous presence in state capitals in order to keep track of a complex body of legislation and administrative rules and make sure that their interests are protected.

The professional associations establish the basic characteristics of their credential systems in the various states. However, an effective credential system must now have national scope. As I noted in chapter 4, state-chartered institutions—examining boards, professional schools, and the like—tend to join together with those in other states to form regional or national associations concerned with certifying or accrediting training programs and establishing common examinations or degree requirements that all will honor in spite of the separate legal jurisdictions of the various states. In turn, state regulations are written that acknowledge and sustain the official use of those privately created professional standards in lieu of particular state standards. The federal government, too, relies on such accrediting programs to guide its fund granting. Professional associations on both the state and the national level must play a part in initiating and endorsing that movement toward a national system.

PROFESSIONAL ASSOCIATIONS IN FEDERAL LEGISLATION

The second half of the twentieth century has seen a massive increase in federal regulation and financing that has transformed the political milieu of the professions. Whereas once virtually all the action was in state capitals, carried out by state professional associations with aid from their national offices, state action is now dwarfed by what goes on in Washington. Federal military spending has a critical effect on the labor-market status of engineers and scientists, as does federal support for research and development in universities and in industry. Federal policies toward education, whether in the form of grants to institutions, loans to tuition-paying students, or grants to faculty, have serious consequences for schoolteachers and professors, not to speak of the managers of their institutions. Federal health and welfare programs similarly affect deeply the various health, social service, and legal professions. And the special status of the certified public accountant is almost entirely a function of the policies of the U.S. Securities and Exchange Commission.

Virtually no profession is untouched by federal programs, and few have many members who are not heavily dependent on them. So while the federal government in the United States does not create the credential system, its willingness to give it official recognition and support is a matter of profound importance to the position of the professions in the political economy. As a reflection of this shift from state to federal government, many professional associations have either moved their national offices to Washington or come to maintain full-time offices in Washington for their lobbyists and staff.

Given the variety of professions and the enormous bulk and scope of the legislation and administrative law that issues from Washington, it is necessary to be rather general in characterizing the activities of professional associations. Nor does one get much help from the literature. Gilb (1966) produced the only general characterization of the role of professional associations in the legislature that I am aware of, but most of her material was drawn from state legislatures and particularly from the state of California. Furthermore, her materials date no later than the early 1960s, before massive federal financing and subsequent federal attempts to control both financing and performance began, so it is difficult to assume that the details of her analysis still hold true. In the absence of more recent guides, however, I shall have to rely on her as well as on the earlier classic by Truman (1951, 321–478).

One point Gilb makes still seems to hold today, and that is that "the major professional associations do not appear to have as much access to congressional as to state legislative committees" (1966, 215), perhaps because many of the bills considered in Congress tend to have been proposed by administrative agencies of the executive branch rather than by legislators themselves. Indeed, when one examines the literature on interest groups and lobbying in Washington, the professional associations are not very conspicuous. Only one—the American Medical Association—is mentioned in the literature with some frequency, and in its case notoriety was gained almost entirely from its long and highly publicized concern with the single issue of financing payment for health care.

ADVISORY COMMITTEES

There is more to the exercise of power than creating legislation, however, and more power exercised by professionals than professional associations can account for. Individual professionals also exercise power. More widespread than formal lobbying in Congress and perhaps as important is the less conspicuous process of formulating recommendations for legislation and for the substance of the regulations and administrative laws that implement legislation. There is where professional associations in some cases and individual professionals in others seem to have fairly consistent and important influence.

For virtually any area in which the professions work there is a variety of committees whose charge is to give expert advice to the legislative and particularly the executive branches of government on both the federal and the state level. The number and variety of such enterprises in Washington are too great to allow secure generalization, and I am aware of no systematic study of their membership, but it appears to me that the vast majority of those called on to serve on advisory panels are prominent members of both the administrative and the knowledge "classes" of professions, selected for their influence and reputation as well as for the important institutions they represent. Officials of professional associations and practicing rank and file are far less often members.

The extent to which advisory committees have any significant impact on policy is not clear. Primack and von Hippel (1974) show how the findings of some committees dealing with scientific issues were suppressed, distorted, or ignored by the government and urge an independent "public interest science" (cf. von Hippel and Primack 1972, 1166–71; and for educational policy advisors, Cronin and Thomas 1971, 771–79). Their examples, however, were drawn from committees dealing with policy issues of a highly controversial and thus highly visible character. Most committees deal with fairly obscure matters, and there are a great many of them. In the short period between 1957 and 1966, the President's Scientific Advisory Committee alone called into existence some eighty advisory panels (Fisher 1966, 324). Considering the size of the federal establishment, we must assume that at any given time there are hundreds if not thousands of such panels in existence. It is probably no exaggeration to say that, for every advisory committee concerned with issues of broad public import such as whether to build a new ballistic missile, finance a supersonic transport, develop antimissile defenses in space, or ban the use of a carcinogenic chemical, there are hundreds of others concerned with obscure, technical issues that do not interest politicians or the public at all. It is in such largely inconspicuous committees and panels that we might expect fairly decisive weight to accrue to the recommendations of its professional members.

PROFESSIONALS IN GOVERNMENT

Advisory committees are more often peopled by visitors to Washington than by civil servants or politicians. They are composed of advisers and consultants who have a permanent position outside government, whether in universities or in firms. But professionals are also resident in the government, serving on its staff. Professional credentials are virtually essential prerequisites to a number of high-level appointed positions in the federal bureaucracy. The surgeon general of the United States is almost certain to be a physician, as is the attorney general to be a lawyer. The commissioner of the Food and Drug Administration is more likely than not to be a physician, a pharmacologist, or a pharmacist. Appointed positions are far more subject to political considerations than those below them in the bureaucracy are, however, and whether professional credentials are employed as a prerequisite for them seems to be a function of the political strength of the particular profession involved. Powerful professional associations can veto the appointment of someone whom they feel does not represent their position adequately, as the American Medical Association vetoed the appointment of John Knowles as Assistant Secretary of the erstwhile Department of Health, Education, and Welfare and as the American Bar Association pressed successfully for a new director of the Office of Economic Opportunity (Auerbach 1976, 270–71). Some professions have not succeeded in capturing high-level posts. The comptroller general of the United States, for example, has been a certified public accountant only once since the position was established in 1921, the position being filled most often by lawyers (Morse 1978, 124).

For those positions that rank beneath heads of departments and other agencies, there is greater consistency in the employment of professionals as a result of civil service regulations that were certainly influenced by the lobbying of professional associations. Engineers, the largest single professional group employed by the federal government, are found in large numbers in the Department of Defense, the Department of the Interior, the Environmental Protection Agency, the Department of Transportation, the National Aviation and Space Administration, and the Department of Agriculture (Schott 1978, 129; and see Schott 1973). Natural scientists of one stripe or another are likely to be found in many of the same places but also in the National Institutes of Health (cf. Uyeki and Cliffe 1963; Marcson 1966; Lambright and Teich 1978). Most widespread of all are lawyers. As Wollan put it, "They are unique among the professionals in government because of their official presence, as lawyers, in virtually every agency, as a kind of 'final filter' for major proposals and transactions. Few agencies have a military attache or a medical officer or a chaplain or environmentalist with that function and the omnipresent budget and information officers do not make much policy, but most agencies have a chief counsel or general counsel" (1978, 106). Indeed, it is with good reason that Mosher (1978, 145–46) singles out law as being the profession with access to a much broader variety of powers than is available to other professions. Lawyers are virtually the only incumbents in the federal judiciary, and legal credentials mark a majority of presidents and legislators (cf. Eulau and Sprague 1964) and a plurality of high officials in the executive branch. Lawyers also constitute a large proportion of the staff serving members of Congress (Malbin 1980, 19–24).

As Mosher notes, "the control of a specialized professional agency is the most frequent, and probably most important channel of professional influence" in government (1978, 146). Most of the major professions have one such agency whose second, third, and fourth levels of administrative positions are filled by their members. The powers they exercise are largely invisible to the public and, for that matter, to Congress, for they are technical and bureaucratic: their jobs consist in writing the concrete rules by which programs established by legislation are realized and in administering or supervising the administration of those programs (cf. Summerfield 1974, 155). Since, however, the administrative law that they formulate after legislation is passed must be made available for public comment before it can be established, representatives of both professional and trade associations become deeply involved in efforts to assure that the proposed rules do not damage their interests. As Gilb notes, "the administrative agencies . . . work closely with . . . professional associations" (1966, 216). Indeed, as Truman noted (1951, 442), where public concern may neutralize the influence of interest groups on the writing and passage of a piece of legislation, those groups may nonetheless be able to influence the subsequent administration of the act.

Since those writing the rules for implementation of an act tend to be members of the professions involved, it would appear at first blush that they would be eager collaborators with representatives of their professional associations. Summerfield (1974, 157) points out that bureaucrats in the erstwhile U.S. Office of Education were members of former employees of such professional associations as the National

Education Association and the American Association of School Administrators. This would imply that they would be eager to write rules that are desired by their professional association. Certainly political expediency alone would lead to modifying rules or procedures that may be strongly protested, but it would be a mistake to assume that the powers that professionals in the government bureaucracy exercise are always or mostly guided by the formal policy positions of the professional associations that purport to speak for them. Physicians in the Department of Health and Human Services, the National Institutes of Health, the United States Public Health Service, and elsewhere may share with the officials of the American Medical Association a general faith in the value of medical science to humanity, but they are unlikely to have the same perspective on how that value can be best realized.

Like the charge of corporate capture of regulatory commissions (cf. Freitag 1983; Quirk 1981), it is much too simple to assume that, because those in government share professional credentials with those outside, they are captives of their professions and will advance the position of their official professional association on legislation and its implementation. Many professionals in government deviate markedly from their colleagues outside: that may be why they enter a government career. Consider, for example, the case of Dr. Jere E. Goyan, commissioner of the Food and Drug Administration in 1980 and a pharmacist. He was in favor of an administrative regulation requiring druggists to provide to consumers of commonly used prescription drugs a leaflet that informed them of their proper use, side effects, and risks. However, that regulation was successfully opposed by massive lobbying on the part of the American Pharmaceutical Association, the National Association of Retail Druggists, and others (Reinhold 1980, 96 ff). They did not agree with Dr. Goyan, who is in theory one of them.

If we acknowledge the fact that every profession contains a number of different ideological and technical segments, some even diametrically opposed to others on particular issues, we cannot assume that professionals in government are automatically in agreement and allied with the official positions of their associations. Indeed, if one may generalize across the varied professions and agencies of the federal government, one may suspect that professionals who are bureaucrats are likely to have rather different perspective on policy issues than do the professional associations that advance the perspective of the majority of their members who work outside the government. At the very least, they are likely to have a "macro" rather than a "micro" perspective—that is, a policy rather than a clinical or practical orientation (cf. Scott 1982). They do wield important powers by virtue of their positions in the bureaucracy, but the policy position adopted by the executive branch that employs them, the substance of the legislation that it is their duty to implement, and their own perspective on the issues are all likely to influence their use of those powers. Their own positions no doubt influence the outcome wherever there is any discretionary leeway, positions that we may not assume correspond automatically to those of their professional associations and that may even be in opposition to them.

THE MANY VOICES OF PROFESSIONS

Clearly, we cannot restrict our pursuit of the exercise of professional powers to examining professional associations alone. Professionals as individuals can also have influence when serving in government positions and on advisory committees. Furthermore, it is not possible to assume that those individuals will express the position espoused officially by the association that purports to represent the profession as a whole. No professional association can be taken to be a unified body whose members are all in agreement. The body of formal knowledge an association purports to advance tends to become institutionalized into different specialty practices that often represent conflicting intellectual perspectives as well as different policy positions and political-economic interests. Both intellectually and economically, professions and their associations are divided internally.

There are serious limits to the capacity of professional associations to speak monolithically and forcefully. They tend to be federated rather than unitary in form and thus often have difficulty preserving sufficient cohesion to prevent some of their members from taking a different public position (cf. Truman 1951, 115–34). The very diversity of the membership may in effect prevent them from developing a consensus that allows adopting any public position at all on controversial issues, as a study of the Chicago bar suggested (Heinz et al. 1979, 771). This does not mean that professional associations cannot undertake any activities of significance, however. Halliday (1982) has demonstrated how the bar could adopt a strong position against McCarthyism on the basis of a common concern with "legalism." Nonetheless, in light of its diversity, associations must be concerned that support from the membership will shift from them to another (Truman 1951, 157–85). After all, the American Public Health Association is available to speak for physicians in a different voice than the American Medical Association, as the National Lawyers Guild is available as an alternative to the American Bar Association.

Differences in the positions of associations representing different segments of the same profession thus often (but by no means always) preclude the assertion of a unified professional position on legislation and implementation. More important than such differences is the fact that equal and even greater influence on the legislative process can be exercised by individual professionals who have no official position in professional associations but who are distinguished by high personal accomplishments. Officials of commercial and industrial organizations can speak officially for their firms without fear of contradiction by any but the rare whistle-blower. But professional associations cannot exercise such control over their members. So long as they claim to speak only for themselves, professionals can speak as individuals independently of their association. And when they have established reputations as exceptionally creative or productive researchers, practitioners, or administrators, they can speak with great authority even though it is not official authority. Many members of advisory committees and some of those who volunteer their opinions at hearings have considerable authority by virtue of their accomplishments. The formal representatives of a professional association express an official opinion that represents the consensus of either the membership or an official committee, an opinion that may sometimes be viewed as that of a special interest. A distinguished individual can contradict the official consensus and be equally, if not more, influential by virtue of a personal reputation for cognitive authority, public service, or strategic institutional responsibility.

The most conspicuous of such individuals are the professional celebrities that Goodell (1977) calls "visible scientists," citing as examples Margaret Mead, Carl Sagan, and Barry Commoner. They are individuals who, like popular actors, musicians, and others, have the symbolic authority of a celebrity (Keller 1983). They are people who can be "outsiders, even sometimes outcasts among established scientists" (Goodell 1977, 6), in part because of their efforts to speak directly to the public and to politicians on both professional and policy matters. Their influence stems as much from their capacity to gain attention from the mass media as from their personal accomplishments as professionals.

In addition to them, however, and probably more consistently influential, are insiders who have had exceptionally distinguished careers in research or practice and who have become involved in issues of public policy. Often called on to serve on major advisory panels, they may also take the initiative in seeking to influence policy by volunteering testimony and by organizing special interest groups on issues they believe to be of overwhelming importance. Unlike professional celebrities, they are not "popularizers" who speak directly to the public in their writings on professional subjects. Greenberg notes that the ranking science "politicians" during the 1940s and 1950s almost always demonstrated scientific or technical creativity before rising to be leaders in the politics of science (1971, 15). Until recently, at least, legislation bearing on science seems to have been influenced far more by individual scientists of distinction and the public policy committees they formed than by scientific societies themselves (cf. Lapp 1965; Greenberg 1971). The importance of individuals in the formation of science-related policy could be attributed to the deliberate policy of restraint in addressing political issues that scientific societies have been inclined to exercise, in part for fear of having their tax status changed (Rich 1974), but I believe that the heart of the matter lies elsewhere.

The power of professional associations (and of their officers) seems to be seriously circumscribed by the limits of what can be official positions in the light of differences among members. In broad matters of immediate self-interest the membership can be sufficiently agreed to launch the leadership on a strong political campaign for or against proposed legislation. On occasion the membership can be unified around issues that go beyond monopoly and material self-interest, as Halliday (in press) demonstrated in the case of the Chicago bar. But there are relatively few issues that unify the membership. In those instances in which professional associations may not be able to formulate official positions, individual professionals can advance their own with impunity. If they are sufficiently distinguished, they can exercise weight in the political process that their associations' leaders cannot, for the officers of professional associations are not consistently distinguished as individuals.

THE INSTITUTIONAL EXPRESSION OF FORMAL KNOWLEDGE

Thus far I have described the various professional actors in the formal processes of policy formation and implementation, the legislative and administrative arenas of government in which they operate, and some of the factors that must be taken into account when appraising their potential influence. Apart from referring to licensing laws in the states, however, I have had to be vague about the content of the policy on which professional associations and individuals can have important influence. This vagueness is an inevitable consequence of the task of generalizing across the broad scope and vast variety of the affairs of such diverse professions as accounting, engineering, medicine, law, social work, and teaching. In the case of licensing and related issues of credentialing we may be sure that the officials of professional associations are concerned in part with improving or preserving the economic position of their members. Economic interest is also pressed in other areas—the subsidization by government of professional education, its continued or increased support of the industry or sector of the economy in which professional work takes place, and the like.

The importance of activities concerned with the professions' economic interest cannot be denied—indeed, I began this book by pointing out that we cannot gain a very clear idea of how those who possess formal knowledge can possibly wield power if we have no adequate understanding of the institutions that provide them with a regular living as well as with political resources. The bulk of this book has in fact been devoted to analyzing those institutions. But it would be a vulgar mistake to dwell on economic interest alone, for it represents only one part of the equation. The other part is represented by the institutions through which formal knowledge is translated into human activity and by the power of professions to serve as agents for the application of their formal knowledge to human affairs.

As I noted in chapter 1, some of the most influential writers concerned with the power of knowledge and with the powers of professions have been preoccupied not with economic power but with the power to shape the direction and substance of policy decisions that affect the way national life is constituted, the power to shape the lay world itself. As we saw in chapter 8, professions engaged in rendering services on an everyday basis to laypeople exercise a considerable range of powers that influence their clients' lives in a number of important ways. Those everyday powers are contingent in part on policy decisions made by those who manage the organizations in which they work. Even more important, they are contingent on the powers granted to those who possess their credentials and on officially recognized and enforced standards employed to specify their activities. In part through legislation, but far more often through less conspicuous administrative law and the activities of private bodies, the professions are deeply involved in the process of establishing the official standards that structure the production of both goods and services.

PRODUCT STANDARDS

The special history of the United States is such that it can be said unequivocally that most standards are chosen by government officials rather than created by them. Most are created by private groups or researchers and then endorsed by government. Whatever uniformity and reliability there is to be found in manufactured goods is due far more to the standards created by private associations than to the initiative of the state.

Consider the following: "A 1981 Congressional amendment to the Consumer Product Safety Act requires that the Commission 'shall rely upon voluntary consumer safety standards rather than [itself] promulgate a consumer product safety standard . . . whenever compliance with such voluntary standards would eliminate or adequately reduce the risk of injury addressed and it is likely that there will be substantial compliance with such voluntary standards'" (Bureau of Consumer Protection 1983, 35). That congressional amendment urges on a government agency the use of product standards affecting the safety of consumers that have been formulated by private (or "voluntary") associations. While it represents the activity of an administration seeking to reduce governmental formulation of regulatory standards, it nonetheless reflects what has always been the case in the vast majority of circumstances. In essence, privately established standards are routinely adopted and given the force of law by public agencies. Those standards underlie the very constitution of much of the material world in which we live.

As Sinclair (1980, 54) notes, "the history of standards in America is not only extremely complex, but almost totally unwritten and easy judgments are unwarranted." No detailed and well-informed description of both the origin and the substance of product, service, and personnel standards in the United States exists today, though a recent Federal Trade Commission report provides a glimpse of product standards and the process by which they are created (Bureau of Consumer Protection 1983). One can only guess at a phenomenon of staggering size and complexity that is all the more obscure because it is created outside the purview of the state or the public by private trade and professional associations and merely ratified by federal, state, and even local agencies. There are some twenty thousand product standards now in use in industry; there are more than four hundred groups that have literally thousands of committees and subcommittees that set standards for manufactured articles ranging from screw threads to safety devices for steam boilers to computer software. The economic power of such standard-setting organizations is enormous, capable of ruining those whose products do not conform to their sometimes arbitrary and self-interested specifications, as the recent case involving the Hydrolevel Corporation and the American Society of Mechanical Engineers indicated. (For a brief sketch of the case, written before the Supreme Court upheld the liability of the Society, see Sinclair 1980, 214–26.)

All the professions are involved in one way or another in setting standards of one sort or another. Product standards involve manufactured goods or materials used in manufacturing, however, and so it is that they tend to be established by committees in which both professionals—particularly engineers but also chemists, physicists, architects, and the like— and representatives of industry—who are often engineers in executive positions—are involved. (See the information on the composition of committees in sixty-four associations in Bureau of Consumer Protection 1983, 113–41.) Representatives of industry and of the American Dental Association establish standards for dental materials and equipment, which are published under the auspices of the American National Standards Institute. The venerable boiler-code committee of the American Society of Mechanical Engineers includes both engineers and representatives of industry. (For a history of the boiler-code committee, see Sinclair 1980, 51–54, 146–57; and Greene 1953.) It is the American Society of Mechanical Engineers, the American National Standards Institute, and the American Society for Testing and Materials that provide the auspices for drawing up and promulgating the bulk of the product standards now in use (Wines 1981, 1718). The American Society of Mechanical Engineers alone publishes over four hundred codes and standards; its annual income from the sale of such publications was over ten million dollars in 1979 (Sinclair 1980, 217).

Not all product standards are industrial, however. The American Bar Association has long been involved in creating model legal codes. In conjunction with lawyers appointed by the governor of a state, its Commission on Uniform Laws develops standardized or uniform statutes or codes on a variety of issues and offers them to state legislatures for adoption. Beutel (1955) estimated that, by the middle of this century, over 1,350 separate statutes were adopted in various states through the efforts of the commission, which began its work in 1889. The activity, he claimed, is wholly dominated by the bar, for while governors appoint the commissioners who draft the statutes (who are members of the bar association serving without pay), they do not assert any control over their activities. State legislatures in turn tend to adopt the statutes as drafted because the underlying aim of uniformity discourages tinkering.

Finally, I may note that another form of product standard is to be found in that portion of the professional credential system concerned with the education of professionals and in state educational systems in general. An accredited or approved educational program presupposes that minimal standards for a curriculum are being met—that schoolchildren will be taught a minimal amount of arithmetic, for example, or that medical students will be taught anatomy, physiology, and other subjects believed to be essential for their proper education. In the case of elementary and secondary education, state boards of education issue the minimal curricular and program standards, with the roles of professional and local school-board associations no doubt varying from state to state and from standard to standard. In the case of professional education, however, the roles of professional associations and those representing the professional schools are determinative, with the state merely ratifying their standards.

Personnel Standards

In a sense product standards are professional service standards, for what they do is establish the minimally acceptable characteristics of a product that an engineer, architect, or other professional can design. The professional service of designing a product or a production process is constrained by and tested against those specifications. A product standard is, at least indirectly, a specification of both procedure and outcome. For most kinds of professional work, however, neither procedural nor outcome nor product standards are promulgated with any degree of frequency. It is true that there are generally recognized standards of procedure that exist in medicine and law, for example, and that they become the focus of attention in civil malpractice suits or in the appeal of an unfavorable verdict, but they are rarely officially codified. Nor are service outcomes. If they were, of course, professionals would have considerably less discretion in performing their work.

By and large, professions attempt to establish and defend personnel standards for professional work. Personnel standards accomplish an economic function by providing a market shelter for professionals and at the same time leave the actual determination of the way work is to be done to them. The presumption is that, by virtue of possessing the requisite credential testifying to successful completion of a course of training in the discipline or formal knowledge represented by the profession, the work will be performed in a satisfactory fashion. So it is that the formal knowledge represented by the professions is institutionalized and is assumed to be employed in dealing with the issues with which professional work is concerned. To the extent to which professional efforts to establish their own personnel standards are successful, one might assume that, in their positions in the various institutions that employ them, professionals will be inclined to conceive of the problems they deal with in the terms that their discipline advances, with the intellectual tools that they have been taught are proper. Just as material product standards shape the material world of manufacturing, so personnel standards may shape the social world of professionalized services.

PROFESSIONS AND STANDARDS

It is in standard-setting committees that the professions in general and professional associations in particular can have the most unequivocal influence. Such committees are usually small, their work appears to be technical, and their position is inconspicuous. Most do not work in the public eye or in the political arena. (For an important exception, see Grossman 1965.) Only when there is a public scandal, as in the case of the Hydrolevel Corporation, or widespread public concern, as in the case of nuclear power and toxic-waste safety, does any awareness of those committees' activities spread beyond the industries and professions they serve. In general, one finds a good deal of freedom on the part of such standard-setting committees to establish codes by the standards of the participants alone. They are then inconspicuously incorporated into legislation or, more commonly, into the rules and regulations or administrative law designed to implement legislation.

Those standard-setting functions are performed more often than not by official committees or subcommittees of professional associations, their members selected from among those who are active in them. Neither the mavericks of the profession nor the especially distinguished are likely to be members. This is where the good, gray members of the profession, often of only nominally respectable technical or intellectual accomplishment but deeply involved in the politics of official association affairs, have their greatest influence. And in the case of material product standards, this is where those members employed by industry and expected to represent their employers' interests are most likely to be influential. Academics and independent members of the relevant professions are less often active on committees setting product standards, perhaps because firms can pay for the considerable costs of participation, while individuals and university employers cannot (Bureau of Consumer Protection 1983, 20–22, 154–55).

The question is, however, whether those standards and the professions' influence in government may be explained primarily by reference to the professions' own efforts and desires. While the professions may be seen to participate in the formulation of policy-making legislation, in the implementation of legislation, and in the promulgation of the standards that shape the constitution of the material and social world of modern society, it is by no means self-evident that they are the prime movers of those processes. Nor is it self-evident that, once placed in their positions, their members employ the substance of their formal knowledge faithfully and systematically. Here, as elsewhere, we need to look more closely at the detail.

References

Akers, Ronald L. 1968. The professional association and the legal regulation of practice. *Law and Society Review* 3:463–82.

Auerbach, Jerold S. 1976. *Unequal justice: Lawyers and social change in modern America.* New York: Oxford University Press.

Begun, James W., and Ronald C. Lippincott. 1980. The politics of professional control: The case of optometry. *Research in the Politics of Health Care* 1:55–103.

Beutel, Frederick H. 1955. Law making by professional and trade associations. *Nebraska Law Review* 34:431–46.

Bureau of Consumer Protection. April 1983. *Standards and certification: Final staff report.* Washington, D.C.: Federal Trade Commission.

Cooper, Cary L. 1980. Dentists under pressure. In *White collar and professional stress.* edited by C. L. Cooper and J. Marshall, 3–17. New York: John Wiley & Sons.

Cronin, Thomas E., and Norman C. Thomas. 1971. Federal advisory processes: Advice and discontent. *Science* 171:771–79.

Eulau, Heinz, and John D. Sprague. 1964. *Lawyers in politics.* Indianapolis: Bobbs Merrill Co.

Fisher, C. W. 1966. Scientists and statesmen. In *Knowledge and power,* edited by S. A. Lakoff, 315–58. New York: Free Press.

Freitag, Peter J. 1983. The myth of corporate capture: Regulatory commissions in the United States. *Social Problems* 30:480–91.

Gilb, Corinne Lathrop. 1966. *Hidden hierarchies: The professions and government.* New York: Harper & Row.

Goodell, Rae. 1977. *The visible scientists.* Boston: Little, Brown & Co.

Greenberg, Daniel S. 1971. *The politics of pure science: An inquiry into the relationship between science and government in the United States.* New York: New American Library.

Greene, Arthur M., Jr. 1953. *History of the ASME Boiler Code.* New York: American Society of Mechanical Engineers.

Grossman, Joel B. 1965. *Lawyers and judges: The ABA and the politics of judicial selection.* New York: John Wiley & Sons.

Halliday, Terence C. 1982. The idiom of legalism in bar politics: Lawyers, McCarthyism, and the civil rights era. *American Bar Foundation Research Journal 1982* (Fall): 913–88.

————. In Press. *Beyond monopoly: The politics of expertise in a nature profession.* Chicago: University of Chicago Press.

Heinz, John P., Edward O. Laumann, Charles L. Cappell, Terence C. Halliday, and Michael H. Schaalman. 1979. Diversity, representation and leadership in an urban bar: A first report on a survey of the Chicago bar. *American Bar Foundation Research Journal* 1979: 717–72.

Keller, Suzanne. 1983. Celebrities as a national elite. In *Political elites and social change*, edited by Moshe M. Czudnowski, 3–14. Dekalb: Northern Illinois University Press.

Kissam, Philip C. 1983. Antitrust law and professional behavior. *Texas Law Review* 62 (August): 1–66.

Lambright, W. Henry, and Albert H. Teich. 1978. Scientists and government: A case of professional ambivalance. *Public Administration Review* 38 (March/April): 133–39.

Lapp, R. E. 1965. *The new priesthood: The scientific elite and the uses of power.* New York: Harper & Row.

Malbin, Michael J. 1980. *Unelected representatives.* New York: Basic Books.

Marcson, Simon. 1966. *Scientists in government.* New Brunswick, N.J.: Rutgers University Press.

Morse, Ellsworth H., Jr. 1978. Professional accountants in government: Roles and dilemmas. *Public Administration Review* 38 (March/April): 120–25.

Mosher, Frederick C. 1978. Professions in public service. *Public Administration Review* 38 (March/April): 144–50.

Primack, Joel, and Frank von Hippel. 1974. *Advice and dissent: Scientists in the political arena.* New York: Basic Books.

Quirk, Paul J. 1981. *Industry influence on federal regulatory agencies.* Princeton, N.J.: Princeton University Press.

Reinhold, Robert. 1980. Pills and the process of government. *New York Times Magazine*, November 9, 96 ff.

Rich, Daniel. 1974. Private government and professional service. In *Scientists and public affairs*, edited by A. H. Teich, 3–37. Cambridge, Mass.: MIT Press.

Schott, Richard L. 1973. *Professionals in public service: The characteristics and education of engineer federal executives.* Beverly Hills, Calif.: Sage Publications.

———. 1978. The professions and government: Engineering as a case in point. *Public Administration Review* 38 (March/April): 126–32.

Scott, W. Richard. 1982. Managing professional work: Three models of control for health organizations. *Health Services Research* 17 (Fall): 213–40.

Sinclair, Bruce, with the assistance of James P. Hull. 1980. *A centennial history of the American Society of Mechanical Engineers.* Toronto: University of Toronto Press.

Summerfield, Harry L. 1974. *Power and process: The formulation and limits of federal educational policy*. Berkeley: McCutchan Publishing Corp.

Truman, David D. 1951. *The governmental process: Political interests and public opinion*. New York: Alfred A. Knopf, Inc.

Uyeki, Eugene, and Frank B. Cliffe, Jr. 1963. The federal scientist-administrator. *Science* 139 (March 29): 1267–70.

von Hippel, Frank, and Joel Primack. 1972. Public interest science. *Science* 177 (September 26): 1166–71.

Wines, M. 1981. Should groups that set standards be subjected to federal standards? *National Journal* (September 26): 1717–19.

Wollan, Laurie A., Jr. 1978. Lawyers in government—the most serviceable instruments of authority. *Public Administration Review* 38 (March/April): 105–12.

Chapter Ten

The Institutional Transformation of Formal Knowledge

In this book I have shown in as much detail as is possible how professions are established in the political and economic order of the United States. Such institutional detail produces a picture that belies the accuracy and analytic value of sweeping statements about the decline, loss of sovereignty, deprofessionalization, or proletarianization of the professions in the United States. The scope and depth of the credential system directly established by law in some cases and supported by legally recognized custom in others provides a firm even if not comprehensively secure framework to assure some credential holders of every profession positions by which to gain a living. Those positions, furthermore, characteristically allow professionals a degree of discretion or autonomy at work that marks them off from other workers. And their expertise can gain them special privilege in the courts that marks them off from ordinary people. The activities of their associations in legislatures and of individual members in committees created to formulate policy recommendations for various agencies of government and in committees that in effect establish national standards for the manufacture of products and the staffing of critical services testify to a position that can have considerable influence on national affairs. It should be clear that professions have deep roots in the political economy of the United States.

It may appear that, insofar as I reject theories of professional impotence, I accept and advance the notion of professional power implicit in the theories of such writers as Ellul and Foucault discussed in chapter 1. My analytic description may imply that the professions are in a position to exercise great power over both policy formation and the concrete ways policy is implemented. The professions' position in committees that formulate the basic standards governing the production of both goods and services may seem to support a conception of influence that is so pervasive as to set the very terms of the material and social world, a conception that it is the "discipline" or "technique" of the professions that shapes the world and controls daily life. But that theory of professional power or, in Illich's usage, "professional dominance" (Illich 1980), like the theories of deprofessionalization and proletarianization, cannot be sustained when one takes a closer look at the professions and at their position in the political economy.

When we consider the consequences of differentiation within the professions and of the professions' relation to other forces in the political economy, we find that they are often constrained by countervailing powers and that, even when they are in a position to exercise power, the formal knowledge or discipline that they claim to represent is not employed consistently or uniformly. Formal knowledge is systematically transformed by professionals with differing perspectives created both by the particular demands of the work they do and by the demands of their particular clients. Thus while we are able to show that the professions can exercise some powers by virtue of their place in the political economy, it does not follow that the formal knowledge they represent figures uniformly and consistently in guiding or shaping that power. Exactly what knowledge is employed is problematic: it cannot be predicted from the formal knowledge ascribed to them. In this final chapter I shall discuss the systematic sources of variation in the use of formal knowledge so as to be able to conclude by appraising the nature of professional powers and the place of formal knowledge in them.

Intraprofessional Divisions of Position

Once one takes a close look at the credential system of the professions, it becomes clear that one cannot understand how the system is sustained without recognizing the critical place of formal role differentiation within the professions. Most occupations can be characterized as a mere aggregate of practitioners or jobholders. Their members have received a general education in school and are then recruited and trained for their particular jobs by employers. What they must know to do their jobs is supplied by their general education and by the specialized instruction given by their employers. It is different for professions. First, they have an occupational community that extends beyond any particular workplace, a community sustained by a common credential, common interest in preserving shared privileges, common specialized training, a shared occupational identity, and the like. (Compare Goode 1957; and Salaman 1974) That occupational community is often divided internally by specialties or segments with conflicting interests and ideologies focused around knowledge, technique, and task in the division of labor (Bucher and Strauss 1961). It is also frequently stratified by differential prestige, income, and power (Abbott 1981).

These characteristics of professions are generally recognized, but they are not enough to allow understanding of how professions maintain their position. Professions could not be what they in fact are if they were composed solely of practitioners joined by an occupational community and differentiated by specialty and variable career success. They could not maintain control over the knowledge and skill they bring to their work, nor could they maintain control over the organization of their work. Professions are also systems organized by a division of authority over the content and organization of professional work. Unlike the crafts, professions have been able to control technological innovation by having their own teacher-researchers to produce and legitimize new knowledge. And they have been able to control working conditions by having some of their own members serve in supervisory and executive positions in work organizations. Their teacher-researchers control the recruitment, training, and certification of their members and, as important, formal knowledge itself. Their administrators preserve for them the power to supervise, direct, and evaluate the work of practitioners as well as to participate in the determination of organizational policy. Their elites work with their associations to shape social policy.

Differential Interests within Professions

The differentiation of members into practitioners, administrators, and teacher-researchers is thus a central characteristic of the organization of professional occupations. It also represents critical division bearing on both professional powers and the use of formal knowledge. Located in different positions in the system, with different duties, each has different interests and perspectives. Practitioners are preoccupied with coping with day-to-day problems of work. Administrators are concerned with having the practitioners' work carried out in such a way as to satisfy the political and economic forces on which their organization depends. They must represent their organization's policies and interests, not only those of the practitioners. In the course of their work administrators are also responsible for formulating and administering a formal body of rules representing the organization's policies as well as requirements imposed by public and private authorities. Given the finite character of the resources available to them, they must make decisions that allocate resources differentially. They must therefore assume the onus of creating some of the major work contingencies against which the rank and file may chafe. Some tension between practitioners and administrators is therefore inevitable.

The division of perspective between academic and practitioner is rather different and has a longer tradition. Even today in virtually every profession there have been complaints that professional education is too academic, theoretical, or unrealistic, that it fails to prepare novices for practice (cf. Hughes et al. 1973). The practical contingencies of day-to-day work so vary from the ideal or hypothetical circumstances assumed or demanded by academics in professional schools that novices are said to suffer reality shock or burnout on entering practice. Those who survive adapt their expectations and actions to the practical exigencies of work by using compromised situational judgments informed but not always dominated by the standards they were taught in school. As survivors they cannot fail to develop a certain skepticism, if not hostility, toward the assertion of cognitive authority by professors and researchers who create standards under considerably more protected circumstances and with more abstract goals than that of coping with daily work. Indeed, the very choice of a teaching or research career implies more concern for the ideal and the abstract than for the practical. Even in such an ostensibly applied discipline as engineering, Ritti (1971, 210) noted that, when a businessman complained that engineers were "over-trained," an engineering school dean stated that he could not attract a good faculty without allowing them to pursue a science- rather than a practice-oriented curriculum and research program.

The difference in interest and perspective between administrators and teacher-researchers is rather more difficult to characterize. Both are inclined to adopt a broader perspective than the rank and file on the aims of their common profession. Both are also concerned, though possibly for different reasons, with exercising control over the performance of practitioners. But academics are likely to be concerned with the way practitioners deviate from cognitively defined performance standards and goals, while administrators are more likely to be concerned with deviation from administratively defined standards and goals that are adapted to the organization's needs rather than concerned with the integrity of knowledge itself.

Differential Powers within Professions

Insofar as practitioners, administrators, and teacher-researchers are located in different places in the professional system and perform different tasks, it follows that there will be variation in the amount and kind of power they have. Paul Wilding (1982, 19–58) distinguished a number of areas in which power can be exercised by professionals. There is power in policy-making and administration, power to define public needs and problems, power in resource-allocation, power over clients, and power to control work. The differentiation of professions into academics, administrators, and practitioners represents a differentiation of access to those powers.

Down at the level of everyday work, practicing professionals have little control of policy-making, little capacity to define general public needs and problems, and little power over the allocation of resources except those immediately at hand. But they do have some variable power over individual clients, and they do have a significant but by no means uniform degree of power to control their work. One source of leverage practitioners have over their clients is their capacity to serve as gatekeepers of desired resources—whether school grades, drugs, financial benefits, or whatever. In this sense they have power over the situational allocation of resources. But it is the administrator who has the power to allocate those resources to the practitioners. Other resources administrators control, such as personnel, equipment, space, and assistance, make particular kinds of professional work possible and condition the way professional work can be performed by practitioners. Furthermore, the administrator formulates and transmits rules specifying what resources the practitioners can dispense to clients and under what circumstances. In this sense, the activities of administrators condition how and whether practitioners can exercise power over clients. They have the power to allocate what resources are available to the organization and to specify the needs and problems the practitioners are supposed to serve. Teachers and researchers, in contrast, exercise virtually no direct power over anything that goes on in professional workplaces, though their work may form the basis for both organizational rules and the decisions at work of its individual practitioners.

Clearly, the power that is exercised in the interaction of professionals with clients at the level of everyday professional work and the power exercised by administrators over that interaction cannot be understood without examination of the broader context in which it takes place—both the organization in which it takes place and the political economy in which the organization is embedded. Ordinary members of the professions—academics, practitioners, and workaday administrators in particular practice organizations—do not routinely contend with the larger forces of the political economy and so do not participate in policy-making, the allocation of national resources, or the political definition of public needs and problems. Rather, it is the leaders of professional associations as well as elite practitioners, administrators, and academics who do so by formal advice and testimony to those who hold the ultimate political power, by drafting the legislation, by influencing the formulation of the administrative rules that implement legislation, and by formulating the product, personnel, and procedural standards to be employed in serving what have been defined as public needs.

INTRAPROFESSIONAL TRANSFORMATIONS OF FORMAL KNOWLEDGE

Given differences in perspective and interest, it follows that the division of tasks between administrators and practitioners influences the formal knowledge each is engaged in organizing and using. Administrative professionals must often formulate procedural and substantive rules addressed to the way professional work is to be performed. Promulgated more as guidelines than as detailed rules, those directives establish a basis for evaluating, even if not closely controlling, the work of the rank and file. But though the individual superordinates may have some cognitive authority of their own, the ultimate legitimacy of their cognitive criteria can be established only by reference to the formal knowledge of the profession that is to be found in textbooks and professionally recognized publications. In the course of invoking and employing the knowledge of teacher-researchers for laying down guidelines for practitioners, however, administrative professionals must selectively transform it.

The formal knowledge of any discipline can be characterized by a single, central paradigm, and one can employ its textbooks as the authoritative source for portraying it (cf. Elias 1982, 38). However, in reality there is always a good deal of intellectual untidiness and indeterminacy in what goes on in disciplines. There is never only one textbook or manual; under a single paradigm will be found a variety of competing views. Normal science or scholarship is neither a mechanical enterprise nor one without passionate disagreement. Some of the formal knowledge of any discipline is often expressed as alternative opinions or theories; other elements are expressed in probabilistic terms rather than as laws or eternal truths. This means that formal knowledge can be applied to human affairs and practical action only by making arbitrary and selective decisions. Faced with a particular problem, which school of thought, which opinion should be followed? Equipped with authoritative knowledge expressed probabilistically, should one deal with an individual, concrete problem as the mechanical odds suggest, or should one follow an informed, firsthand guess that the case is a possible, even if statistically improbable, exception? Those are the questions that face the practitioner.

Guided in part by the practical institutional contingencies that limit the time and resources that one has to choose and in part by direct, firsthand experience with the concrete type of problem confronting them, rank-and-file practitioners are inclined to follow their own individual situational judgment even when it may contradict received opinion and practice. Part of the formal knowledge in which they were trained, therefore, may be ignored or even contradicted by them in their choices. Zussman (1985, 70) notes the "primacy of experience over theoretical knowledge" for engineers. Thus the formal body of knowledge they actually use during the course of their work becomes something considerably less consistent and systematic than the formal knowledge purveyed by academics, becomes something considerably more individual and idiosyncratic. In contrast, administrative professionals transform formal knowledge into something considerably more formal and consistent than it in fact is. When they promulgate guidelines designed to influence the way professional work is to be performed or evaluated, they must assert a definite standard. What is only one of several opinions or schools of thought is selected to become the established school; what are only probabilistic findings or assertions become the acceptable, usual, and even mandatory norms.

Both types of transformation of formal knowledge are essential: some choice among alternatives must be made if one is to act, and the practical action required of an administrator has different requirements than the practical action required of a practitioner does. Since the formal rules are promulgated by those in administrative positions to guide the performance of subordinate practitioners in the organization, we must see their version of the profession's formal knowedge, adapted to relevant legislation and the policies and resources of the particular organization, as authoritative. The rank and file, therefore, must simultaneously take those formal rules into account, take their understanding of their discipline's formal knowledge into account, and cope with the practical exigencies of their work situation. Just as they are likely to take liberties with the formal knowledge they learned in school and read about in professional journals, so are they likely to take liberties with the guidelines promulgated by their supervisors and managers.

Thus Foucault (1979, 170–94, 306) is mistaken in assuming that either the formal knowledge of a discipline or the formal rules of organizations can be employed to understand how the "functionaries" will apply them, particularly when we take into account the relationships they have with the clients over whom they are attempting to exercise power. Knowledge cannot be treated as some fixed set of ideas or propositions organized into a discipline that is then employed mechanically by its agents. It lives only through its agents, who themselves employ ideas and techniques selectively as their tasks and perspectives dictate. There is no assurance what knowledge will be used to guide the use of institutional power. No "one best way" is predictable from the formal body of knowledge itself.

When we take a close look at the professions, then, we find important forms of differentiation that force us to qualify our view of the powers available to them and of the substance and manner of use of the knowledge employed in exercising power. While each profession may be said to represent a particular discipline or formal body of knowledge, that knowledge is used selectively and transformed in the course of its use. The professional agents of knowledge differ in how and why they select and employ it because of the different perspectives and needs of those serving different functions in the organization and performance of professional work. Those differences are also frequently reflected in the policy orientations of professional associations, those representing practitioners often being at odds with others representing the administrators and the teacher-researchers, all members of the "same" profession. The American Medical Association, for example, taking the practitioners' side, lobbied against support for a federal agency established to review the safety and costs of medical procedures and technology, arguing that it was "trying to dictate the practice of medicine" (Sun 1983, 37). The Association of American Medical Colleges, representing the institutional interests of teachers and researchers, unsuccessfully supported the agency.

PROFESSIONAL POWERS AND THE PUBLIC

Professional control over work requires some control over clients. It presupposes that the professional, not the client or the employer, determines at least a good part of what work is to be done and how it is to be done. The critical variable thus becomes the relative power of each. Some professions characteristically serve clients who are powerful, sophisticated, and well organized. Such clients are in the position to define their own problems and needs and expect practitioners to serve them. Engineering, architecture, and, increasingly, science cannot be practiced without large amounts of public or private capital, so as professions they are typically dependent on clients who possess capital and who are therefore powerful. The Big Eight accounting firms and the large law firms serving corporations are also in the service of powerful clients. Under those "patronage" circumstances (Johnson 1972) professionals will, because of their expertise, be able to determine many of the tactics or methods of the service they provide but not the strategy or the goals of the service itself (e.g. Heinz 1983). Rather than exercising power over their clients on the basis of professionally generated conceptions of what their needs and problems are, these practitioners serve and advance their clients' conceptions.

The professions that provide personal services to a broad heterogeneous mass of unorganized clients exercise considerable power over their clientele, though when individual clients happen to be wealthy or powerful, we may be sure that the behavior of practitioners is markedly constrained. In general, the practitioners of personal service professions control clients by employing a number of institutionally generated means. But even this should not be overestimated. Since "discipline" for schoolteachers, "compliance" for physicians, and "cooperation" for lawyers and others are constantly cited by practitioners as central problems in their work, we cannot assume that they have sufficient power to be able to impose all their demands on their clients without resistance. Indeed, we must assume that they are obliged to accommodate in some way the lay preconceptions and desires of all but their most incapacitated clients. Accommodation to lay ideas is in fact one of the elements leading them to deviate from the formal knowledge advanced by academics and researchers.

One must also note that, while those receiving personal services from professionals do not generally have much power in their interaction because they enter it as isolated individuals or, as in classrooms, as relatively small, poorly organized batches of individuals, the client population represents an external source of pressure on practitioners. A considerable amount of power can be generated in the United States by public opinion, mobilized and focused by the mass media and culminating in political actions that can markedly constrain the degree and manner in which practitioners and their administrators can control professional work and their clients in the United States.

Not all professions are equally vulnerable to the pressure of public opinion because not all professions' work excites the same amount of interest. In the United States it seems to be illness that excites the greatest amount of public interest and concern and that therefore attracts a great deal of attention by mass media seeking to increase their circulation. Indeed, the public, or at least specially concerned lay groups drawn from the public, is an active and often powerful force in influencing policy and allocating resources independently of the health professions. (For case histories, see Troyer and Markle 1984; Johnson and Hufbauer 1982; Culliton 1972.) A close reading of Conrad and Schneider's (1980) review of the history of the "medicalization" of a number of personal and social problems shows clearly the powerful role that laypeople and lay associations have played in establishing policy and defining public needs and problems. To take another example, we may note that Mrs. Lasker's plan for a "war on cancer" was not supported by any professional association. However, she interested the syndicated columnist Ann Landers in writing a column on the idea, after which over a quarter of a million letters were written to members of Congress. Aided by the American Cancer Society, a committee of lay and medical advisers, and extensive lobbying, she gained her end in the Senate and came close to doing so in the House (cf. Rettig 1977; and see Strickland 1972).

Thus organized lay groups mobilizing public opinion

through the mass media can be seen to be an important factor in influencing the type and substance of power that professions may exercise in the United States. They are especially important for professions that characteristically provide personal services to broad segments of the public. They are considerably less important for such professions as engineering, industrial science, architecture, and the corporate service sectors of law and accounting. In the latter cases the issues are generally too technical and specialized to excite general public interest and have little immediate relevance to daily life. While it is true that public concern has been aroused by such matters as the safety of automobiles, nuclear power plants, toxic waste, and the like, the overwhelming bulk of the work of engineers, architects, corporate lawyers, and accountants escapes public notice. Indeed, they are rarely held responsible as professions. When something goes wrong, as it did at Three Mile Island, the public does not single out nuclear engineers as the culprits, as it would single out physicians in health issues. Instead, it singles out the corporations that employ or retain the profession or the government agency established to regulate them.

SUBSTANTIVE TRANSFORMATIONS OF FORMAL KNOWLEDGE

I have already suggested that, by the nature of their different perspectives, administrators and practitioners each transform in different ways the formal knowledge produced and advanced by academics and researchers. The freedom each has to work such transformations varies, however, for in some professions practitioners are in a considerably weaker position than others, and administrators are more powerful. Professions like engineering, architecture, and industrial science (particularly chemistry) do work that can often be structured systematically in a manner that is not possible for the work of professions like medicine or schoolteaching. Accounting or auditing is also amenable to such formal structuring (cf. Montagna 1973). In such professions the administrators' selection of the relevant formal knowledge to be used at work is likely to have more weight than the practitioners' conceptions.

But for both administrator and practitioner the substance of the formal knowledge selected or rejected for use is likely to be strongly influenced by the power, interests, and knowledge of the clients they serve. In engineering, for example, the client is primarily private capital. Practitioners have a relatively weak position, while administrators can be very powerful because they become chief executive officers of huge corporations and of heavily capitalized engineering firms serving corporations. In engineering a comparatively large amount of research is done under direct corporate auspices outside the nominally independent professional school (Weingart 1982; Whitley 1982; Dickson 1984 notes a trend toward this in science in general). The engineering profession's fragmented associations are also heavily influenced by those of its members who are high-level administrators in corporations and by the trade associations representing the industries in which their members work.

The academics and academic researchers of engineering have some influence on the shape of public and corporate policy, largely, one may suspect, through the advisory and consulting activities of their elite members. They share with the administrative elite positions of leadership in professional associations and their standard-setting committees, in the National Academy of Engineering, and on government advisory committees. However, the administrators of the profession seem to possess the overwhelming balance of power in influencing the affairs in which the profession is involved, and since their major members are executive officers who are understandably committed to the fortunes of their corporations, their perspective on the use of formal knowledge is weighed by the aims and interests of those corporations, which, in the United States, are concerned with profit on capital. It is from that perspective that they direct the activities of practitioners.

On the whole, available evidence suggests that the practical needs of their firms lead the administrative leaders of engineering to aim somewhat short of the standards that the formal knowledge of their profession makes possible. Such standards are likely viewed as impractical or perfectionistic, unfitted for the real and complex world of managing men, meeting a payroll, and turning a profit. It was probably on such grounds that corporate management resisted for some time adopting

Taylorism, or scientific management (Galambos 1979, 275–77), and even then never accepted the system in its full-blown academic form. Similarly, more recently, those determining corporate policy, who, by the 1940s, included a considerable number of engineers in executive positions, resisted the introduction of the numerical control machine-tool automation that was urged by Air Force and Massachusetts Institute of Technology scientists (Noble 1984). What was represented by scientists as the most desirable method was rejected in favor of the established way of the firm. Furthermore, what was established as "the one best way" of controlling boiler pressure by the American Society of Mechanical Engineers subcommittee in the Hydrolevel case was not established on the basis of "technique." Rather it was established on the basis of the vested interest of executives connected with the McDonnell and Miller firm, who used their position on the subcommittee to interpret standards in a way that reflected adversely on a competitor's device.

Available formal knowledge, therefore, is used selectively, its selection guided by the perspective of those identified with private firms and their fortunes. Historically, it has been the academics of the profession who have stressed professionalism and the need to serve the general public welfare rather than particular corporate interests (Layton 1971, 10–11). And is no accident that the academics of engineering have also stressed basic rather than applied research—that is, what they, not clients, regard as important. However, those in a position to exercise the greatest amount of power over both public and corporate policy and over administration, the specification of public needs and problems by legislation and standard setting, and the allocation of resources to the manufacture of the material world are the profession's administrative members. By virtue of their commitment to private capital they select from and develop formal knowledge in ways that advance the interests of capital, as do accounting and law firms that serve corporations.

The very knowledge that engineers can undertake to develop or elaborate becomes a function of the interest and judgment of those who control the capital that makes it possible. In this sense both the particular formal knowledge that is employed in shaping a large part of the material world and the particular areas in which new formal knowledge is developed are determined selectively not by engineering as a profession or by some logic drawing it toward one best way but rather by elite administrators of engineering who are as much, perhaps more, agents of their corporations as of their profession's knowledge. In other political economies they are the agents of the state or of the Party. The formal knowledge that can be used is limited by that constraint, and so is the formal knowledge that can be shared by the profession as a whole, for much of what is developed under corporate auspices is proprietary and protected as trade secrets. And insofar as knowledge becomes patented it is closely held property that others cannot use without a license to do so (cf. Noble 1977, 84–166; Nelkin 1983).

In contrast to professions like engineering, in professions that provide personal services to individuals or batches of individuals and whose work is not amenable to detailed formal structuring, organized public forces have greater influence. We can see this clearly in the case of schoolteaching, which, like engineering, is composed of a very large practitioner group that operates within broadly defined bureaucratic constraints. The profession's administrators are, as in engineering, fairly numerous and include immediate supervisors, executive officers of individual schools, heads of local school systems, and heads of large state systems. Unlike engineering, the major employer is the state and the immediate employers for most teachers a local school district.

Schoolteaching is not a strong profession, however. Its weakness stems from interaction between the insecurity of its academics and the formal knowledge they assert and the power of the public and the state. The profession's failure to establish firmly based cognitive authority is only partly a function of the objective quality of its formal knowledge. Of almost equal importance is the fact that the work it does revolves around issues that are of widespread public concern. Nor can it ever be inconspicuous and hidden because everyone at some time is exposed to it as pupils and then again, later, as parents of pupils.

Since education in the United States is not organized and

administered by a central national authority, as it is in many other nations, and because it is primarily scrutinized and financed by localities, its practitioners and administrators must contend directly with local publics and their children. Local school boards, influenced by pupils and parents, can exercise considerable leverage over at least the balance if not the content of the curriculum that teachers can present, though professionalized state agencies do limit how far they can go by formulating state standards.

Furthermore, as in the cases of health and criminal justice, about which the American public is also deeply opinionated, education is subject to cyclical waves of public alarm. Political pressures follow that strongly condition the allocation of resources to the schools. They also strongly influence policy formation and definitions of the needs and problems of schoolchildren. Both the content and methods of the profession's work, including the guidelines laid down by state agencies, show the heavy impact of such movements. Administrators in education have far less power than those in engineering. Its academics have some voice in educational reform movements, but researchers and writers from other disciplines, lay enthusiasts, media celebrities, and politicians all seem to be able to develop some authority over educational policy and the proper way to administer schools, allocate resources, and define public problems and needs.

The outcome in practice is that the substance of what is asserted as the formal knowledge of the profession has a rather unusually tenuous relation to power over educational affairs and even what is done by the teacher in the classroom. In the classroom, where the relationship between professional and client is sustained by the gatekeeper function as well as by bureaucratic authority, teachers must adapt and compromise what they do in the face of the strength of student and parental values, unable to exercise specifically professional judgment freely (cf. Bidwell 1965, 990). Situational judgment seems to far outweigh formal knowledge, making it highly dubious to use textbooks to serve as evidence of what goes on in schooling, as did Lasch (1979). The empirical circumstances of schoolteaching in the United States cannot sustain efforts to impute the stable and standardized "tutelary complex" imposed on schoolchildren that Donzelot (1979) did for France, where there is a centralized state system of education.

INSTITUTIONALIZATION AND KNOWLEDGE

What, then, of professional power? As human institutions, professions can manifest different kinds of power. As associations they are interest groups that can exercise economic and political power. As credentialed incumbents in key positions in agencies and organizations they can exercise bureaucratic, even state, powers. But the same can be said of a variety of nonprofessional occupations. The key question for the professions is whether the exercise of those powers also advances or imposes the formal knowledge by which they distinguish themselves from other occupations. Is professional power the special power of knowledge or merely the ordinary power of vested economic, political, and bureaucratic interest? That is the critical question.

It should be clear from my discussion that the term *knowledge* is as problematic as the term *power,* however. To speak of it globally, as to speak of power globally, is a convenient way of avoiding any possibility of determining whether what one ascribes to it is true. There is no place to stand, no definite content that one can trace through the interaction among professionals, the actions of their associations, legislation, organizational rules, and the actual production of goods and services. In order to create a place to stand, an orientation point, I have chosen to restrict the term to that which is associated with universities and their business of creating and systematizing knowledge. I distinguish formal knowledge as specialized knowledge that is developed and sustained in institutions of higher education, organized into disciplines, and subject to a process of rationalization. It is composed of organizing ideas and theories and of systematic substantive statements about both the nature of that portion of experience it addresses and the human activities that are appropriate to undertake in dealing with that experience. So delineated, formal knowledge may be found empirically by examining the literature produced by its creators and custodians—the professions' teachers and researchers, who are usually located in universities. This definition of formal knowledge may be crude and mechanical, but it has the virtue of definiteness that allows us to locate something concrete and to be able to trace it through institutions.

Merely to delineate formal knowledge, however, does not provide any evidence of its being employed to guide or otherwise influence the activities of human beings in the world of action outside universities. Nor can it tell us who employs that knowledge in the exercise of power, how it comes to be so employed, or whether it is employed in whole or in part, in pure or in corrupt form. At the outset of this book I argued that by studying the agents of formal knowledge one can begin to understand how formal knowledge can exist and have some connection with power. Now, after my analysis of professional institutions, it is possible to suggest that the nature of the institutionalization of various bodies of formal knowledge or disciplines allows us to identify in an organized fashion the differentiation to be found among the agents of knowledge, the methods of employing knowledge, and the sources of selectivity in the use of such knowledge in the exercise of power.

Taking the formal knowledge of textbooks and disciplinary publications as the point of reference, which excludes general, extradisciplinary publications addressed to a broader public, I have suggested systematic sources of both structural and substantive transformation when that knowledge is employed to influence human affairs. I suggested that, when the "pure" knowledge to be found in textbooks and disciplinary publications is put to use, it is transformed by the administrators and practitioners of the professions. Administrators make arbitrary selections from the formal corpus that best fit what they believe to be the practical situation of the organizations for which they are responsible and proceed to reduce what they select to an artifically limited and consistent set of rules, guidelines, or procedures. Issues of state regulations, income, and client pressure figure in their plan. Formal knowledge is simplified and rationalized, given greater formality than it actually possesses. It is arbitrarily made into "the one best way." Practitioners, on the other hand, accept that portion of the formal corpus and of the guidelines of administrators which is useful to them in their variable day-to-day work experience, while rejecting that which is not, in the light of their pragmatic judgment, based on the work situation confronting them. The resistance of clients composes an important part of that work situation. Formal knowledge is employed inconsistently and informally. In each case a different transformation of formal knowledge into "working knowledge" (Kennedy 1983) takes place.

Apart from the general difference in perspective between administrators and practitioners that leads to structural transformation, there are specific differences in situation that vary from profession to profession. Those differences influence the substance of the formal knowledge that is employed in exercising power. The most important difference stems from the nature of the professions' clients and the relative power they have. I have tried to show, albeit briefly, that formal knowledge is used highly selectively by powerful clients, with administrative professionals employing only that which is believed to be in the interest of those clients and supporting only the development of new knowledge that is thought to be in their clients' interests. Academics and many practitioners would like to pursue the "interesting"; administrators pursue the practical and the profitable. Where the professions' clients are heterogeneous, scattered, and relatively weak, formal knowledge may be subject to less substantive selection and the authority of academics and researchers stronger and more independent of the lay world. But there, both the power of politically organized lay opinions in the United States to resist and confound the cognitive authority of the profession and the stubborn resistance of clients at the level of everyday institutional activities make it difficult to support the view that formal knowledge is imposed by its professional agents like some mechanical stamp on human life. Only where we find standard setting does that seem remotely possible.

In the largely hidden process of standard setting we come closest to circumstances in which Foucault's use of the word *pouvoir* (power) may be relevant. It delineates a force so pervasive as to shape the world and control systematically the content and process of human life without having to rely on physical coercion. The personnel, service, and product standards of the United States set the official parameters of the material world of buildings, highways, consumer goods, and the like, of the qualifications of professionals in organizations that deal with laypeople, and of how they are expected to perform at work. Are those standards heavily structured by the disciplines whose members participate in their creation? Are they embodiments of formal knowledge into a powerful unilateral, formal scheme organized around the dominating ideas of disciplines?

When we look closely at the detail of standard setting, we find the dilution and compromise that is the price of institutionalization. All who have commented on accreditation standards in the United States have noted their minimal, permissive character. This flows in part from the fact that in the United States they are formulated by private associations. Such associations must tread a delicate line of compromise between their stronger and their weaker members, being careful to avoid offending so many of the latter by asserting overdemanding standards as to lose them as members and to lose the capacity to claim to represent them. Similarly, critics of licensing, certification, and registration standards have pointed to their crudeness, precise in their formal credential requirements but permissive of the varied qualities of the institutions that produce them. On the other hand, procedural or performance standards are not widely established for professionals, but when they are, they are as often as not "community" standards—that is, what is widely accepted and performed by practitioners rather than what is recommended by the theory and research of formal knowledge. And finally, product standards, like accreditation, are forged into something that is not much more than the least common denominator of what representatives of various competing firms of an industry are willing to accept. Thus, by the nature of the process by which they are formulated and agreed on, the vast majority of all professionally produced standards permit a significant amount of variation in products, services, and personnel policies on the part of the concrete organizations and professionals who are supposed to be governed by them. It is true that a norm is officially adopted, but it is not very restrictive.

It should be clear that the way knowledge is expressed in human activities is not easily inferred from the documentary sources available to those who cannot themselves observe living human actors. To assume, as do many who analyze documentary sources alone, that textbooks and other publications of academics and researchers reflect in consistent and predictable ways the knowledge that is actually exercised in concrete human settings is either wishful or naive. The least that can be done to test that assumption is to compare those expressions of formal knowledge with legislation and with the rules of institutions whose operation is believed to be influenced by formal knowledge. Even that necessary step is not enough, however, for empirical studies of armies, factories, hospitals, schools, prisons (e.g., Thomas 1984), and even concentration camps have shown, without exception, that organizational rules and regulations do not predict with an acceptable degree of accuracy how activities are actually undertaken. The formal plan, based on some tidy set of academic or political hopes, becomes transformed when it is institutionalized as a set of administrative rules; the administrative rules become transformed again by those who must carry them out. Short of firsthand study, only documents produced by the rank-and-file practitioners and their clients can show us the ultimate transformation by which a considerably modified, even contrary, version of formal knowledge is finally expressed in living practice.

I have tried to illuminate the character of the professions of the United States by looking at as much detail as was feasible for a view across them all in so many different contexts. This has made it possible to see where those varied terms for people connected with knowledge may find concrete referents. *Technicians* cannot be other than practitioners divorced from policy determination—particularly those whose work is amenable to formal structuring. *Technocrats*, on the other hand, cannot be other than those with professional credentials serving as high-ranking administrators or advisers to those in power, their aims and purposes as identified with the aims of their firms, organizations, agencies, or employers as with their professions and nominal professional colleagues. And insofar as *intellectual* refers to any distinctive position, it must be that of those who gain sinecures in universities by virtue of their disciplinary credentials and who then, their living assured, ignore their disciplinary commitments and address instead a lay audience and general issues.

Furthermore, when we render the idea of knowledge into tangible human institutions and credentials, we see that the institutionalization that permits knowledge to be employed in human affairs presupposes empirical processes positioning actors into different places in a system, with different tasks and perspectives. Their concrete work in those varied places, the impact on that work by clients of varied capacities, by capital, and by the state, and the differences they have among themselves by virtue of their different perspectives evoke a complex and subtle picture of interaction and negotiation by active human beings. All have distinctive privileges, even the rank and file. And all use some of the formal knowledge of their disciplines. But the reality seems sufficiently fluid and complex to call into serious question the value of such grand and colorful words as *technique, social control, hegemony, domination,* or *monopoly of discourse* to characterize it. Remembering the quotation with which this book began, perhaps I may end by saying that such notions show us color but not line, allow us to see the purple velvets and lilac silks but not the false beards. And so we do not perceive the props, do not suspect that the purples and lilacs may not even be true velvet and silk, do not understand the performance as a production of many prior rehearsals, and do not realize that no two performances are even the same. This may not be a serious handicap inside the theater, but as Babel's story went on to show, when we are outside, out where "streetcars lie like dead horses in the street," the grandiose illusions of color without line are fatal guides for action.

References

Abbott, A. 1981. Status and status strain in the professions. *American Journal of Sociology* 86 (May): 819–35.

Bidwell, C. 1965. The school as a formal organization. In *Handbook of organizations*, edited by J. G. March, 972–1022. Chicago: Rand McNally & Co.

Bucher, R., and A. Strauss. 1961. Professions in process. *American Journal of Sociology* 66 (January): 325–34.

Conrad, P., and J. W. Schneider. 1980. *Deviance and medicalization.* St. Louis: C. V. Mosby Co.

Culliton, B. J. 1972. Cooley's anemia: Special treatment for another ethnic disease. *Science* 178 (10 November): 590–93.

Dickson, D. 1984. *The new politics of science.* New York: Pantheon Books.

Donzelot, J. 1979. *The policing of families.* New York: Pantheon Books.

Elias, N. 1982. Scientific establishments. In *Scientific establishments and hierarchies*, edited by N. Elias, H. Martins, and R. Whitley, 3–69. Dordrecht: D. Reidel Publishing Co.

Foucault, M. 1979. *Discipline and punish: The birth of the prison.* New York: Vintage Books.

Galambos, L. 1979. The American economy and the re-organization of the sources of knowledge. In *The organization of knowledge in modern America, 1860–1920*, edited by A. Oleson and J. Voss, 269–82. Baltimore: Johns Hopkins University Press.

Goode, W. J., Jr. 1957. Community within a community: The professions: Psychology, sociology and medicine. *American Sociological Review* 25 (December): 902–14.

Heinz, J. P. 1983. The power of lawyers. *Georgia Law Review* 17 (Summer): 891–911.

Hughes, E. C., B. Thorne, A. M. DeBaggis, A. Gurin, and D. Williams. 1973. *Education for the professions in medicine, law, theology and social welfare.* New York: McGraw-Hill Book Co.

Illich, I. 1980. *Toward a history of needs.* New York: Bantam Books.

Johnson, M. P., and K. Hufbauer. 1982. Sudden infant death syndrome as a medical research problem since 1945. *Social Problems* 30 (October): 65–81.

Johnson, T. J. 1972. *Professions and power.* London: Macmillan Press.

Kennedy, M. M. 1983. Working knowledge. *Knowledge: Creation, Diffusion, Utilization* 5 (December): 193–211.

Lasch, C. 1979. *Haven in a heartless world.* New York: Basic Books.

Layton, E. T., Jr. 1971. *The revolt of the engineers.* Cleveland: Press of Case Western Reserve University.

Montagna, P. D. 1973. The public accounting profession: Organization, ideology, and social power. In *The professions and their prospects,* edited by E. Freidson, 135–51. Beverly Hills, Calif.: Sage Publications.

Nelkin, D. 1983. *Science as intellectual property—Who controls scientific research?* New York: Macmillan Publishing Co.

Noble, D. F. 1977. *America by design: Science, technology and the rise of corporate capitalism.* New York: Alfred A. Knopf, Inc.

————. 1984. *Forces of production: A social history of industrial automation.* New York: Alfred A. Knopf, Inc.

Rettig, R. A. 1977. *Cancer crusade: The story of the National Cancer Act of 1971.* Princeton, N.J.: Princeton University Press.

Ritti, R. R. 1971. *The engineer in the industrial corporation.* New York: Columbia University Press.

Salaman, G. 1974. *Occupation and community.* Cambridge: Cambridge University Press.

Strickland, S. P. 1972. *Politics, science and dread disease.* Cambridge, Mass.: Harvard University Press.

Sun, M. 1983. Fishing for a forum in health policy. *Science* 219 (7 January): 37–38.

Thomas, J. 1984. Some aspects of negotiated order, loose coupling and mesostructure in maximum security prisons. *Symbolic Interaction* 7 (Fall): 213–31.

Troyer, R. J., and G. E. Markle. 1984. Coffee drinking: An emerging social problem? *Social Problems* 31 (April): 403–16.

Weingart, P. 1982. The scientific power elite—a chimera: The deinstitutionalization and politicization of science. In *Scientific establishments and hierarchies,* edited by N. Elias, H. Martins, and R. Whitley, 71–87. Dordrecht: D. Reidel Publishing Co.

Whitley, R. 1982. The establishment and structure of the sciences as reputational organizations. In *Scientific establishments and hierarchies,* edited by N. Elias, H. Martins, and R. Whitley, 313–57. Dordrecht: D. Reidel Publishing Co.

Wilding, P. 1982. *Professional power and social welfare.* London: Routledge & Kegan Paul.

Zussman, R. 1985. *Mechanics of the middle class: Work and politics among American engineers.* Berkeley and Los Angeles: University of California Press.

Index

Abbott, A., 211
Academy of Certified Social Workers, 69
Accounting profession, 53–55; autonomy vs. bureaucracy in, 160, 162–63; client power over, 218, 220; gatekeeping powers in, 167; professional control in, 87; and professional corporations, 128
Accreditation, 73–77; conflicts with management involving, 151–52; and employment policies, 77–82; and professional class system, 82–87. *See also* Credentialing
Administrators: as census category, 49–52; and credentialing, 83–87; as professionals, 60, 83–87, 211–30. *See also* Managers
Advertising, ban on, 113–14, 116–18, 188
Advisory committees, 191–92, 197, 204–5
Agriculture, and self-employment, 120, 121–22
Airline pilots, 54, 58, 60
Akers, R. L., 188
Amateurs, 22–24
American Assembly of Collegiate Schools of Business, 81
American Association of School Administrators, 194–95
American Bar Association, 193, 197, 202–3
American Cancer Society, 219
American Chemical Society, 151
American Council on Pharmaceutical Education, 75
American Dental Association, 202
American Library Association, 76, 164
American Medical Association, 191,

193, 195, 197, 217; Committee on Allied Health Education and Accreditation, 80
American National Standards Institute, 202
American Pharmaceutical Association, 195
American Public Health Association, 197
American Society for Testing and Materials, 202
American Society of Mechanical Engineers, 201–2, 222
Anderson, J. G., 161
Andrews, F. M., 165
Angel, M., 143, 146
Antitrust law, 113–19, 129
Architects, 53, 60, 166; client power over, 218; and professional corporations, 128; self-employment of, 123
Armor, D. J., 161
Armytage, W. H. G., 8
Aronowitz, S., 119, 134
Arterburn, N. F., 104
Artists, 54, 60
Association of American Medical Colleges, 153, 217
Association of Schools of Music, 153
Atlantic Cleaners and Dryers, Inc., 115
Auerbach, J. S., 82, 193

Baar, C., 164
Babel, Isaac, x–xi, 230
Bacon, Francis, 4, 8
Bailes, K. E., 10–11, 15
Baldridge, J. V., 162
Bank officers, 51
Barber, B., 28, 110
Barron, J. F., 63

233

DATE DUE			

Freidson   203731